Canadese

A PORTRAIT OF THE
ITALIAN CANADIANS

Canadese

A PORTRAIT OF THE ITALIAN CANADIANS

By

Kenneth Bagnell

Macmillan of Canada
A Division of Canada Publishing Corporation
Toronto, Ontario, Canada

Canadian Cataloguing in Publication Data

Bagnell, Kenneth, date
    Canadese : a portrait of the Italian Canadians

Bibliography: p.
Includes index.
ISBN 0-7715-9386-4

1. Italian Canadians – History.*   2. Immigrants – Canada – History.
3. Italian Canadians – Biography.*   4. Immigrants – Canada –
Biography.   5. Canada – Emigration and immigration – History.
6. Italy – Emigration and immigration – History.   I. Title.

FC106.I8B33 1989   971'.00451   C89-094623-X
F1035.I8B33 1989

Text and jacket design: Jean Lightfoot Peters
Jacket illustration: Richard Whyte

MACMILLAN OF CANADA
A Division of Canada Publishing Corporation
Toronto, Ontario, Canada

Printed and bound in Canada by
T.H. Best Printing Company Limited

FOREWORD

I first learned of Kenneth Bagnell almost a decade ago upon coming across his first book dealing with immigration to Canada, *The Little Immigrants*, which dealt with British orphans sent to the Dominion between 1870 and the Great Depression. The study filled an important lacuna in the saga of Canada's peopling and I recommended it to students in my Canadian immigration history class.

Some years later I was pleased to learn that the author was working on a second volume on immigration, this time dealing with Italian Canadians. Mr. Bagnell contacted me for information, and, impressed by his sincerity in wishing to present a balanced account of the Italian-Canadian experience, I soon came to have high regard for both the man and the project.

Over the last six years Mr. Bagnell has been a regular participant at the annual lectures and various conferences sponsored by the Elia Chair in Italian-Canadian Studies at York University. On these occasions, Mr. Bagnell would patiently take notes or tape-record the proceedings, occasionally asking a question or making an incisive comment. The author's open-minded willingness to learn as much as possible about Italian Canadians shone through and he gained not only my trust and respect but also that of many members of the community, from students to professionals, from working people to writers and artists.

In preparing his manuscript, Bagnell has waded through a substantial body of scholarly studies dealing with Italian Canadians, consulted primary sources and documents, visited various Italian-Canadian communities as well as Italy itself and, best of all, along the way he has accumulated a rich stock of oral testimony which provides the study with its vitality.

In writing about immigration and ethnicity, one must deal

with the complexity of human nature and social interaction, and a number of perspectives are possible. As a social historian, my own perspective, choice of facts and characterizations would, in a number of instances, have been different from those of Bagnell's, a seasoned journalist. But one does not have to agree with every detail and interpretation within a book to endorse its overall tenor.

This volume marks an important juncture in the study of Canada's fourth largest ethnic group. At three-quarters of a million, Italian Canadians follow the British, French and Germans. There is little doubt that in the major cities of central Canada — foremost among them Montreal and Toronto — as well as in small towns such as Glace Bay, Nova Scotia, Sault Ste. Marie, Ontario, and Trail, British Columbia, the Italian presence is part and parcel of the local history and society. A particular strength of the book is the manner in which the author skillfully blends the specificity of the Italian experience with the more general, mainstream events of Canadian history.

Since almost seventy per cent of Italian Canadians are post-World War II immigrants or their descendants, the group's role as a major ethno-cultural influence in Canada is more recent than others'. This perhaps helps to explain why it has taken so long for a comprehensive book on Italian Canadians to appear. Mr. Bagnell's effort marks the first narrative to appear in English dealing with Italians on a national level. That it was written by someone not himself of Italian background is testimony to the increased interest and receptivity on the part of charter-group Canadians towards the new multicultural reality that has emerged as a hallmark of post-Centennial Canadian identity.

In writing a book that combines the facts of history with anecdotal material, Mr. Bagnell both complements scholarly work and adds to our understanding of the Italian contribution to Canada. His book deserves a wide audience.

Franc Sturino
Mariano A. Elia Chair in Italian-Canadian Studies
and Department of History, Atkinson College
York University, Toronto

CONTENTS

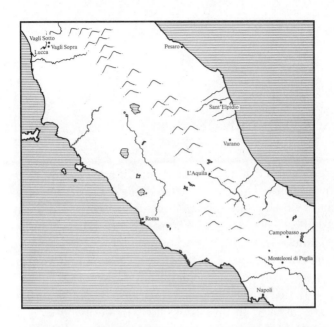

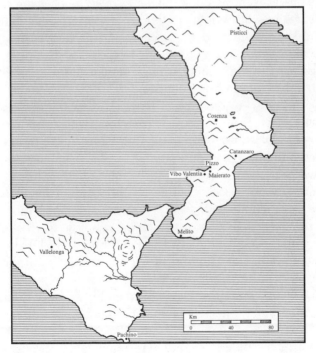

ACKNOWLEDGEMENTS

My first acknowledgement must rightly be to the Multiculturalism Directorate of the department of the Secretary of State which expressed support for the work in its early stages and offered encouragement through the years to completion. I am indebted, as always, to a number of people who have assisted me with archival and manuscript research at various periods of my work, in particular Enid Lesser and Patricia Smith of Toronto. I am also grateful to Barbara Regan of Aurora, Ontario who assisted in invaluable ways by verifying facts in numerous passages of the book. Diane Forrest, a colleague of former years, has offered her editorial guidance at certain points, and Mary Rutherford, my researcher on an earlier book, *The Little Immigrants*, has also provided assistance. My appreciation also goes to Maria Bergamin of Alitalia Airlines, Montreal; and to the Ontario Arts Council.

Several specialists in the area of Italian-Canadian life, past and present, have been unfailingly generous with time and insight, in particular Franc Sturino of York University, Toronto, whose thoughtful introduction to these pages is deeply appreciated. Two postgraduate students in Italian-Canadian history at the University of Toronto, Nick Forte and Luigi G. Pennacchio, have provided me with various forms of assistance, especially in the book's final stages. The manuscript has been produced with the help of Pina Circosta and Judy Powell. I also wish to acknowledge the support of various colleagues in the public affairs department of Imperial Oil Limited in Toronto, specifically Wynne Thomas, David Wetherald, Patricia Ruddock, Suzanne Tidey, Sheila Donohue and Jean Suiker. To my editor at Macmillan of Canada, Sheldon Fischer, I extend my gratitude for the consideration and care which he has brought to this task.

PREFACE

It will soon be a full half-century since those early days of summer in 1940, when, as a child of six in Glace Bay, Nova Scotia, I suddenly became aware — in a way that was dramatic yet vague — of the lives of people who were Italians in Canada. In the second week of June with World War II well underway, the police, acting on behalf of the federal government, descended swiftly, taking into custody a number of Italian men from nearby communities, putting them aboard trains and sending them to Petawawa, Ontario, where they were interned as suspected aliens. The shock of that Draconian event, with its incalculable emotional injury, reverberated through the town, leaving its scars on the imagination even of a child. Today, the events of that week, so little known to most Canadians, remain a vague, permanent imprint in my memory, like a hazy snapshot from childhood.

Later, when my work brought me to Toronto in 1961, I became witness to new tides of history for Italians. Their immigration in the fifties and sixties had changed not only the face and personality of Toronto but the nature and destiny of Canada. When in 1986 Prime Minister Brian Mulroney told the visiting Italian president, Francesco Cossiga, that first-generation Italian Canadians built Toronto's skyline and the second-generation owned it, he was exaggerating but not misleading. Still, the Italian presence in Canada is not measured solely in commerce and its experience has not been free from deep pain.

This is a book about Italian Canadians in this century. Although they had come in smaller numbers in preceding years, the main waves of immigration occurred in this century, from 1900 to the beginning of the first war, and from 1950 to 1970. This is a journalist's book and as such draws its life mainly from the lives of people, and I am indebted to hundreds of them who have, often at considerable cost to themselves, spent many hours with one who might be considered an outsider, but who has been received, without exception, with unfailing goodwill. Many such people appear in this book, but a large number of others, whose names are part of my memory if not these pages, have offered me their invaluable experience and insight. (Perhaps their recollections will receive a fuller treatment in a second book which I am considering.)

A number of the people who have spent time with me are academics in Italian-Canadian history, and while I acknowledge my debt to many of them elsewhere, I must mention here in particular the most distinguished academic on Italian immigration to Canada, Robert Harney of Toronto. Dr. Harney's work and insight have informed an entire generation of scholars, and he leaves all of us — those whose ambitions are academic and those such as myself whose writing is journalistic — deeply indebted.

This book bears my name, but its content and spirit carry the imprint of my researcher, Alberindo Sauro of Toronto, a former executive director of COSTI-IIAS, the immigrant aid society created by Italian Canadians, and a man held in wide esteem and affection within Toronto's Italia. He has been with me on my long quest since it began in 1981, accompanying me on many interviews and visits to Italy where, acting as my interpreter, he arranged numerous meetings, and finally reading the entire manuscript and offering his corrective views. Whatever compassion and sensitivity there are in this sometimes painful story is a reflection of his abiding affection for his heritage.

My friends, Jack and Jean Free, have graciously made available to me their country home above the quiet Beaver Valley north of Toronto, where, beginning each spring for the past few years, I have overlooked the valley, the coming and going of the seasons, and written most of the words that appear here. And of course, as in the case of my previous book, *The Little Immigrants*, I owe an enormous debt to my wife Barbara. It has been, for me and for her, a large task and a long journey. I thank her.

Kenneth Bagnell
Eugenia, Ontario
May 1989

To

Pasquale Allegrezza, 27
Giovanni Correglio, 45
Giovanni Fusillo, 27
Allesandro Mantella, 25
Guido Mantella, 23

who met death together in the evening,
March 17, 1960, Toronto.

"O Eterno, ascolta la mia preghiera, e porgi l'orecchio al mio grido; non esser sordo alle mie lacrime; poichè io sono uno straniero presso a te, — un pellegrino, come tutti i miei padri."

Salma XXXIX

"Hear my prayer, O Lord, and give ear unto my cry; hold not thy peace at my tears: for I am a stranger with thee and a sojourner, as all my fathers were."

Psalm XXXIX

PART ONE

CHAPTER ONE

CONFRONTING CORDASCO

One July morning in Montreal many years ago — a morning when the sun was high and hot and fell upon streets and buildings with the heat of a furnace — a couple of dozen men could be seen arriving, each on his own, and climbing the steep, broad stairway of a domed building which stood at 155 Notre Dame East and was known to everyone as The Montreal Courthouse.

They were, by any measure, striking in their diversity. A few, in winged collars and sombre suits, climbed the steps with the confidence born of familiarity. There were others, however, short men in sleeveless shirts, ragged trousers, and shoes cracked from rain and heat, who stood for long moments staring up at the large portico and pillars in apparent bewilderment. They were young, they were Italian, and on July 21, 1904, they were penniless: Giuseppe Mignella, Pompeo Bianco, Vincenzo Sciano, Salvatore Mollo, and a score of others.[1]

These men in tattered clothes, with vague confusion on their faces, would strike onlookers as the most irregular of the men entering the courthouse on that morning. But it was two others, quite different, upon whom the arriving journalists would fix their attention. It was these two, who in the end, would bring to the event now beginning, its drama and decision.

The first was a tall man, courtly in style, with a thick, trim beard and small spectacles which seemed to rest most comfortably near the tip of his strong nose. This was Judge John Winchester, who had arrived by train from Toronto the previous day. He was then fifty-five years old, the son of an immigrant shoemaker from Scotland, and a man who by reason of his legal gifts, public reputation and Liberal affiliations, had been appointed a judge of the high court in Toronto.[2] He was beginning to head numerous inquiries and commissions, the first of which had just been completed in Toronto, where his findings on ballot-box stuffing in a civic election had led to criminal charges. A Toronto newspaper described him: "A judge with industry, common sense, knowledge of human nature, conscientiousness and courtesy."

No, Judge Winchester's sense of duty would never be questioned. In fact, there may have been those among his friends who wondered to themselves at his zeal in leaving his Toronto home — where he lived beneath the great shadowing trees of High Park — at the height of summer and traveling to Montreal, arriving on the very day *The Gazette* noted the city was in the midst of a heat wave, so that on the afternoon he stepped down from his coach at Montreal station, the temperature was ninety degrees in the shade. "It was the hottest day Montreal experienced in three years," said *The Gazette*. In the minds of some people, the purpose of his coming was rather insignificant, unrelated to major events in the mainstream life of Montreal. It was, to the men who managed that city's affairs, a marginal matter, merely a social nuisance, but one that had to be faced: the questionable dealings that brought thousands of Italians to Montreal where they found no work and cluttered the streets. One of the leading lawyers of the city put a telling perspective upon it when he said the situation had to be dealt with because of the embarrassment it caused to municipal authorities. The effect it had on the disenfranchised workers seems to have escaped his attention. Thus, John Winchester arrived at the steps of the Montreal Courthouse carrying with him authorization from the Deputy Governor General of Canada to conduct a Royal Commission to Inquire into the Immigration of Italian Laborers to Montreal, and the Alleged Fraudulent Practices of Employment Agencies.

It was when a second man arrived, however, a thick-chested man in his middle forties, with eyes that were bright and riveting beneath heavy brows, that the gathered reporters could feel their curiosity quicken, and could sense the possibilities his presence could bring to the ten days of the hearing. His name was Antonio Cordasco, and as events would soon reveal, he was an incarnation of some of the more primitive instincts to surface in Canada's immigration history.

Cordasco, who had left Italy years earlier, going first to the United States, and then to Montreal, was by his own description, a banker, a steamship agent, and the operator of an agency that provided work for immigrant laborers. This last occupation was to make him the centre of attention at the Royal Commission. He was, he would tell anyone who would listen, dedicated to helping men from his native country find jobs in North America, in mining, in forestry, and in construction, especially railway construction.

He would tell them he had the very best contacts among those building the lines of steel in Canada and the United States, that they trusted and respected him. Really, he said, he was serving not just his fellow countrymen, but the energetic cities and the great companies of North America. Indeed, that spirit was reflected in his advertisements in newspapers published in Montreal but sent in large quantities to small towns and villages in the remote parts of Italy, to be read by men who knew nothing but poverty and dreams. One advertisement, run in *La Patria Italiana*, conveyed not only his vision of himself as a man of standing, but his aplomb and his abundant self-confidence:

> *A. Cordasco*
> *If you want to work on railways, canals, waterworks and other kinds of work of long duration and guaranteed — payment sure — at the price of $1.25 and $2.00.*
>
> *If you want to be respected and protected either on the work or in the case of accident or other annoyance, which may be easily met.*

Apply personally, or address letters or telegrams to

Antonio Cordasco
441 St. James St.
Montreal

*Sole Agent, who may find with every security and guaranteed
employment for labourers and foremen who know how to do
their duty. He is fully trusted by all the greatest companies and
contractors, who continually request his services.*

In the first five months of 1904, over six thousand men, most of
them leaving families behind, came to Canada hoping like
those who preceded them, to earn enough to go home and
support their families at least for a few years. So, in hundreds of
villages throughout the south — mostly in Calabria — men rose
while it was still dark and began the long trek by cart to port
cities, often Naples, where they put down their life savings for a
ticket on the steamship for Montreal. They would arrive, in the
cold of January and February and March, imprisoned in their
own language, with a pittance of money and no skills, only the
flimsy piece of newsprint carrying the name and address of
Antonio Cordasco. They would go in groups to his office on St.
James Street, and hand over everything they had — usually
three or four dollars — in return for the work he promised he
would find for them: good work, with good pay. Far too often,
there was no work. And so the men huddled six and seven to a
room in cold flats or hostels from which they would emerge in
the morning cold to wander the streets, fearful, hurt, and with
rising anger. When they ate, they ate remnants of food provided
by a charity set up for Italian immigrants.

Now and then, of course, one of them would be angry and
courageous enough to return to Cordasco's office and confront
him. One day that very spring a young man named Michele
Cilla, who had come from Calabria, walked in on Cordasco and
as politely as he could, asked if, since he had gotten no work, he
might have his money back. Cordasco said no, he could not.
Then he took a revolver and looked straight at Cilla. "If you ask
any more for your money," he said, "I will pull forty drops of
blood from your forehead."

Judge John Winchester did not know on that July morning, as he entered the second-floor courtroom and prepared to open the commission, of the more sordid and bizarre acts of Antonio Cordasco's career, but he knew enough of Cordasco's work to hold him in deep suspicion. On the train from Toronto, as it glided through the green fields beyond the city, passing the old genteel Loyalist homes of Cobourg, and on through the gentle Ontario summer, Winchester read and reread a slim sheaf of papers which, unknown to everyone around him, contained a report that for years to come would remain highly confidential. It had been compiled by a young man working for the federal government, who, on instructions from Prime Minister Sir Wilfrid Laurier, had spent many days in Montreal trying to piece together the reasons for the vast number of out-of-work Italians and the facts behind their pathetic circumstances. Winchester knew the young investigator, a scholarly, reform-minded man named Mackenzie King, then thirty years old, and as he read his report he felt nothing but confidence in its veracity. It had the ring of truth.

"The primary cause of the large influx of Italians in the present year," King had written earlier in May, "is, I believe, to be found in the work of certain Italian agencies in that city, and in the methods pursued by these agencies in co-operation with railway and steamship companies or their agents, to induce immigrants to come to Canada." He said that Antonio Cordasco had more to do with the hiring of such laborers than any other man. But it was a later sentence that stayed in Winchester's mind and gave focus to his questioning of Antonio Cordasco throughout the Royal Commission hearings: "The amount of fraud," wrote Mackenzie King, "which appears to be practiced by these employment agencies in securing men in the first instance, and in securing from them their money afterwards, is almost incredible."[3]

Cordasco had gone to considerable length to build himself a reputation as the great benefactor of Italian laborers. The means he used were, by any standard, audacious. On January 25 of that year, for example, *The Gazette* had carried the story of one of his more inventive schemes, in which he contrived to have himself ordained as King of Italian Laborers:

One band, three national flags, six carriages, and 2,000 Italians constituted the procession which started from 376 St. James Street Saturday afternoon and wandered along McGill, Craig, St. Lawrence, St. Catherine, Windsor, and back to the starting point via Little St. Antoine. The parade was given in honor of Mr. Antonio Cordasco, who has been named by his countrymen 'King of the Laborers.' Before the parade, a crown and basket of handsome flowers was presented to Mr. Cordasco who is very highly thought of in the Italian colony.

Then, just a month later, the paper carried another story detailing a banquet said to have been given by the Italians of Montreal in honor of Antonio Cordasco. "Mr. Cordasco," *The Gazette* said, "has won the admiration of his countrymen in Canada, owing to the interest which he takes in them on their arrival and during their stay here." The events, like the articles themselves, were a reflection of the imagination and audacity of Antonio Cordasco, a man of limited education, but with sufficient skill in English and sufficient friends in high places in Montreal that he would wield immeasurable influence over the lives of thousands of working men he invited from his native land to Canada.

Now, on this sweltering July morning in 1904, Cordasco sat near the back of the Montreal Courthouse in a corner seat, his broad, thick frame draped in a black suit, and his usually expansive face subdued and wary. One person sat with him, a wisp of a man named Antonio Ganna, a secretary of sorts for whom the days ahead would be filled with humiliations. Cordasco looked up as the judge began speaking: "This inquiry is open and I will begin calling witnesses."

In the courtroom, in seats not far from Winchester, were three lawyers, Jerome Internoscia, a graceful, dignified man, the first Italian-born lawyer to practice in Montreal, who was representing The Italian Immigrant Aid Society of Montreal; A.J. Walsh, a little-known man who had given legal advice to Cordasco in his business and now came to observe the case on his behalf; and finally, H.M. Mowat, a respected courtroom lawyer and Liberal, who was there on behalf of the federal government.

Mowat rose first. In his opening words, the distinguished lawyer revealed something of the spirit that would prevail throughout the hearing; but he also revealed a sense of the issue's importance to the leaders of early Canada. He had intended, he explained to the judge, to open by calling upon two witnesses who could explain the problem: "the embarrassment caused to municipal authorities by the large number of Italians brought in during the months of April...." Unfortunately, he went on, the two men he wished to call, Hormisdas Laporte, the mayor of Montreal, and Honoré Gervais, a Montreal member of parliament, were not there. They were, he said, too busy.

The first Canadian inquiry into discrimination against Italian immigrants was underway. John Winchester looked out upon the spare room and its random gathering of men — so few of whom could even understand the language being spoken. He felt that the hearing he was presiding over had been inspired less by a longing for justice than by social propriety on the part of the leaders of Montreal — English and French. He had in his briefcase, the contents of a letter written on the last day of the previous May by Montreal's mayor to the Prime Minister himself, Sir Wilfred Laurier, complaining of the large number of indigent Italian men walking the city streets: "A sentiment of fear pervades our citizens that those people who have been enticed to Montreal, may commit some excesses, because we have not sufficient employment to give them. We are of the opinion that a serious investigation should be made in order to shoulder the responsibility for such a state of things upon those at fault, and our citizens will esteem it a boon if you will kindly consent to take the initiative in stopping this influx of unemployment and in repatriating all those already here." In a matter of days, Winchester had been appointed, and gone to Montreal.

Indeed, as the federal lawyer Mowat called his first witness, Alberto Dini, a man who ran an agency of his own bringing Italian laborers to Canada, the politics behind the hearing — most certainly invisible to the men who were its subject — were confirmed immediately in front of Winchester. Mowat turned to Dini, a stylish middle-aged man, and asked casually how long he had been in Montreal. Thirty-two years, he was told. "How long have you been conducting, among other things, an employment agency for laborers?" Mowat, of course, was fully

aware — though he did not bring it out — that Dini was indeed
engaged in other activities that while honest, were highly influential and political. He was vice-president of The Italian Immigrant Aid Society, whose president was none other than
Montreal's most respected Italian Canadian, Charles Honoré
Catelli, creator of the nation's largest macaroni company,
founder of The Italian Orphanage in Montreal and recipient of
Italy's highest honor for his service to his fellow Italians in
Canada.

For a long time Montreal had been home to one of the
country's earliest Italian colonies, some of its members, in the
hotel trade, having come as early as the late 1700s, but most of
whom — laborers, artisans, craftsmen of various kinds —
started to arrive in the late 1800s, drawn by relatives already
there. Montreal was then Canada's magnet for work, either at
the harbor, the freight yards, the railway junction, or the maintenance shops. The community was already mature enough to
have created its professional class, the *prominenti*, who led in
forming its immigrant aid society.

Men like Catelli and Dini and the lawyer Jerome Internoscia
were annoyed at the articles in the newspapers, especially *La
Presse*, in which Italian laborers — sometimes almost a hundred
of them jammed in a single boardinghouse on Ste. Agathe or St.
Timothée — were depicted as coarse, cunning men, quick with
their tempers and their knives. In one article, about the murder
of a man named Domenico Camino in a boardinghouse fight,
the journalist provided this background: "A stinking, filthy
street where hundreds of Italians live, men of the lowest class."

John Winchester had absorbed this background before he
began to listen to the first words of testimony from Alberto Dini
who spoke at times vaguely and hesitantly, and here and there
in outbursts that clarified nothing and left an air of pathos over
the courtroom. But when Jerome Internoscia, the lawyer for the
Italian Immigrant Aid Society began gently and sympatheti-
cally to question him, Dini burst out with a claim that brought
embarrassed anger to Internoscia's face. Dini said the Italian
working men were not poor, they were simply pretending.
Immediately, A.J. Walsh, the lawyer representing Cordasco,

asked him: "Did I understand you rightly a few moments ago, did you mean to say that the Italians were not poor, but were simply making believe?"

And Dini, despite the report of Mackenzie King, said yes, that was his opinion. No, he could not prove it, but he believed that they spent their money on liquor.

The kind of work and the wages the immigrant men dreamt of finding in Canada was made clearer when a man named John Skinner took the stand. He was in his early forties, a lawyer from Ontario, who had come to work, about a year before, for the CPR at its headquarters on St. James Street. He described himself as a labor agent of the company, a job in which he supervised all workmen on the CPR, once they'd been hired. He was careful to explain that another man, his manager, George Burns — who would be appearing later — was responsible for the hiring arrangements.

Skinner testified that the CPR had been the main employer of Italian laborers during the years leading up to 1900 and immediately afterward. They would arrive in Montreal — some directly from the port of Naples, others after landing in New York — find lodging with friends or relatives, and then look for work. They would clear the woods, lay the ties, drive the spikes, in the hard bush country through which the CPR was pushing its way to the great Northwest. It was always heavy, often lonely, without female companionship, or comfort. A traveller in the bush country north of Lake Superior once came upon a young boy from a village in Calabria sitting alone in the bunkhouse, having, as he said, no one for company but God.

According to John Skinner, over three thousand Italian men had been employed in 1903. Winchester asked how many men had been available. "Well, the total number of unskilled laborers was something in the neighborhood of six thousand," Skinner answered. Since the country brought in twice as many men as could be employed, wages were conveniently driven down, so that most of the men would work for as little as $1.50 a day, not only because it was the going rate, but because compared to the 25 cents a day they made at home, it was good pay. They would dream of a year or two of work, saving their pay, and then returning to the village they came from. But many, perhaps most, did not get the money or the treasure, for they never got the jobs. Instead, like the handful of men listening to Skinner, they ended up getting 30 cents a day from the Italian Aid Society of Montreal, then as their numbers increased, 15 cents, and finally, as the society began running out of funds, a single loaf of bread.

In time, Winchester asked Skinner the question most people were waiting for. "Now," he said, "who is your employment agent, who employs Italians for you?"

"Antonio Cordasco."

"His office is?"

"375 St. James Street."

"Adjoining yours?"

"Yes."

The extent of the CPR's liaison with Antonio Cordasco — a liaison suspected by both Mackenzie King and John Winchester — began to be revealed when John Skinner's boss, a mild mannered Scot named George Burns, took his place and faced Winchester's unrelenting questions. Burns, who had been in charge of the railway's labor department for four years, began by admitting that he engaged Italian laborers exclusively through Cordasco. He further admitted that his relationship with Cordasco included trips taken together to the United States where he helped Cordasco secure a new arrangement: Cordasco would represent certain steamship lines in order to be able to sell men prepaid passage from Italy. "I took some steps," Burns admitted, "to get these agencies for him." He did not make it clear, nor did he appear anxious to explain what this had to do with his job with the CPR in Montreal.

Winchester asked him how much he paid Cordasco to locate the men who would be sent to the hinterlands of the CPR line. His answers throughout the hearing were vague and conflicting, less perhaps out of willful deceit than out of a casual under-standing of his responsibilities. He said that in the beginning, in 1901, he'd paid Cordasco a dollar a man for all the men he could secure. Later, he claimed, he made him sole agent in order to simplify hiring practices, and paid him five dollars for every day he worked. This meant that for hiring activities alone, Cordasco netted four thousand dollars a year, at a time when, in Montreal, one thousand dollars was a handsome salary. "I was desirous of getting business arranged so as to have the least possible trouble," Burns said lamely.

Winchester was not convinced he was hearing all that he ought to hear. He recalled Burns for questioning based on the suspicion that money no one knew of had passed from Cordasco to Burns. Winchester was concerned about Cordasco's many avenues of earnings, including the supply of provisions to the men in distant places. He asked Burns about gifts from Cordasco, about their close friendship, about certain allegations. "And you swear on your oath that you have never received any share of any profit or any sum of money in connection with any Italian labor?" Burns replied in the affirmative.

But that was not the end. In a day or so, Burns was back before Winchester, and this time Winchester pressed him further still. He had Burns produce his wife's bankbook, and after examining it suggested pointedly that his wife deposited money above and beyond Burns' regular CPR salary: "Where did these two sums come from? These two sums form a larger sum than your salary." Burns fumbled, said he did not draw his salary, that he had no recollection of the deposits under question, that he could not be sure.

"November, $120, December, $160," continued Winchester, his bushy-browed eyes staring into the small book in his large, muscular hands. "January, 1904, $225. This is again larger than your salary?" Again, Burns pleaded that he had a little spare money here and there which he gave to his wife but that no, he had no income other than the CPR. Winchester heard him out (in the end, he would say nothing conclusive) but his suspicions hung in the quiet air of the courtroom. "That is all I want from you," he concluded, "These are your bankbooks."

George Burns fared no better at the hearing when another witness took the stand. A man named Rodolphe Candori, a clerk in the Italian Immigrant Aid Society office, said that the society had been convinced Antonio Cordasco, as well as making thousands from the CPR, was at the same time overcharging the Italian laborers. Candori met Mr. Burns one day and they went together to Cordasco to try to straighten things out and get the truth. "It was raining," recalled Rodolphe Candori, "and Mr. Cordasco was not in his office and we were standing on the corner of Little St. Antoine and St. James Street, and he said to me exactly this: 'I don't give a damn what Cordasco charges provided the business goes on thoroughly well.'"

The hearing was into its third day when Winchester and his fellow commissioners called upon Antonio Cordasco himself. He was a jowly man, in a dark, three-buttoned suit, with which he usually wore a vest, and a heavy chain and ornate pocket watch. His fingers were like sausages. He was neither arrogant nor retiring.

"I am a labor agent," he replied to Winchester as soon as he was sworn in, "ship Italian money, and sell some steamship tickets." For five minutes he drew a picture of what he did: he had been bringing men to Canada for six years, originally men from Britain, Scotland and Ireland, but for the past three years, only from Italy, the country from which he himself had come.

"You *claim*," said Winchester, "to be the sole agent for the Canadian Pacific Railway for the employment of Italians?"

Cordasco, his large frame overfilling the chair, shifted as the air in the room thickened with tension. He hesitated, then deliberately fumbled: "I put that in the papers, and did not find anybody to interfere."

"You claim to be sole agent?"

"You see I was employing."

"Are you sole agent for the Canadian Pacific Railway?"

"As far as I see nobody else is."

"Were you employed as sole agent?"

"I do not know if . . . "

"You must answer my question: are you sole agent for the Canadian Pacific Railway?"

"Yes, I am."

"Why did you not answer at first? How long have you been sole agent for the Canadian Pacific Railway?"

"About three years."

Thus Cordasco set the tone for his next three appearances before the commission: never nasty or arrogant, but reluctant, his answers hidden in deliberately opaque English.

He received, he admitted, five dollars a day, beginning in October of 1901, which was a tidy sum, but of course he made more than that. Each of the men he recruited — mostly from Italy, but also from among Italian immigrants to the United States — paid him sums which varied with what the traffic would bear. Cordasco tried at first to obscure the fact that along with the railway, the men, so many with next to nothing to begin with, also paid their supposed benefactor. John Winchester, knowing already from the report of Mackenzie King that indeed Cordasco was making a healthy income from the men, framed the question deliberately:

"Mr. Burns swears that the agreement between you and him was this, you were to be paid one dollar for each man employed by the Canadian Pacific Railway, on the condition that you would not charge the men a single cent. Is that agreement right as Mr. Burns says? There cannot be two ways of understanding it."

"Not right, we . . ."

"Where," asked Winchester, his skepticism written on his face, "is it wrong?"

"It is wrong in this," replied Cordasco. "At the time I worked in my office, in the office belonging to me, when a man registered in my office, and when the CPR asked for one hundred men I make the contract and I charge nothing to the CPR."

Winchester ignored the evasive tactic and patiently restated his question in words it would be impossible to deflect.

"How many in round numbers," he asked, "paid ten dollars?"

"I cannot remember," Cordasco hedged, "but my books will show."

At that point Winchester paused, and, reaching among the papers spread before him, located a long ledger, opened it, and began to read a list of names, sixty-one in all — Pellingrino, Poliseno, Del Vecchio, Bertone, DeCiccio, Spinosa, Farina — and after he pronounced each name, he looked at Cordasco asking for the amount each had paid, usually for no work at all. Cordasco put on the record that not only was he paid hundreds of dollars by the CPR for recruiting Italian laborers, but indeed he was paid hundreds of dollars more by the men themselves, each one of whom, from his starvation savings, gave an amount usually of ten dollars. When Winchester asked how many men, foremen, and laborers passed through Cordasco's office in a six-month period beginning the past November, a man who worked for Cordasco gave the number: 3,863.

The reasons why so many men from every corner of Europe (and elsewhere) were coming to Canada was not the subject of the inquiry, but formed the background without which this drama could not have taken place. The surging strength of the national economy of the time, which despite periodic recessions was still moving forward, was measured in the scores of new towns opening in Ontario and on the prairie frontier, in the hundreds upon hundreds of miles of fresh track that had cut through the cold wilderness of the northland during the 1890s. All of this created a powerful attraction for the men from Italy.

What Winchester did not know was that in addition to Canada's need, there were in Italy itself numerous men in business offices and editorial rooms encouraging emigration and trade as a promising path into the future for Canada, for Italy, for Italians. A 1901 report to Rome by the Italian consul in Montreal, Giuseppi Solimbergo, recognized that many arriving Italians were facing hardship, but felt that if immigration could be conducted under decent arrangements, Canada held out great commercial potential for the immigrant, and, because of his attachments to his homeland, the country that he left.[4] From their jobs as fruit vendors, or in cotton mills and iron mills and quarries, the sojourning laborers remitted much of their money home to waiting families.

Thus, because the pressure from abroad was not fully known to the commissioners, and the politicians and people of Montreal, the full reason for the enormous number of men who came from Italy, even when there was no work so that they wandered the streets in desperation, remained hidden to them. Winchester began by asking simply if, in the early winter of 1904, Cordasco had advertised, by newspaper or letter, in the United States or in Italy that there were jobs, plenty of them, in Canada, enough for ten thousand men, and that he, Antonio Cordasco, was the man to contact.

Cordasco did not hesitate. "I do not remember that I ever wrote such a letter," he replied, "if you can show it to me." For a few minutes, Winchester persisted and Cordasco evaded, and then Winchester produced a single piece of paper and began to read from it, his eyes seldom lifting from the wrinkled page: it was, he said, addressed to a man named Antonio Paretti, of 94 Aquila, Udine, Italy. It was dated March of that same year, and it read in part:

> At the end of the present month there will open up great and important works, and I must supply about 10,000 laborers. If you have any passengers, you can send them without any fear — I am able to give them immediate work. The salary will be $1.50 a day. . . . The work will last long and the payment is sure. Each man gets a contract in Italian, containing clear conditions under which they have to work, on which is specified the length of time and salary. In one word, there will be no tricks or schemes. I am always ready to defend the interests of compatriots. . . . If you wish to send us any men, you need not have any fear, and send them all to my address.
>
> The letter was signed: "Antonio Cordasco."

It was false in almost every claim, and Cordasco, sitting impassively, seemed resigned to its being put before the commission. Winchester simply looked at him and waited. Cordasco did not waiver; he denied writing the letter. "I never sign this letter," he said, "never authorized anyone to sign it." Then he went further, on a tack he would take for the entire hearing: he put the blame on his secretary, the pathetic, harried Antonio Ganna who sat furtively in a nearby chair. "I blame him," Cordasco began, "for the whole thing." Time after time, Winchester would produce a letter or advertisement promising thousands of jobs — almost always ten thousand — over the name of Antonio Cordasco, only to hear that he, Cordasco, had not authorized it, nor written it, nor approved it. "Mr. Ganna got these up," he would say, pointing in the direction of his minion, "There is the gentleman who did the work."

But the bold evasions reached their zenith one morning when Winchester, referring to the great parade in which Cordasco was lionized by Italian workingmen, and the subsequent banquet on February 27, 1904 at The Italian Hotel, where he was declared King of Labor, inquired politely if, in fact, Cordasco himself had produced the invitation, and distributed it in Italy among men desperate for work. "That was in February," he smiled. "Did you get that printed?" Once again, Cordasco blamed it all on Ganna, who sat quietly wrapped in humiliation.

Late one afternoon, when the first twilight fell through the windows, Winchester's questioning began to reveal that Antonio Cordasco had no restraint on his desire to profit from the vulnerability of the Italian workingman, and others as well. Cordasco, it became clear, not only made money from the laborers — whether he got them jobs or not — or indeed from the CPR, but also by supplying provisions, mainly food, for the men on the working gangs, and he did so at a rate of profit that astonished.

"You charge," began Winchester, "for provisions bought for Chinese going to the coast?" Cordasco said he did, but at the request of George Burns, his good friend at the CPR; he simply ordered food supplies from a retail grocer a few doors from his office. He said he did not forward the grocery account to the CPR, but handled it himself, then charged the railway for his work as a supplier. No, he told the Judge, there had never been any complaint against him. Winchester asked about the amount Cordasco realized from his role of provisioner:

"You charged about sixty percent, sometimes sixty-two percent and sometimes more?" Cordasco said he thought that was fair enough, and when Winchester looked at him calmly and said that, when he shipped sardines to the men, he marked them up an enormous 150 percent, Cordasco replied that when it came to sardines he was not that aware of their true market value. He said that 150 percent was not unreasonable.

For the remainder of the hearing he was aloof, arriving alone and leaving early, the man who personified the exploitation, though of course it was not he alone. The men from the CPR would always be in a shadow in the mind of John Winchester. Winchester did his best to prove that in the case of George Burns, there were monies in his bank account that totalled more than his CPR salary and for which he gave no plausible explanation. Still, it was Cordasco who remained the living embodiment of a system full of moral ambiguities, if not outright evil. The hardship was made most vivid not in the arguments of the lawyers but in the testimony of the Italian men who one by one, came forward and, in shy, low voices, told what happened. Giuseppi Agostino came from the region of Calabria. He had been two years in Montreal.

"Did you apply to Cordasco for work?" asked Winchester. Agostino said he did, on December 23, paying Cordasco the sum of two dollars for himself and his son. The boy was fifteen.

"Did you receive any work at all?"

"I worked only two days because I was waiting. I spent all the money I had made last summer waiting for work." For the one day he did work, he was charged an extra levy by Cordasco.

On July 26, shortly after three in the afternoon, John Winchester suddenly looked out over the handful of men who had been in the courtroom for the entire hearing — a few reporters, several clerks and a small scattering of Italian workingmen — and announced that he would be adjourning to study the evidence and arrive at a recommendation.

That same evening he sat alone and enveloped in thought in Windsor Station, then climbed aboard the train bound for Toronto. Twilight fell over the city and the lamps were lit in the train, throwing an amber glow over the soft, plush seats.[5]

As he relaxed over a dinner of roast beef, vegetables, and a modest wine, Winchester glanced once more at his papers. Most were from a batch of over a hundred letters written by Cordasco on his florid letterhead (a coat of arms, a crown and a cross, and the words, "Antonio Cordasco, Banca Italiana"). They verified all that had been said, and all that Winchester had

been told of Cordasco's method. A typical letter to Angelo de
Santis, who had already arrived in the United States, and was
living in Buffalo, boasted: "I need this year nearly ten thousand
men but all of them must be able to work with pick and shovel."
And to others, in the United States, and Italy, it was the same: "I
send men to work for the CPR and other great companies and
contractors and this year I shall be in need of 10,000 men. The
first shipments will be sure in spring according to the weather
and the first to start are those marked in my books."

Two letters aroused Winchester's deeper suspicion. One was
from C.C. Mariotti, the secretary-treasurer of the Italian Immigration Society, the group that in the crisis of 1904 had provided a pittance of money to the men who had been so
exploited by others. The letter had been written on March 5,
1903, and addressed to D. McNicoll, General Manager, the
CPR. It was a plea to permit the society to help in supplying
laborers, so that their numbers would never exceed demand,
and so that Italian men would not be the pawns of either
business or brokers. Part of it read:

> As our principal aim is to protect our countrymen against any
> kind of swindlers, of whom they have been victims until now, we
> try to secure the goodwill and cooperation of all the companies
> that engage Italian laborers, the CPR first, as the most impor-
> tant of the Dominion, offering our services for the allotment of
> the men. Two months ago we sent to the CPR 50 copies of our
> by-laws and as perhaps they did not reach you, we beg to send to
> you another one of them, from which you may see that our work
> is highly moral and deserves to be taken into consideration.[6]

On March 16 an official of the CPR replied to Mariotti, saying in
effect that although the society had the highest credibility, there
was no opportunity for it to share its knowledge and integrity
with the railway. Besides, "our present system of employment
has given entire satisfaction so far. . . ." The letter was signed
"George Burns, Special Agent."

For the rest of that humid summer in Toronto, John Winchester spent many of his days in the large, shadowy study of his
home on High Park boulevard, finding more and more that the

evidence from the hearing confirmed, in principle and in fact, all that he had felt from the very beginning. While others may have concluded that it was simply a moral ambiguity inevitable in the larger enterprise of nation building, to Winchester, it was a scandal. By autumn he had begun to write his report, with conviction that grew stronger as summer rusted into autumn. Two of the testimonies in particular remained vivid in his memory. One was that of Charles Catelli, the dignified leader of Montreal's Italian community who, though a shrewd business-man, understood that immigration should not be a business. The commission had asked Catelli: "Would you go so far as to say that private agencies should be prohibited?" And Catelli had said yes, he would go that far.

"You think," Winchester remembered asking him, "that the cause of this excessive immigration was that if a man is inter-ested in making money he can be trusted to make as much as he can, business is business you would say." And Charles Catelli, whose own business acumen was already building a famous food empire, replied again with brevity that reinforced his cer-tainty: "Yes, Sir."

The other influential testimony was that of a member of parliament, Honoré Gervais, from the riding of St. James in Montreal. Gervais had appeared before the commission to urge that the problem so apparent on the streets of his constituency be cleared up. Gervais' urgings were not so much humanitarian as they were practical, political — and perhaps elitist. But in Winchester's mind, Gervais was right in saying:

> The class of immigrants that Canada wants to be brought here are picked up by the proper officials of the Dominion Government, by the proper agents of our government, and I do not recognize the right of any private individual to speak in the name of Canada to the foreign laborers and induce them to come here. We have our proper officials who will not deceive the foreign laborer and, consequently, I would say that these private agencies should be checked. Special legislation should be incor-porated defining those who shall have the right to represent Canada abroad, because the good name of Canada and the credit of Canada may be imperiled.

Well into the winter of 1905, Winchester finished his report. He wrote that there was no doubt that the thousands of poverty-stricken men from Italy who came to Montreal had been induced to come by the misleading advertisements of Antonio Cordasco. But Winchester did not spare George Burns of the CPR:

> In my opinion, Mr. Burns had control of Mr. Cordasco's actions and was well aware of the sums that were being paid by the men employed by the Canadian Pacific Railway Company as also for the provisions supplied, but instead of preventing the collection of these extortionate sums, he refused to interfere when requested to do so.

He concluded with a one-line recommendation that the federal government put a stop to the activities of brokers such as Cordasco by permitting only federal officials to speak in the name of the country in encouraging potential immigrants. Sharing a language and country was not then, and seldom has been, proof against exploitation of fellow human beings.

Winchester went to Ottawa that March on a day when the capital was still encrusted in ice. The snow crunched beneath his feet as he walked to the offices of his political compatriot, Sir William Mulock, the minister of labor. They talked briefly of politics in Toronto, where Winchester had once been president of the Reform party, and then of his report. The following day, after Mulock had spent the night reading it in his suite at the Château Laurier, he called in several of his officials from the department of labor, and in a matter of days they drafted a new clause, to be inserted in a piece of law called The Alien Labour Bill. While the bill did not go as far as Honoré Gervais had envisioned, it sharply disciplined the activity of private entrepreneurs. Anyone making and circulating a false representation to induce immigration to Canada would be liable to a fine up to one thousand dollars for each occurence. It was passed in the House of Commons, and entered the statute books the following year.

In Montreal, Antonio Cordasco seemed to vanish back into anonymity. He was never directly punished, though perhaps obscurity was punishment enough for a man who had called himself the King of the Workers. As for his good friend George Burns, he continued to hold his job as a minor functionary in the CPR, though an official decree from the office of D.K. McNicoll, the railway's general manager, forbade him to continue his former associations.

But the most important result of the Cordasco years was an indirect one, one that would influence the immigration of Italian citizens to Canada for the rest of the century. For many of the men who came in answer to Cordasco's promise, intending to return in a year or two to Italy, did not return. They stayed, either because they could not afford to return, or because they slowly began to discover that despite the hardships of their first years, Canada still held opportunities, if not in Montreal, then in the towns and cities of Ontario and beyond. And they managed, some becoming workers and tradesmen, respected members of various Italian communities. Some, who went to northern Ontario to work with the gangs that pushed the railway through the bush, became early and honored citizens of the North's Little Italies. At home in Italy, hundreds of men and boys continued to rise before dawn, in mountain villages as old as Genesis — Pisticci, Vallelonga, Azzano Decimo — where, surrounded by prayers and tears, they crowded into horse-drawn carts and rode the paths to the sea and to Canada. Here they would find fathers and brothers and cousins, settlers who would welcome and embrace them in the warmth of their own sunny land.

CHAPTER TWO

THE TWIN CITIES AND THE DEPRENZO BROTHERS

Almost six months to the day after he had received John Winchester's report on the dealings of Antonio Cordasco, Prime Minister Wilfred Laurier left Ottawa by train and began the long journey through the pine and rocks of northwestern Ontario, beyond Timmins and Sudbury and on to the rim of Lake Superior. On September 15, 1905, just as the mid-evening mist began to blur the window of his private car, he arrived in the town of Fort William. The station was empty; even the streets seemed unusually still.

Next morning, after some three hours at work reading, signing documents, and writing letters, he prepared for his imminent meeting with local politicians and businessmen before the main event of the day: the sod-turning for a third railway into Fort William. This town, like its neighbor, Port Arthur, was filled with the promise of prosperity. As the gateway for grain to the world, its stability and growth were assured. Moreover, the two towns were a microcosm of the racial and cultural diversity that were to characterize the West in the century just underway — their populations expanding by over one hundred percent since 1900, almost entirely through immigration from southern Europe, and much of that Italian.[1]

The cities had a long history of rivalry. Fort William, set

23

alongside the brooding Kaministikwia River, and close to a wide inlet on Lake Superior called Thunder Bay, had been a point of rendezvous for the North West Fur Company, in the late 1700s, the only company that had come close to challenging — in the end unsuccessfully — the continent-spanning monopoly of the Hudson Bay traders. Port Arthur, its rival, came into being around 1859 when S.J. Dawson, the famous surveyor and explorer, chose its location over Fort William because of its deeper waters, and used it as the starting point of his land and water route to the West's Red River.

But as Laurier knew only too well, railways rather than water-ways became the pathway over which Canada traveled in the nineteenth century to the East and West. Thus, both the Cana-dian Pacific and Canadian Northern chose "the Lakehead" (as the cities were jointly called) as their point of departure to the West. The CPR's coal handling facilities were the largest in North America. Laurier recognized the Lakehead's promise as a great metropolitan centre.

His secretary drew back the velvet curtain in the entry to the car, and spoke softly. The delegation had arrived. They were three: Edward Saunders Rutledge, 42, Mayor of Fort William, who ran a store and built houses; James "Fighting Jim" Con-mee, 57, a firebrand Liberal, once Mayor of Port Arthur and newly elected member for Thunder Bay and Rainy River in Laurier's government; and finally, the man who would do most of the talking, S.C. Young, 39, President of the Fort William Board of Trade, a former CPR conductor and a man of reform convictions within the Liberal Party.[2] The three joined Laurier in his dining car, at a table of sparkling linen and gleaming silver. Laurier said little. Instead, in the manner of a wise politician, he let his visitors use the two hours to lay the eco-nomic opportunity of Fort William before him.

They began prudently, by commending Laurier and his min-isters for establishing policies for opening the West, aiding settle-ment, building railways, and encouraging immigration. "They have brought to all of Canada," S.C. Young said in his clipped and formal manner, "unprecedented prosperity, particularly to that part of the Dominion west of Lake Superior, of which Fort

William is the connecting link between the East and the West."
Young continued: the growth of western prosperity would continue to create a need for more railway construction and more
product manufacturing in the East. "The West," he said, "will
mean an ever-growing market for the product of Canadian
factories." Then, as Rutledge and Conmee nodded in support,
Young pressed home with his vision:

> Prime Minister, we are now witnessing the commencement of
> an era similar to that experienced in the United States when the
> tide of immigration from the Old World flooded into the West-
> ern states. Similar conditions to those which built up Chicago,
> St. Paul, Minneapolis and Duluth, will now build up Winnipeg
> and Fort William.[3]

The optimism around the table that day left no room for doubt.
After all, the land of the West was barely broken but already its
wheat and grain flowed like a mighty river through Fort William, on its way to the markets of the East and the waiting
vessels of Europe. Over 160 million bushels had moved through
in the previous year. The golden era was just beginning.

Shortly before the end of their time with the Prime Minister,
the three men repeated their opinion that the government's
immigration policy was sound, that it should be expanded,
that, to be specific, it should encourage immigration from the
British Isles. "It is a practical and necessary expedient," one of
them told Laurier, "bringing out a class of people who will
speak English and are desirable from all points of view." There
was no mention of bringing more of the men who were already
in Fort William and Port Arthur in such large numbers —
working for a few cents an hour, unloading the grain from the
West and then, staggering like packhorses, moving it into the
holds of trains and vessels that would carry it eastward.

They were immigrants too, mostly Italian, truly essential men
in Fort William's future. There were at that time about 350
Italians in the twin cities. Most lived in a gloomy, swampy
section of Fort William known as the coal dock. There was no
thought of having them represented in the delegation to visit the
Prime Minister, or to sit near the front while he spoke that
afternoon. Only occasionally were they publicly recognized.

The Italian workers, read one editorial in the *Port Arthur Daily News*, were "a horde of ignorant and low-down mongrel swash-bucklers and peanut vendors." The paper did not find it worth-while to report the arrival, the hopes, the ambitions of these uprooted men and their families.

Outside the dining car on that September afternoon in 1905, a silent expectancy filled the streets of Fort William. Barbershops closed; general stores emptied. Here and there, curtains were drawn, locks clicked, and then, just after two o'clock, men in groups of three or four and women moving quickly with chil-dren in tow emerged. They climbed into buggies, or walked along Syndicate Avenue and Brock Street on their way to West-fort, a spare, open space where the Prime Minister was to speak. There, he was to turn the sod for the building of a new railway into Fort William: the Grand Trunk. His speech was brief.

Laurier pointed to the West and said it was not just the place of the prairie but the gateway to the Pacific. Fort William and Port Arthur were also gateways, through which people and produce would flow east and west, today and tomorrow. The future was as golden as the autumn day. "I think and hope," he said, as well-mannered applause rippled through the crowd, "that Providence may spare me a few years more that I may see that hope realized and Fort William and Port Arthur become the Chicago of the North." He sank a small spade into the ground, and announced that the building of the Grand Trunk line through Fort William and Port Arthur was under way.

The flow of men from the hill towns of Italy to the hard soil of the Lakehead had begun years earlier. The men came from a country that offered a rich culture but a poor existence. Italy had a tremendous surplus of people. Moreover, it was young, having been formed less than half a century earlier, and its people, especially those who lived in the poverty-ridden regions south of Rome — Campania, Calabria, Sicily — were caught on a treadmill of poverty. For tens of thousands, emigration — to Argentina, to Australia, to America, to Canada — was not a matter of youthful dreams, but of rational ambition. For many southern Italian young men, emigration was a virtual rite of passage, as much a part of their culture as baptism into the bosom of the faith.

The flow had increased dramatically in 1901 when Canada's economy had suddenly turned buoyant, its outlook optimistic and its need for workers strong. There were jobs to be filled in Fort William and Port Arthur — at the freight yards, the grain elevators, and the coal docks. The men came, as they would for years, hoping to work for a year or two, but staying a lifetime. In 1905, there were hundreds of them, living nine and ten together in plain wood boardinghouses once the properties of earlier settlers who had left the land beside the sheds and elevators for more choice areas. Meanwhile, the predominantly Italian residents lived on narrow lanes with Highland names: McDonald, McTavish, McLaughlin, McIntosh, McLeod, McPherson and McBain. Here, on land segregated by railway tracks and sheds, where life had once been as regular as tea time, a new society was being born, with new rituals, but also with reverence for the country its members had chosen. By the time of Laurier's visit, the Italians of McIntosh and McBain had formed the Societa Italiana Di Benevolenza to help each other make their way in the new country and to become, as their charter put it, "more acceptable to the Great Country that has received us."[4]

The communities of Port Arthur and Fort William in which they earned their meager living were called "the Twin Cities" not only because they were roughly the same size (about four-by-five miles) but because of their similar makeup. Above all, they were alike in character and industry. Each had a majority Anglo-Saxon class which produced the community's leaders in politics, business, and labor. In fact, most of those who held office or headed the small business of both cities were British immigrants. They had begun as laborers themselves in the sheds, yards, and railways, and climbed quickly into leadership, but retained a basic sympathy for the labor movement which had supported them in Britain and given them their start in Canada.

But Port Arthur and Fort William also had a strong segment of European immigrants, roughly a quarter of the total population. Italians were the largest single group, the majority of them in Fort William's coal docks, just steps from where they worked, the remainder on some of Port Arthur's bleaker streets, where their frame houses with tiny windows stood on wet land, and only the occasional spruce tree broke the rocky horizon. The land was low, so that for months at a time, water settled upon it. There was no sewage disposal; in summer the stench fouled the air; in winter the streets and yards were frozen in slabs of ice. There was one tap for the entire district so that in the extreme cold, men with axes hacked at the ice to provide water for the families to drink.

As in Fort William, Port Arthur's immigrant community was also called "the coal docks", and authorities regarded it as a menace to health. But despite the pleas of its residents, that they paid taxes and deserved better, the politicians did nothing to provide basic services. Few of the residents spoke any English. One could only wonder about the inner feelings of these men returning at night to cramped and freezing rooms, men who in those very years, when they formed their benevolent society, described their beloved Italy, the land they had left behind forever, as "a land envied by all nations, the garden of the world."

In the spring that followed Laurier's visit and his historic prediction of 1905, over a thousand men were at work in the railway sheds and grain terminals of both cities — freight handlers who shouldered goods from the ships to the sheds, and from the terminals to the trains. They were called porters or dockers or coal handlers, but whatever the designation, their work was hard, dirty, and long. The pay was about 17 1/2 cents an hour, less than two dollars for a day's work. The trade union movement, strong only in spirit, was struggling to survive within the companies that employed these men.[5]

They would rise long before dawn and troop through the dark to stand in silent clusters in drab clearings near freight sheds, hoping that when the hiring call was made, they would get at least a week's work. Then, just before dawn, a company officer would climb atop a platform, shout out the number of men required for the day, and would fling hundreds of metal disks in every direction over their heads. The men would scramble, shove, and grab for the piece of metal that was the ticket to work. Always, there were far more men than disks, so that Italians were pitted against Italians, as well as other nationalities.[6] Moreover, the companies used a bonus system (usually one cent an hour) paid at the close of the navigation season, but only to those who had worked the entire period. Thus, men were kept from leaving to search for other work, even if it paid better.

But something ominous was taking place in the shacks and streets of the coal docks to which the men returned in the winter evenings of 1905 and 1906. The primitive and degrading hiring practices of the railways and shipping companies were creating a deepening anger that would soon vent itself. There had been minor skirmishes and strikes in the opening years of the century, but now, in early 1906, the anger among the laborers reached its depth. It was about to erupt into some of the ugliest episodes in Canadian history.

In the final week of April, 1906, the freight handlers at the Canadian Northern Railway sheds in Port Arthur, about one hundred and twenty-five men in all, submitted a petition to the railway's local superintendent. They asked for a raise of five cents an hour, bringing their regular rate to twenty-five cents an hour on weekdays and thirty cents an hour in the evenings and on Sundays. The superintendent told them their demands were highly unreasonable. If they struck, he said, he would have no trouble bringing in workers from Winnipeg to take their places. The chief of the railway police and the chief of Fort William's city police were advised to keep an eye on things.[7]

Then on May 4, W.A. Brown, General Superintendent of the CNR, arrived in Port Arthur from Winnipeg, told the men that their demands could not be met, and that they should return to work at the regular rate. They did. A local paper reported a little prematurely, but with satisfaction: "General Superintendent W.A. Brown came, saw and conquered."

A few months later, on October 1, when the cities were feeling the first grip of frost, a day when a travelling evangelistic team from Toronto called Crossley and Hunter began a revival campaign at St. Andrew's Presbyterian church, the men at both the

CNR sheds in Port Arthur and the CPR sheds in Fort William, suddenly walked out en masse. In all, several hundred men were on strike, once again seeking an increase of five cents an hour. They encouraged others to walk out in sympathy — machinists, elevator men, even city workers. "The strike," wrote one reporter from the *Daily News*, "from its commencement, threatened to spread until today (October 1) at noon, the situation had developed proportions of a stupendous nature." Within days one thousand men were out.

The people of Port Arthur and Fort William had other events and issues to which they would have preferred to give their attention in those October days. But the strike overwhelmed their communities because of its strength of numbers. And for the first time, violence seemed to lurk in the air. A few minutes past one o'clock in the afternoon of the strike's first day, a number of Italian freight handlers gathered at the site of a civic excavation — a local improvement project — and began to explain their plight to fellow countrymen working for the city. They urged them to lay down their tools in sympathy. "About this time," reported the *Daily News*, which took a dim view of both Italians and strikers,

> Officer Charles Symons appeared on the scene and unaccompanied sprang into the midst of the yelling mob. The presence of the officer for a moment had a quieting effect on the Italians. But it was for a moment only. One of the mob, all of whom had receded from their advanced position back to the station platform, advanced in a defiant attitude toward the officer. Symons didn't scare. Leaping from a rock he closed with one Italian and threw him to the ground. The officer, having drawn his baton, and receiving another instrument of defense in the shape of a 6-shooter from the CPR offices, the mob slinked away.

There was no evidence that any of the strikers used or threatened to use a weapon. A few probably had knives and clubs, believing they would need them if conflict broke out. Nonetheless, the excitable *Daily News* editor attacked the laborers for using their weapons as an offensive threat:

> There are however, features to the lockout which command attention. The chief of these is the circumstance that among the

strikers are a majority of foreigners, chiefly Italians, who are reported to have prepared to meet opposition to their demands at the point of the knife, the national weapon of the 'dago'. . . .

On the following morning, a Tuesday, the air was deceptively calm and clear. CPR Superintendent G.R. Bury of Winnipeg arrived at noon at the Fort William station. With him were four railway cars filled with strikebreakers.

Suddenly, Bury's car and those holding the strikebreakers were surrounded by about a hundred Italian laborers, who had come running from their homes in the coal docks after word had spread that, once again, the CPR was importing strike-breakers. They drew their homemade weapons, mostly clubs; a few had rifles. The railway police ordered them to clear the way for the strikebreakers. They refused. The police began firing. The men scattered behind sheds and barricades and returned the fire. Over a hundred shots were fired, in what the papers called, "a reign of terror." Two strikers were injured and one police officer. Finally, after ammunition ran out, the shooting ceased and the mobs dispersed. Port Arthur and Fort William were in hysteria. Fort William mayor E.S. Rutledge appealed for volunteer police officers to help maintain the peace. But then, as suddenly as it had blown up, the conflict subsided.

The mayor and one of his councillors, both former labor men, urged Superintendent Bury of the CPR to make a conces-sion on the issue of pay. The rate of 17 $1/2$ cents an hour for day work and 20 cents for nights, became 20 cents and 22 $1/2$ cents. On October fourth, the men were back at work.

But despite the modest increase and the exterior calm of the next few months, the men seethed. Through the blizzards of winter and the insect-ridden days of summer, tension grew stronger. The events of October had shown the Italian laborers that the compan-ies viewed strikebreaking — with its imported labor and armed police — as a routine way of treating the demand of their workers for a decent wage. But something else had been impressed upon them: shot at by the police and insulted by the newspapers simply because of their heritage, they were regarded as the enemy by some of the Anglo-Saxon leaders of the Lakehead. The atmo-sphere was set for the explosions to come.

On the morning of August 9, 1909, when the drizzle that had fallen all night made the houses of the coal docks almost invisible in the grey light, five hundred men, mostly Italian, working in the freight sheds of Fort William, walked out. Despite the three-cent raise of 1906, their wage was back where it began, the result of a company edict. The walkout was orderly. Bosco Dominico, a bright young Italian interpreter who had once worked in the courts but whose English had made him a leader in the coal docks, put the case of the strikers in temperate words.

> All men of all nationalities are on strike in the CPR freight sheds in Fort William. It came to the time when they were not getting enough wages for the work they were doing. And they were not being treated right. Now, to secure better conditions, they are trying to organize a union. They intend to give the company fair treatment. If the company will give the men the small raise asked for, the men will be thankful, for living here is very high, and they work hard for the money they are asking for. The men also ask the CPR to recognize the union.

Thus began another of the six strikes of the freight handlers between 1902 and 1912.

For three days, hundreds paraded quietly, sometimes singing the songs of the old country, up McTavish Street, along a section of CPR track, down McLaughlin, along McNaughton, and up McTavish again. The drizzle lifted, the air lightened and the August sun fell like a benediction through the trees in front of their small houses. In the evenings they sat on their front steps singing, smoking, and talking. "The strike," commented one local journalist, "is remarkable for the absence of disorder."

The authorities may not have noticed, however, that despite their good nature, the men kept a keen eye out for those they viewed as the enemy. Several of them checked the arrival of each train in Fort William, ready to signal every Italian laborer in the coal docks should one be carrying the armed railway police mobilized in almost deliberate provocation against them. On a Thursday morning shortly after 10:30, a rail car holding twenty armed CPR police pulled into the station.

The first shot, according to impartial witnesses, was fired by the company police. Once again, the workers understood that they were indeed the enemy, to be put down by any means. That first shot reinforced the belief of many Fort William and Port Arthur citizens, that the CPR was not only an oppressive employer, but in the matter of a strike, a blundering one.

Within minutes after the first shot, McTavish and McDonald Streets were battlefields, with the railway police out of control and scores of Italian laborers taking up positions with rifles, shotguns and revolvers. They drove the police toward the railway bunkhouse. They shelled the building and smashed every window. They were ready to storm it when, in a momentary lull, Fort William's Police Chief, who commanded a measure of trust, appealed for a truce. It was temporary.

Into the evening, the firing erupted again and again, until over a dozen men were wounded, and the fact that no one was killed seemed a tribute to the good fortune of poor marksmanship. "Lawlessness such as caused the streets of Paris to run with blood at the inception of the French Revolution," screamed the frantic *Times-Journal*, "prevailed all morning in the coal dock district."

By mid-afternoon, the mayor, L.L. Peltier, had read the Riot Act, which was also carried that evening on the front page of the *Times-Journal*: "Our sovereign Lord the King, charges and commands all persons being assembled to disperse and peaceably to depart to their habitation or to their lawful business upon the pain of being guilty of an offence on conviction of which they may be sentenced to imprisonment for life." The whole day long — Friday, August 13 — the air cracked with wartime tension; soldiers paced the coal docks streets, officers met in groups of three and four, and messengers darted through backyards, as if picking their way through the trenches.

It was the mayor, a fair if somewhat naive man, who brought a rough and temporary peace to Fort William. On Sunday afternoon, August 15, at the corner of McTavish and McIntyre Streets, Mayor Peltier climbed upon a makeshift platform of two packing cases and, looking over the crowd of men that stretched beyond his view, pleaded with weary sincerity.

First he appealed for order, not just on behalf of Fort William, but on behalf of the men and their economic future. Then, he explained that he had met with officials of the company, who had assured him that they were ready, on condition that the men returned to work, to have the issues of wages and the hated bonus sent to an arbitration board. The officials would abide by its decision. "My dear fellow citizens," pleaded Peltier, his voice ragged, "return to your jobs. Trust the government to give you justice and the Mayor to help you all he can. The company has given me its word and name signed that it will do all I say to you and I promise you that it will keep its agreement." The following morning, the men obediently returned to work.

In weeks, a conciliation board did consider the issues. It found in favor of the men on all counts. Throughout Fort William and Port Arthur, the news surprised no one, for support for the men was widespread from the business community, the pulpit, and newspapers from outside the Lakehead. "The surprise," said a paper in Winnipeg that week, "is that more than 1,000 able-bodied men can be found regularly applying for this work on the basis on which it is conducted when the whole West is demanding labor on a more normal basis." Throughout the winter of 1909 and the early months of 1910, the spirit of the coal docks community seemed raised by apparent victory.

But in the first weeks of early spring, at the opening of the new shipping season, there came an announcement that shattered the new optimism: the CPR said it would cease hiring Italians. Mayor Peltier's trust had been misplaced; the company had agreed to conciliation to get the men back to work, to get goods moving, knowing that if it did not like the findings of the conciliation board, it would simply refuse work to Italian laborers.

Thus in April, 1910, the Italian laborers of Fort William and Port Arthur stood by as imported labor, mostly from the West, arrived to do the work Italian immigrants had been promised. If any thought of venting their anger, the CPR police were at the ready. "The police department of the CPR is organized this year," said its chief, "and just now enough constables would be mustered to compete with a bunch of soldiers, let alone a bunch of foreigners who would not stop running if they saw a redcoat walking down the coal docks streets."

Two years passed before the CPR began once more to hire Italian immigrant workers, in April of 1912. It was destined to be the bloodiest of all seasons, this time at the coal docks of Port Arthur; the employer was the CNR. As before, the issue was pay. The men asked for an increase of about five cents an hour, which was rejected in the second week of July. On July 29, when the papers were full of the findings of an inquiry into the sinking of the *Titanic*, the men struck. About two hundred went out and passed the day parading calmly through the streets of their neighborhood. Late Monday afternoon, an Italian striker named Tony Shumacke was on picket duty along with a hundred others on Fort William Road, near the entrance to the CNR coal dock. Two men, apparently imported strikebreakers, tried to cross the line at Shumacke's position. He turned them away. But a Port Arthur police constable, John Silliker, tried to arrest him. Immediately, Silliker was surrounded by angry strikers, some with clubs, who demanded he release Shumacke. Silliker did so and quickly departed for the police station to summon help. In minutes a car arrived carrying Police Chief Angus McLellan and five constables. McLellan got out first.

For a moment he stood silently surveying the strikers and the gathering, silent crowd. Then he strode over to Shumacke, intent on arresting him. One of Shumacke's neighbors, a tall, muscular man of thirty named Domenic Deprenzo, who was carrying a water-soaked club, went to Shumacke's side. McLellan placed his arm on Shumacke's shoulder. There was pushing and shoving, and suddenly, McLellan was on the ground bleeding from a club wound. Constable Hjalmar Peterson grabbed his pistol. He shot at Deprenzo once, twice. The worst riot in the history of Fort William and Port Arthur was under way.

Meanwhile, in another part of the city, a Baptist preacher, the Reverend W. Madison Hicks, a visitor to Port Arthur and a man famous for his socialist convictions and oratorical prowess, was leading a parade. Two hundred men, most of them Italian, were shouting slogans, singing songs, and marching to the beat of the Italian band. Hicks, a dapper man with a flowing mane of hair, was waving to the crowd along Arthur Street, when suddenly he was met by Port Arthur's mayor, S.W. Ray. Ray was flushed with anger. He had just heard of the violence at the coal docks and suspected it had been incited by Hicks' presence in Port Arthur. He ordered him to disband the parade: under the Riot Act, he told Hicks, any such parade was unlawful. Hicks listened courteously, but, knowing that the wisest course of action was to keep the marchers together and prevent them from heading to the coal docks, he told Ray he would lead them to another, safer section of the city. As the Italian band struck up a Souza march and the parade changed direction, the events at the coal docks turned ugly.

The police constables who had accompanied their now-wounded chief — Peterson, Silliker, Thurlow, Burleigh, and York — were in a pitched battle with the strikers. Most of the strikers stood back passively almost as if, despite their rage, they were unwilling to throw punches, much less swing clubs. A small number, their frustrations at the years of humiliation boiling over, stood their ground, and then closed in for battle.

The police met the strikers' clubs with gunshots. Peterson had fired three times on Domenic Deprenzo but Deprenzo was on his feet, still wielding his club. Peterson shot him again, and then again, the fifth shot hitting Deprenzo in the abdomen. Deprenzo fell, whereupon his brother Nicholas raised his club and started for the constable. But suddenly, horrified, he saw another officer rush to his brother and hold him erect while Peterson took aim and fired. Peterson turned and shot Nicholas too, hitting him in the leg. Both brothers were bleeding profusely — Domenic from six shots, Nicholas from three. The chief of police and three of his officers were heavily bruised from club wounds. Throughout the city, panicking residents barricaded themselves in.

In the hospital that evening, just after 7:30, a surgeon named Donald Williamson bent over Domenic Deprenzo. Amazingly, Deprenzo was still conscious when brought into the operating room. Williamson removed the bullets that remained in Deprenzo's abdomen, and sutured the wounds — one in each shoulder, one in the foot, the knee, the groin, and chest. Turning to Nicholas Deprenzo, he plucked the bullets from three places and sewed up four wounds. Domenic Deprenzo remained in hospital for two weeks, his brother for a month. Chief Angus McLellan was released and back at work a week later. While the Deprenzos lay in hospital with injuries that kept them close to death, the police drew up charges of attempted murder against both.

By the evening of that same day, Madison Hicks had led the marchers to an open field and spoken to them of the just nature of their cause, counseled them against violence, and dismissed them with the plea that they return to their homes. An hour or so after midnight, Hicks left the Port Arthur police station. He had been served with a summons and charged with "causing a tumultuous assembly". Though Hicks had marched the laborers away from the scene of violence and successfully urged them to disperse, he was too convenient a scapegoat to be ignored. Next morning, a Friday, at ten o'clock, the slight clergyman, wearing gold-rimmed glasses and the socialists' red tie, rose before the crowded benches in the station to hear the charges read against him:

"That Madison Hicks is responsible for causing a tumultuous assembly to congregate in the city of Port Arthur, . . . that he did march the assembly and invite others to join it, which action was likely to promote a breach of the public peace, such action being also to the fear of citizens living in the vicinity of the tumultuous assembly," and on and on, in terms almost Dickensian. Hicks' powerful voice filled the courtroom: "I am not guilty."

The crown prosecutor called the mayor, S.W. Ray, who recounted his version of the events. Following Ray, Hicks rose and moved to the front of the dock. As a clergyman and a pacifist, he explained, he would not initiate violence nor contribute to it as the charge indicated. As he spoke, a couple of his followers, standing in the entry to the crowded room, began to shout their support. Hicks turned quickly and rebuked them, urging that they recognize the decorum of the court. Even the magistrate looked at him with respect; Hicks was committed nonetheless to stand trial in the same session of the high court that would hear the evidence against Domenic and Nicholas Deprenzo.[7]

The trial of the Deprenzo brothers, by judge and jury, opened on Tuesday, October 8, at 10 a.m., presided over by the dour Mr. Justice Middleton of the Supreme Court of Ontario.[8] The prosecution was conducted by H.D. Gamble, K.C., an eloquent lawyer whose reputation extended well beyond Port Arthur and Fort William. Domenic and Nicholas Deprenzo were represented by A.E. Cole. Cole's name and appearance bespoke his Anglo-Saxon heritage, but his sympathies were widely known to be with the laborers and the immigrants of the Twin Cities.

When Judge Middleton entered the dim courtroom, he looked out on the smattering of spectators — a small turnout, even considering the cold, pelting rain that blew in gusts against the narrow windows. Listening to the witnesses — mostly policemen — Middleton occasionally glanced at these windows; more often he stared at a sheet of foolscap in front of him, scribbling notes as the story of the incidents at the coal docks unfolded.

The first to speak was John Silliker, the large, raw-boned man who had been on the police force during the riot but had subsequently left to take up carpentry. He explained how, on the evening of July 29, at about 5:40, he got word of trouble brewing in the coal docks. He found little trouble when he arrived, about a hundred men standing around or picketing. Suddenly, Silliker said, he saw Tony Shumacke, a striker, move toward the railway office to prevent two strikers from entering. He approached Shumacke. In the face of strong objection from the defendants' attorney, Silliker claimed he had felt a gun in Shumacke's pocket. "Come with me," he said to Shumacke, "You're under arrest."

Silliker went on to describe the tumult from which he retreated to the Port Arthur police station for reinforcements. At 7:30 p.m. he was back, this time with five others, including Police Chief Angus McLellan. Silliker reported that McLellan strode up to a group of strikers demanding that they hand over their clubs (pieces of whittled wood the strikers insisted were made for sport, but also, if needed, for self-defense). Many gave them up. Then Silliker tried to arrest Shumacke once again. On McLellan's orders, Silliker took Shumacke to the paddy wagon. The strikers, incensed that Shumacke could be arrested for resisting strikebreakers, surrounded McLellan, shouting and shoving. A tall, dark Italian, Domenic Deprenzo, moved to the centre of the melee. Someone — never identified for certain — struck McLellan, who began bleeding profusely. Immediately, an officer armed with a .32 revolver opened up. He pumped ten bullets at Deprenzo, six of which found their mark.

When police officer Harold Burleigh took the stand, he testified that when Nicholas Deprenzo saw his brother writhing on the ground he took off after the officer who had fired. At this point, Burleigh began to shoot at Nicholas. He fired four shots, he said, at a range of about six feet, two of them hitting Nicholas Deprenzo and crippling him.

The string of witnesses extended into the gloomy afternoon. Gusts of rain beat against the windows, almost drowning the words of Mike Pento, the union's president, who gave his testimony in a voice so low even the translator strained to hear him.

"There were," Pento recalled, "about one hundred and fifty men. Maybe two hundred. The police chief said to drop the sticks. He took them away. He had quite a bundle. Then they went for Shumacke, to arrest him. I said to the chief, 'This man has done nothing.' He said to me, 'That makes no difference.' Then I saw nothing until the chief was knocked down. All the police were suddenly shouting and shooting. Domenic had no club. But they shot him. Then he fell. I heard him scream to his brother 'Come and help me. I am dying . . . ' "

Others that day testified that, in fact, the police had not only opened fire first, but, in the case of the Deprenzo brothers, had acted with wild abandon. When Nicholas Deprenzo stood in the dock, he too, recalled his brother screaming on the ground. He described how, at that moment, a policeman went to his wounded brother and held him erect, so that another officer could take better aim: "One of the police raised my brother from the ground. He held him sitting up. Then a police shot him again."

There were those in the courtroom who felt that under the circumstances revealed, Judge Middleton could not help but feel that the Deprenzos — who had no guns and were even said to have had no clubs — had been wronged. But if Middleton agreed he gave no sign. While he took copious notes as the policemen spoke, he took none at all while the Deprenzos testified, and none while their lawyer A.E. Cole made his rather curious defense.

Cole, speaking quietly, and with an air of resignation, told Judge Middleton that the Deprenzos should be objects of sympathy. They did not know the laws. They did not speak the language. As he put it, they were rough, coarse, and uneducated. They were peasants from southern Italy. Their only advantage was that they had strong frames. That made them valuable acquisitions to Canada, he concluded.

By five o'clock that afternoon, Nicholas Deprenzo had given the last testimony. He had explained that he had no club, that he had gone to the aid of his brother, that he had been shot several times, the final shot hitting him in the hand that reached toward his brother; that he had been hospitalized many weeks, near death.

When Deprenzo stepped down, Judge Middleton shifted slightly on the bench, and turning to one side, gave his instructions to the jury, advising them on the points of law they should keep in mind as they weighed the evidence and considered the verdict. The point they must keep in mind, he said, was that foreigners must not be allowed to take the law into their own hands. Foreigners, he stressed, must not be permitted to throw aside the customs of civilized society. It must be brought home to them that violence would not be tolerated.

The jury reached its verdict quickly: guilty of resisting arrest and unlawfully wounding. On October 9, Middleton sentenced each of the Deprenzo brothers to ten years in prison. The following day, the jury also found the Reverend Madison Hicks guilty of having held a riotous procession. Middleton gave him a suspended sentence. Later that week, Domenic Deprenzo, 30, and Nicholas Deprenzo, 25, were put aboard the CPR for the desolate village of Stoney Mountain, a train stop fourteen miles north of Winnipeg, where a penitentiary had been built in the midst of the stone quarries. Each would serve his full ten years.

On the day they left, their fellow immigrants in the coal docks — who would fight for years to have them released — filed a petition with the municipality of Port Arthur, requesting that something be done about the dreadful conditions of the services in their community. Their petition was duly noted in the Port Arthur *Daily News*, with no list of the men and women who had filed it. It said simply that the petition had been signed by "twenty unpronounceable names."

The Reverend James Shaver, a lean man of thirty-five, whose serious face was warmed by friendly eyes, stepped down from the train in Fort William that tumultuous autumn of 1912. It was only a few years since he had been ordained to the Methodist ministry. He and his wife, whom he met while she was studying at Queen's University, were both dedicated Christians and reformers. She had accompanied him many evenings, summer and winter, on his visits to the poor near Fred Victor Mission in Toronto, where he had a small room.

In Toronto, Shaver was the man chosen by Methodist leaders when, in 1912, in the wake of the labor unrest, they decided that their ministry to the immigrant community of the Lakehead had to be strengthened. In cooperation with Fort William's affluent Wesley Church, they planned to open a mission in the coal docks, to be called Wesley Institute, and designated Shaver its director. He was, first and foremost, a minister dedicated not to the well-to-do, but to helping the disadvantaged and working to change the economic system which he, and other democratic socialists like him, felt to be unfair.[9]

In the early years of the twentieth century, there were many young ministers, usually Methodists, who saw in Christianity not only the way of salvation, but the way of societal improvement. One who had influenced Shaver greatly was a fellow minister in Winnipeg, James S. Woodsworth. Woodsworth worked among the immigrants of that city in All People's Mission, until he left (and was succeeded at the Mission by his friend Shaver) to help launch a federal political party, the Cooperative Commonwealth Federation, later to become the New Democratic Party; he was the first leader of the CCF.

Shaver began his mission work in a Fort William frame house and converted pool room beside it, set alongside a broom factory on McTavish Street in the coal docks. He brought with him a progressive, enlightened attitude and a readiness to work hard for the creation of a better society — one in which poverty would be replaced by opportunity, and the abundant life of the gospel would flourish. His approach to Italian workers was the approach taken by the brightest and best of his generation, and expressed clearly by the leader of the social reformers of the day, the Reverend James Woodsworth.

In 1909, Woodsworth wrote a small booklet outlining his beliefs concerning Canada's bursting immigrant population: *The Stranger Within Our Gates*. In it, he discussed immigration not so much as a national opportunity but as a national problem: "There is a danger and it is national," wrote The Reverend J.W. Sparling, Principal of the Methodist Church's Wesley College of Winnipeg, in the introduction. "Either we must educate and elevate the incoming multitudes, or they will drag us and our children down to the lowest level. We must see to it that the civilization and ideals of Southeastern Europe are not transplanted to and perpetuated on our virgin soil." Woodsworth himself wrote that "We need more of our own blood, to assist us to maintain in Canada our British traditions and to mould the incoming armies of foreigners into loyal British subjects."

When James Shaver wrote that he went to Fort William because the city had a "terrible foreign problem on her hands" and that Methodists were anxious to tackle it, he was in line with the advanced thinking of his day: Italians were the raw, rough material out of which, if Anglo Saxons applied their best efforts, outstanding citizens could be made. Immigrants should be given the opportunity to learn, to adapt, to become above all part of the middle class of Canada, shaped on the anvil of Anglo-Saxon values and Protestant virtue, just as Shaver and the reformers had been shaped. The foreign problem, as Shaver called it, would vanish in the broad brotherhood he and others envisioned: "Every move we make is toward the end of bringing the foreigner and the Canadian together."

If, in this coming together, the customs and culture of the immigrant were lost or diminished, at least his lot in life — his economic well-being — would be improved. While Shaver's approach was colored by his generation and his upbringing — he saw assimilation of Italians as in their welfare — he was different from many other Protestants of the day. Most leaders of Protestantism were alarmed at the enormous increases in the foreign populations of Fort William and Port Arthur. Shaver had scarcely begun his work when a delegate to an assembly of the Presbyterian Church in Toronto said: "Either we must raise them or they will lower us; we must 'Christianize' them, or they will 'paganize' us."

For his part, Shaver, in his nine difficult, rewarding years in Fort William and Port Arthur, never gave in to such fear, nor did he lose his affection and optimism for the Italian immigrants. He welcomed them, worked with them, helped them in their homes and in their disputes, even those that went before the courts. He did not try to win converts; in fact he went out of his way to assure Catholic priests — often indifferent to the social needs of their people — that he had no interest in stealing their flock. Shaver once told some friends that Canadians too easily believed they were the chosen people and that others were inferior: "The workman calls him a 'damned dago', and even the clergy speak of the 'poor, ignorant foreigner.'"

Almost every evening, dozens of Italian men and women entered the peeling buildings on McTavish Street. Some took English classes in the cheerful front room. Others crowded into the smaller rooms upstairs where women from the city's churches spoke of the value of schooling and showed pictures of missionary work in Africa. By the end of 1913, over five hundred people, adults and children both, were regular visitors to Wayside, some for its educational programs based on English and Civics texts drawn up by Shaver, others for floor hockey or basketball. Wayside had a point of view: Anglo-Saxon, Canadian, and Protestant. But it was then the only institution in the

Lakehead that saw in Italian immigrants, virtually all of them
Roman Catholic, men and women of dignity and purpose.
"Among them," wrote Shaver in 1914, "are many of God's first
gentlemen, seeking, groping, longing for their place in this first
democracy which will never be perfect until they have found
that place."

In the same year that James Shaver was establishing The Wayside Mission in Fort William, an eighteen-year-old named
Hubert Badani left Azzano Decimo, a small Italian town surrounded by brown fields and modest vineyards about three
hundred kilometres north west of Milan, in the region of Friuli.[10]
He had heard his priest say in a sermon that more young people
should emigrate to Canada, for it was the land of opportunity.
Badani was the son of a prosperous businessman, a food caterer
who often worked abroad, but since he was an ambitious boy
who saw little ahead of him, he took his priest's advice. In the
late spring of 1913, he pooled his savings with a contribution
from his father, and bought a ticket on the *Olympic*, sailing from
Milan for New York. He was about a week from New York,
when standing at the rail one sun-filled morning, he fell into
conversation with a few fellow passengers, also from Friuli.
    "So you are on your way to Canada," one said with keen
optimism. "Yes," replied the younger man, "I can hardly wait. I
am going all the way across Canada, to Vancouver."
    The others paused, then together they told Badani of their
plan to go to a city called Fort William, where many people
from Friuli already lived.
    "You should come with us," they argued. "Then, if you don't
like it, you can move later. It is on the way to Vancouver."
    Badani smiled and gazed at the breaking waves. Then he
looked up quickly and nodded. His decision that day to go to
Fort William would have an influence Badani could not have
imagined — upon his own life and the lives of thousands of
others in the Twin Cities and, as well, in the town he left behind.
    In Fort William, Hubert Badani caught the eye not only of the
Italians who had preceded him, but of others who saw in him a
certain native wisdom they respected and a personality they

liked. He seemed destined not for labor but for leadership. Badani went to work immediately in construction, but in December 1915 he enlisted in the 94th batallion and went overseas. There he stayed for four years, working as an interpreter, for along with Italian and English, he also spoke German. When the war ended in 1918 he worked for a time as a construction foreman, building bridges in outlying Ontario communities with men he had rounded up around Port Arthur. By 1920, he was ready to settle in Fort William and make his home there.

That year Vincent Dolcetti, who had come to Port Arthur from Azzano Decimo, approached him with a business proposition: partnership in Dolcetti's Port Arthur automotive business. Badani began his lifelong and prosperous career in automotive sales and service: he and his sons would run Kam Motors (after the Kaministikwia River) for well over 60 years.

As Badani prospered, people close to him noticed that he spent more and more of his time at a number of projects for which he received no financial return. Some involved his fellow Italian immigrants, but most had to do with broader community work — the Church, YMCA, Red Cross, The Rotary Club, and The Chamber of Commerce. But beyond these, Badani developed one of his own: helping hundreds of his fellow Friulani come to Canada, often to Fort William and Port Arthur. "They are," he told his friends in business, "ideal people, genuine, and faithful. They are not after the entertainments, but after work. I don't sponsor them as such; I just suggest they come as I did — and take their chances." Great numbers did, many settling for an entire lifetime in Fort William and Port Arthur and — in the style of many northern Italians — launching themselves in businesses that employed their countrymen.

In the late thirties, a number of Badani's friends, mostly in the business and service organizations in which he had been active, urged him to run for the Fort William City Council; Badani sat as the city's first Italian-born alderman for a decade. In 1948, he stood for mayor, won, and held office for four successive terms. While still mayor, he received a call one winter's day in 1958 from C.D. Howe, the formidable Liberal minister and MP from Port Arthur in Louis St. Laurent's government.

"Hubert," said Howe from his Ottawa office, "I want to see you soon. I'll be in Port Arthur on the weekend. Can we get together?"

They met at Howe's constituency office. Fort William's Liberal MP, The Reverend Dan McIvor, who was over eighty years old, would not be running for re-election. Prime Minister St. Laurent and C.D. Howe wanted Badani to seek the nomination, which, given his popularity, would be assured. Before he left Howe's office, Badani had given his assent. On a rainy evening in June, 1958 — on which John Diefenbaker's Conservatives swept the country and nine Liberal ministers, including C.D. Howe, from office — Hubert Badani was elected. He would be elected four more times until he chose to retire, surrounded by respect and affection, in 1972. In over thirty years of standing for office, he had never been defeated.

During his retirement, Badani was singularly active. He exercised at the YMCA every day into his nineties, and advised old friends and former constituents in his office above the family business.

Often in early spring, he left Thunder Bay to visit Azzano Decimo, the town he had left over 70 years before and where he was honored with dinners and medals and citations. When Badani was ninety years old, a Canadian who found himself in Azzano Decimo, fell into conversation with a leader of the community. He was asked if he had ever met a man in Canada named Hubert Badani. "There is no man like him," the visitor was told. "A man of deep goodness. You know, every Christmas a gift comes to the town from him — a gift of a million lira."

CHAPTER THREE

BUILDING ONTARIO: THE WARD AND JAMES FRANCESCHINI

Victoria Day in Toronto in 1912 was clear and the sun was high. In the neighborhood of Rosedale, the gardens were bright with bloom and the morning streets perfumed with the scent of tulip, lilac and falling forsythia. By noon, the silence which rested like a Sabbath hand upon the city began gradually to vanish. Streetcars, their windows open, their seats crammed with parents and children, clanked in from the city's new suburbs of Deer Park and Wychwood, as families made their way to High Park, to the Island, to Hanlan's Point, where children would race, mothers would watch, and fathers — in high collars and wide suspenders — would savor a cigar. In the evening, they would listen to the Salvation Army Band performing in the open air. Then, as the sun began to fade, they would head once again for the electric car, not to go directly home, but to cool off by riding it right around the belt line — along King, up Sherbourne, over Bloor and down Spadina — all for five cents each. Then, relaxed by the hour's ride, satisfied by those small pleasures of the day, they would head off into the soft spring evening.

Roughly 450,000 people lived in the city in 1912, most of them of British origin or ancestry, giving Toronto an energetic but no-nonsense character and a style subdued to the point of dullness. Aside from Massey Hall, there were few places of

47

serious entertainment, so that a visiting scholar, Ernest Jones
(later the renowned biographer of Sigmund Freud) was prod-
ded to write "it was the dead uniformity that I found so tedious.
One knew beforehand everyone's opinion on every subject, so
there was a complete lack of mental stimulation or exchange of
thought."[1] A generation earlier, in the 1880s, Mayor William
Howland waged such war on sin that the city would be known
forever after as Toronto the Good. Howland's concerns were
reflected in C.S. Clark's book *Of Toronto the Good* in which
Clark worried for many pages about men and women slipping
down to the lakeshore to the immoral pleasures of the boat-
houses: "Houses of ill-fame in Toronto? Certainly not. The
whole city is an immense house of ill-fame, the roof of which is
the blue canopy of heaven during the summer months."[2] The
Victorian moralism of Howland, Clark, and thousands of other
citizens would influence the city for decades to come; in 1912,
Toronto banned Sunday tobogganing in its city parks.

On that holiday evening in 1912, there were hundreds of
other Toronto families whose festive spirit was subdued or lacking entirely, not because of any prim Anglo-Saxon heritage, but
because they felt themselves to be strangers in a strange city,
people who lived on the edge of the city's cold reserve. On
Victoria Day, some of them trailed home alone in the greying
evening, pushing their hurdy-gurdies or peanut stands. They
were Italian, and they were from a neighborhood in the city
known as The Ward.

The Ward was a community of narrow, obscure streets near
City Hall, crowded and heavily Jewish but increasingly Italian,
and bounded to the north by College Street, to the south by
Queen, to the west by University and to the east by Yonge.[3]
Toronto had other Italian settlements — Little Italies, they were
called — farther to the west along College, and to the north near
Dufferin and Davenport. But from the early days of the 1880s, it
was this community that was home to most Italians.

The Ward was also the centre of several controversies, and the
cause of certain persistent worries among Toronto's politicians,
bureaucrats, inspectors, and clergy. A leading Presbyterian clergyman, J.G. Shearer, expressed his concern to the highest body

of the Presbyterian Church, meeting in 1913 in Toronto: "We do not need to go six blocks away from Massey Hall, Toronto, to find a whole city full of people that are at any rate non-Anglo-Saxon, a large proportion of them non-Christian, and a goodly number of them whether non-Anglo-Saxon or Anglo-Saxon, pagan in life . . ."[4]

While just over 1,000 Italians lived permanently in The Ward, so many others came and went that the entire Italian population, at peak periods, was estimated at around 14,000. The itinerant sojourners would spend quiet winters in Toronto and in spring they would be gone, perhaps as many as 10,000 moving on to the United States, or to northern Ontario, for railroad, mine, or logging work. Those who remained lived in small and crowded houses, on unpaved streets with names such as Centre, Chestnut, Elizabeth and Terauley. Here and there among them were entrepreneurs who would open fruit stores or pasta factories or boardinghouses, but for the most part, the men from The Ward were in construction: working on the streets, putting in sewers, or, even more often, helping to rebuild the city in brick, in the wake of the great Toronto fire of 1904.

From the beginning, the people of Toronto were bothered by The Ward and its residents. They disliked several things: the tendency of these foreigners to live among their own people, thus maintaining a close community; their habit of clinging to their cultural traditions in music and cuisine; their social style, including their strange habit of standing in clusters in the evening on the streetcorners, in lively conversation in their own language. And perhaps Torontonians were haunted by the old stereotype of violent behavior. Just before the turn of the century, the Toronto writer Goldwin Smith remarked: "There are scatterings of other races, the last arrived being the Italian with his grinding-organ and, we hope, without his knife."[5]

Usually the men of The Ward worked outside its boundaries, many leaving home while it was still night to push their empty carts southward along Elizabeth and then University, to Union Station. A few years earlier, many of their friends had done the bullwork on the station's foundations and walls as well as the finer masonry on the columns and cornices. There, waiting for the trains from which they would load their carts with potatoes, carrots, beets, and tomatoes, they would talk of family and home. It took a special courage for these men to try to earn a pittance of a living in a land that was deeply strange, in a language they did not grasp, and in a line of work that was far from their ideal. Their outward manner masked a thousand feelings. "The largest British city in Canada," wrote the London writer Rupert Brooke of Toronto during a visit at the time, "in spite of the cheery Italian faces that pop up at you out of excavations in the street . . ."[6]

One day in the autumn of 1912, the people in The Ward noticed a strange woman, a bright-eyed matron with a brisk step, striding earnestly along Walton and Elizabeth Streets. She carried a small notebook. From time to time she stopped, peering into the windows of barbershops and the doorways of fruit stores, beside kosher shops of the Jewish Shocket, from which the smell of fresh lamb and the cluck of chickens floated out to the hot sun-baked street. Sometimes she smiled as she scribbled, then walked on, satisfaction on her face.

Her name was Margaret Bell. She was a journalist, who, that autumn, was on an assignment for the *Canadian Magazine*, a publication which appeared regularly in the city and was read, for the most part, by business and professional people. She spent many days in The Ward — spread over a few months — and while she was not seen actually interviewing anyone, either Jewish or Italian, she took many notes and made many observations. Most of all, Margaret Bell formed a great many impressions, or clarified her previous impressions of The Ward. When it appeared, her article on The Ward was called "Toronto's Melting Pot"; it began with a description of one of the Jewish shops of The Ward, into whose window Margaret Bell had peered several weeks earlier. "You glance up at the shop-keeper as he comes to the door," she wrote, "rubbing his soft hands and showing two rows of yellowish teeth . . . 'Won't you step inside? You need not buy. There are plenty of things — very beautiful things, which are not displayed in the window. And it costs nothing to look. . . .' But you do not trust the cunning shopkeeper who stands in the door, rubbing his hands and showing his yellowish teeth."[77]

It was not, of course, the Jews of The Ward, or the other small immigrant groups, including some Chinese and even Blacks — descendents of slaves who escaped to Canada — who most interested Margaret Bell. She was drawn to the Italians, and throughout her article she sketched them in terms that were revealing not just of them, but of her and the feelings of her community toward Italians. She recalled, she wrote, the Italian operas and the great singers who had graced them. How ironic, she went on, that they came from such a people as she saw swinging pick axes and peddling fruit in The Ward: "There they are, a whole hundred of them, bare-armed, bare-necked, sturdy, brown fellows, forming a cordon in the middle of the street, between the two rows of tumbledown shacks which form the business section of the city's melting-pot!" She strolled past the working men, she reported, and while they paid little attention to her, Miss Bell felt they very much wished they could: "They would like to, you can tell, by the side-glances which are jerked toward you." She took notice, of course, of their family life — always so important to Italian men and women — as it was reflected that day in the activities of their youngsters: "A mob of children come screaming from a small side street somewhere. They are dirty little wretches, with hair uncombed and clothes all torn. You wonder why they are not in school."

Margaret Bell's article was not intended as an attack on Italians, their customs, or their neighborhood. When the people of Toronto read it, there was little they found surprising, and certainly nothing angering. To many of them, her point of view was rather predictable. It did, however, reveal in an unusually clear way Toronto's view of The Ward: an undesirable part of the city, congested, cluttered, and alien.

Many people in The Ward — shopkeepers, scrap dealers, jewellers — did business in their homes, using their front rooms for dealing with customers and the backyards for raising poultry. This seemed peculiar to Miss Bell and struck her not as cluttered, but as unclean: "For the doors stand ajar, letting in the dust from the street. And some air, too, let us hope. Although one wonders how the air from that part of town can be worth the coveting." She was not impressed with their small stores, behind which they lived in bare subsistence: "What should be another living room is a miniature grocery shop, where one may buy ice cream from dirty cones, or cakes which hang in the window, on a bit of greasy brown paper." She noticed a shopkeeper trying to place some of his items in their proper place and, strangely, even this displeased her: "His systematic arrangement of every-thing is sickening."

Her article concluded with a description of The Ward in the evening, with its food aromas wafting through front doors past men who sat sipping wine and listening to music. This, too, distressed Miss Bell; she sensed an idle, dangerous people, albeit a content one. "Lazy-looking workmen lie sprawling on the doorsteps," she wrote. "The gang from down the street comes lurching home, with their pickaxes. Urchins are everywhere, under your feet, peering saucily into your face . . ." She noted the beauty of the Italian girls, their olive complexions and fine black hair, but added, "If it were not for the filth all around!"

Margaret Bell, like many of her fellow citizens of the time, seems to have been intrigued by the Italians, perhaps nearly envious of the mystery that she felt hovered over their lives. But in the end she was unable to accept them, only patronize them, and that at a distance: "They live there," she concluded, "hud-dled up in impossible little shacks, they laugh and dance and sing — and sometimes kill — but they are happy."

In the early months of 1916, concern about The Ward was spreading throughout Toronto. Several of the city's most earnest citizens and reformers, though not given to racial outbursts, agreed that the community of street peddlars, organ grinders and small boardinghouses needed cleaning up. Since the begin-ning of the century, when the small, cramped shacks had housed perhaps a family of six or so each, the number of occupants had now grown to often eight or more. As one investi-gator remarked: "The foreigners cannot always be relied upon to give accurately the number of occupants in the house."

An organization called the Bureau of Municipal Research

had been set up in March 1914 to investigate conditions in the city and act as an independent lobby to improve them. It was easy to understand why the members of the bureau were so concerned with that noxious confusion of streets and yards, full of strange smells and tongues. They seldom ventured into it, relying instead on the reports of those who went there in the line of duty — reporters, inspectors, politicians and others with axes to bring to the public grindstone.

The Bureau's members were among the most informed civic leaders of the day. They had twenty years of exposure to articles and speeches made about The Ward. The *Canadian Magazine* a few years earlier, in a famous piece by Augustus Bridle, had bemoaned the fact that the district, once a stronghold of Methodism, was now taken over by foreigners, mostly Jews and Italians along with Finns, Armenians, and others of the Old World, making it, Bridle wrote, as bad as any European ghetto.[8] They had also picked up copies of *Jack Canuck*, a crusading tabloid, which while not exactly their kind of newspaper, was nonetheless rooted in convictions they shared, and in which Italians were regularly pictured as dirty, lazy, crooked, danger- ous, and a black mark on Toronto: "The Italians are taking money out of the country all the time and giving little in return for it," wrote one contributor.[9] In the same issue, an editorial sharply reprimanded Italian men, claiming that those of their number who made a living as street musicians were taking women and children into the streets with them simply to gain sympathy: "These girls are frequently seized by half-drunken young men in hotel 'snuggeries' and pressed for a kiss or embrace." In *The Globe*, no less a figure than Charles Hastings, the medical officer of health, had sharply condemned The Ward, suggesting its existence was a threat to the rest of the city. "It must be apparent," he summed up in his 1911 study, "that we are confronted with the existence of congested districts of unsanitary, overcrowded dwellings which are a menace to pub- lic health, affording hotbeds for germination of disease, vice and crime."[10] Most of the city's church leaders looked upon The Ward as an affront to virtue in their midst. The Methodist publication *Missionary Outlook* lamented that fact and put its view soberly: "Every city has its four-fold problem of the slums, the saloons, the foreign colonies, and the districts of vice."

Their understanding and resolve strengthened by such public expression, the members of the new Bureau of Municipal Research embarked in 1916 on their landmark study of The Ward — a profile of its character and a solution to the problem it presented. Their findings would stand for generations to come as a window on the attitude of reform-minded Anglo-Saxons toward the newcomers in their midst. The Bureau report, released in 1918, was entitled: "What is 'The Ward' Going to do with Toronto?" with the subtitle: "A Report on Undesirable Living Conditions in one Section of the City of Toronto — 'The Ward' — conditions which are spreading rapidly to other Districts."[11]

The introduction deplored the unsightly appearance of The Ward: "A district where many people, mostly of foreign nationality, exist to the best of their ability in drab old buildings which are usually strangers to the paint brush, usually in a state of dilapidation, with ill-kept yards and anything but inspiring surroundings", and went on to make, almost incidentally, the most telling point of all, the one that would eventually seal the fate of the first neighborhood of Toronto Italians: "It is, in fact, an old residential section in process of becoming a business and industrial district, but now in that intermediate stage where residents either lack or no longer take a civic pride in their dwellings."

There was, of course, no thought given to the possibilities that The Ward might remain a neighborhood of homes and families, or that what bureau reformers saw as clutter was simply the design and character of an old-world village like the villages the Italians had left, or that the backyards they decried were the yards of men doing business from home, like the 'backyards' of any small farmer.

The map of The Ward on the opening pages of the report showed that already, in 1916, the public and business buildings that would spread to obliterate the community were already poised on the edges of the neighborhood. On the southern boundary, at Queen Street, stood The Armouries, Osgoode

Hall, City Hall, and the symbol of commercial influence of the day, the store of the Timothy Eaton Company. On the northern edge, along College, stood the Central Military Convalescent Hospital, the Hospital for Sick Children, and the largest of all the institutions looming over The Ward's future, the Toronto General Hospital, dominating the northwest corner of College and University. The hospital was regarded by Augustus Bridle almost as an advance guard bulldozing The Ward into history. A few years earlier he had written in the *Canadian Magazine*: "The Hospital Board, with a Methodist at the head, had come into its own in that part of the 'The Ward.' Jews and Gentiles fled the streets and the lanes at the approach of the invader. Modern money and enterprise drove them out."

The Bureau of Municipal Research, with its social workers, church leaders, and public-spirited businessmen, was never so flagrant as Augustus Bridle. It simply took the view that any responsible citizens would agree to the obliteration of The Ward. "Should not thought and study be given to the problem by public-spirited citizens," it asked in a lofty tone, "with a view to bettering existing conditions and initiating steps which would mean their ultimate elimination?" The Bureau saw The Ward as a nuisance, and an eyesore to be removed, not a neighborhood, and certainly not as a place where poor men and women lived in conditions not of their own making but visited upon them by circumstances and by absentee landlords, who owned the hovels they lived in and left them in disrepair to await the alluring offer of commercial development.

The Bureau dissected The Ward with clinical detachment. It reported that within its 147.2 acres, dwellings and stores took up 49.5 percent, streets and sidewalks 24.5 percent, and public and other buildings (like Toronto General Hospital, Osgoode Hall and the Hospital for Sick Children) 26 percent. "It is not so much that the total available building space is occupied," said the good leaders of Toronto, "as that the yards which, in an ordinary residential district, would be well-kept lawns or gardens, are in 'the Ward' cluttered with a confused collection of sheds and other frame buildings . . . "

The sheds, of course, were the buildings in which Italian fruit

vendors kept their carts and shoemakers did their repairs. This
was missed — or dismissed — by the Bureau, whose members
regarded a neat lawn as not only a pleasure to the eye but a
confirmation of conformity to the character of Toronto. Children in The Ward, it reported, had insufficient open space for
play, and therefore used the streets, with a loss of decency all the
way around: "It does not create an atmosphere which is likely to
raise the already too-low standard of living of the foreign resi-
dent. . ."

Fortunately, there was one aspect of The Ward's condition
which impressed the Bureau: its changing nature from a place
of homes and people to a place of business and industry. It
noted with implicit approval the fact that houses were being
demolished to make way: "In the period 1909 to 1916, inclu-
sive, the total number of buildings of all classes in the district
decreased from 1,761 to 1,656. This is largely accounted for by
the fact that a great number of smaller buildings were torn down
to make way for the erection of several modern buildings. The
erection of the Toronto General Hospital is an instance of this."
Nonetheless, the report realized that this sign, desirable though
it was, was no reason to feel complacent. The people, after all,
would survive. They could move elsewhere: "It does not prove
that the driving out of the residents of this district by development will abolish 'Ward' conditions in the city. Is it not more
likely that it will simply establish them in another section?"

Midway through the report, the Bureau began to look beyond
property at the people who lived in the houses it wanted
removed. Social workers, it said, had compiled certain case
histories and it was easily seen from these that The Ward was
simply a corridor to trouble. The case histories — actually a
handful of data in the form of charts — mirrored the cool
distance the Bureau kept between itself and those it studied.

In the reports on several Italian families, there was no history
of law-breaking, except for the act of a hungry eight-year-old
boy, who stole some fruit. The rest was a sad litany of illness,
poverty and defeat, for which the people themselves were
blamed. The histories were, at best, an oblique representation
of the citizens of The Ward. They revealed men and women

who had come to Canada with high hopes and witnessed the death of their dreams. Family Number 20 (in the report's cold-shouldered terminology) consisted of a man, a street cleaner, with a wife and seven children, whose income was fifteen dollars a week. "During 1916 and 1917," said the social worker, "the history of this family is one long story of illness and continuous assistance. Father had kidney trouble; one boy sent to hospital; baby girl ill with gastro-intestinal trouble and sent to Hospital for Sick Children; eldest girl has trouble with nose and throat; mother meets with accident, sent to St. Michael's Hospital, ill for several months; boy and girl in Isolation Hospital with diptheria; baby (one of twins), dies of malnutrition." The pro-files portrayed The Ward's Italian citizens as poor, ill, and in a struggle against great odds, a struggle made harsher in that their weakness was seen as a nuisance.

The Bureau's recommendations were: legislation that would permit Toronto to expropriate anyone's property for the purpose of replanning; legislation to permit fire chiefs and medical officers of health to remove buildings; educational campaigns on housing and planning and evening schools for people in The Ward. Throughout the report ran the hope of the Bureau that somehow the people who populated The Ward would learn to rise above the conditions which were so clearly of their own making. As the Reverend Peter Bryce, President of the Neigh-borhood Workers' Association said in the final pages of the report: "Slum conditions are not created by bad housing and imperfect community environment." Rather it was the for-eigner, with his low standards of living, who created them.

When the Bureau report was released in December 1918, it was duly noted at City Hall and in the press. But the wrecker's ball had already begun to swing over the tiny, vulnerable rectan-gle that had obsessed "Toronto the Good" for so many years. Business decreed the demise of The Ward. It was, after all, only minutes from Union Station, the gateway to Toronto for people from east and west, for men on business and the goods that business produced. The land was as vulnerable for housing as it was coveted by business. It was still more vulnerable in that most of the property was owned by absentee landlords (1,100 of the 1,300 houses still standing in 1916) who had no interest in repairs, since the land was daily becoming more valuable as commercial pressures grew. When 1918 came and the war was over and the engine of the economy once more ignited, the homes of The Ward came down quickly, first along Albert Street by City Hall, then up Terauley and along Edward. Before long, they would all be gone, and with them the people who would find new "Little Italies" not far from the streets where they had spent their first days in Canada. In their going, something of value was lost — a community which welcomed thousands of Italians, and reassured them they were not that far from the villages they had left.

Often after Mass in the parish church of The Ward, The Church of Our Lady of Mount Carmel, a few families still living in the neighborhood would set out on foot through the Sunday silence of College Street, crossing Bathurst, and arriving at last in the sunwashed open space of Dufferin, a new street on which hundreds of newly arrived Italians were now living. A new neighborhood was growing around St. Mary's of the Angels. Its residents would be relaxing, on those Sundays after World War I, on the low steps of small houses, their front gardens bright with the yellow sunflower and the blood-red rose.

The new neighborhood grew, as Little Italies would grow for future generations within cities and even the suburbs of Toronto, through a handful of men and women from a specific town, the *comune*. They settled first, then brought others from home to be near them and the always important parish church. Often on soft spring evenings, the neighborhood resonated with the laughter of *paesani*, who had grown up together in a hill town in Italy. On summer Sundays, throngs of them made their way to the *feste* of some neighboring *comune* from the *provincia* back home.

On such Sundays, an elderly Italian man from The Ward, originally from Aquila in Italy's Abruzzi region — a place of great mountains, rocky land and poor farmers — would make his way alone to a boardinghouse on Dufferin Street run by Maria Linzi, who gave room and board to ten laborers.[12] One of them, a young man named James Franceschini, was also from Aquila. The older man, anxious for news from home, passed many Sunday afternoons with the young James.

Sometimes they went with others from the boardinghouse to play *bocce* in the small well-tended park, or else they would sit in the sun, the young man's huge hands holding a letter from his parents, Lucia and Giuseppe Franceschini. James would read it aloud to the older man, who leaned forward, his head at a slight angle, the better to hear the word from the family in Aquila. One afternoon they walked for several miles while Franceschini told his older countryman of his early days in Toronto.

He had, he explained, arrived at Union Station several years earlier, on a cold, rainy evening in May, 1905. He was fifteen. He had been told before he left Aquila that someone from his town — a man named Verocchi who had a good job in construction in Toronto — would meet him and look after him. He stepped down from the train, a boy with a sturdy frame, dark wavy hair and eyes gleaming with innocent confidence. He looked about, expecting that at any moment someone in the crowd of Union Station's hall would step forward, put an arm around his shoulder, and welcome him to Canada and its Italian neighborhood of warmth and opportunity. The crowd drifted away. An hour passed, then two. Midnight came, the station was silent. The boy sat imprisoned in his own language, fear mounting in his throat, when suddenly, he sensed someone standing over him. He looked into the face of a policeman.

The policeman, familiar with stranded Italians who spoke no English, sighed, handed the youth a piece of paper and a pencil, directing that he should write a name, his own, or a friend's. He took the paper and pencil and in large letters (he had had only one year of school in Italy) he wrote the name of the man his father said would meet him: "Verocchi". The policeman read it, folded it and put it inside his jacket. He motioned for the boy to come with him.

Together on that spring night early in the century, the policeman and the teenager walked into the grey Toronto streets. They crossed Front Street, and went up York to Queen, and past City Hall into the jumble of streets of The Ward. There, on Louisa

Street, the policeman knocked on the door of an Italian rooming house. A man, groggy from being wakened, came to the door in his undershirt. The policeman handed him the paper with Verocchi's name on it, and showed the boy into the fetid hallway. "Look after this kid," he said, "and help him find his friends in the morning." The man nodded, closed the door, and signalled with his thumb to an upstairs room where the sounds and smells of nine people sleeping drifted through an open door. He told the boy he could sleep on the floor. James Franceschini spent his first night in Canada sobbing in the dark until he fell asleep.

Listening to the story of Franceschini, now a young man in his twenties, the old Italian smiled softly and said that really, when you come to a new land, the experience is sometimes like a funeral when it should be like a wedding. There was a pause, broken eventually by the old man who stopped suddenly on the sidewalk where they strolled, turned to Franceschini, and, his finger pointing and keeping time with the rhythms of his speech, asked loudly: "And this Verocchi. Where was he? He was to come. Why not?"

Franceschini looked at his elderly friend, whose eyes mirrored his hurt at the carelessness of a man for a boy, and decided it was better not to tell the entire story of Verocchi. Franceschini replied simply and truthfully that the next morning, after his first night in Toronto, he did locate the man. Verocchi worked as the foreman of an Italian labor gang at Canada Foundry at the end of the street car line, near Lansdowne Avenue. "He told me he had not received word I was coming," said Franceschini. "But he offered me a job right there. Pick and shovel. I took it."

The two were, by this time, almost back at the boardinghouse on Dufferin, and their talk turned to other things — Aquila, Franceschini's father's business in silver and china tableware. Before dusk, Franceschini bade his old friend goodnight and watched him amble south on Dufferin, grateful that he had not insisted on knowing more about their fellow countryman.

For Verocchi had done what countless foremen and straw bosses of the day had done. He waited until young Franceschini had settled into the job, then one day demanded a kickback of five dollars a month or else he would fire him. About two months later, he opened a boardinghouse and told the young man he had better move in as a paying boarder if he wanted to hold his job. Franceschini (who was then making $9.60 a week) was expected, along with his fellow boarders, to keep Verocchi in kegs of beer. Only a modest skill in arithmetic was needed to prove that Verocchi was making much more on kickbacks from his men than he was as foreman of the labor gang. Franceschini paid the bribe, and while one part of him seethed, another part of him shrugged; he knew it was a common experience of many immigrants of many nationalities to be exploited by one of their own people in the new land. He looked for a new job, even one that paid less, that did not involve a payoff to the foreman.

In the spring, he did as thousands of other Italians had done and got hired on with a track gang of the CPR. This one was building a line near the small town of Orangeville, north of Toronto. There, he began for the first time to discover a sense of confidence, as his soft hands grew hard and his talent for leadership began to show itself. "There are over a hundred men here," he wrote his father and mother back home, "and I am one of the few who can write." He began writing letters home on behalf of dozens of men from every region of Italy, who were helping to build an historic piece of Canada, yet were unable even to sign their names. The men looked up to him. So did the CPR superintendent. When the foreman took ill, James Franceschini stepped into the job.

During his first years in Toronto, James Franceschini went from construction site to construction site, sometimes to the north of Ontario, sometimes to obscure streets within the city itself. Usually, though he was younger than everyone in the gang, he was made foreman. And almost always, as he had discovered in his first weeks as a laborer, he had to face the petty cheating of the straw boss. Once, while working on city sidewalks along Queen Street, just at the edge of The Ward, his superintendent, a Scot, took him aside to acquaint him with the devious practice in place. The cement used for the sidewalk extension was mixed with the necessary sand and water on a low board set beside the sidewalk. The job called for four bags of cement to each mix.

"This job's inspected," the Scotsman said, "so when the city's man comes about, make sure that four bags are at the ready. When he leaves, make it three bags, and put the fourth over here and I'll look after it."

The superintendent, so the rumor went, had a side line selling city cement on the cheap. Yet his dishonesty, and that of others in construction, did not warp but rather strengthened the resolve of James Franceschini. In the Scotsman's case, it so repelled Franceschini that he quit, convinced that cheating would be found out, and that it served only to diminish the quality of work and the workers themselves.

It was in the middle of winter, in his third season in Canada, when he was working in a foundry, that he met Jack Gould, a middle-aged tradesman who operated a crane, and who took an interest in Franceschini that was to have great influence upon his life and work. Gould and his wife welcomed the young Italian into their home for Sunday dinners, sensing in him a native intelligence and a degree of ambition that deserved opportunity. At the Gould's table in middle-class Toronto, Franceschini saw a style to which he aspired, a way of living beyond the sweat and grime of the labor gangs and the dark rooms of boardinghouses.

One day that winter, Jack Gould opened the *Toronto Star* and found a small advertisement, placed by a man building a house who was looking for someone to dig his basement. Gould set the ad aside for the following Sunday, when Franceschini — by then known as "Big Jim" — would be visiting. Over the dinner table, he urged Jim to make the man an offer for the excavation. "You can do that kind of work," he said, "you know the ropes. Things are quiet in the winter, so why not make an extra dollar?" The next day, Franceschini located the man and offered to do the job.

He was met with a question which he couldn't answer: "How much will you charge me?" Franceschini shook his head. But he was set on getting the work. "I'll do the job," he offered. "You check it. If you're pleased, pay me what you think."

The next morning, he borrowed five dollars, bought two wheelbarrows, and with two of his fellow laborers started digging. A week later the builder measured the excavation, approved it and wrote a cheque which Franceschini split three ways. Each man had been paid about fifty cents an hour. Franceschini bought himself a bicycle, and when he finished each day's work on a construction gang, he pedaled around Toronto answering ads for excavation work.

He built a house on Dufferin Street and sold it for an enormous $4,000, feeling his first surge of success and the affluence that goes with it. The Goulds, always his supporters, kept clipping ads, so that almost every evening Jim Franceschini could climb on the bike and pedal to Rosedale or Deer Park to offer his services digging basements and pouring concrete. Soon he had a dozen men working with him, then horses and wagons and a large stable in which to keep them. Then Jim Franceschini stepped out in front of almost any other excavator in the city: he bought a steam shovel, imported from the United States. It was one of only two in Toronto.

James Franceschini built not just houses, but stores, with small apartments upstairs which he now rented. He married Annie Pinkham, a bright young Anglo-Saxon woman, with a shy smile, whom he had met at the Goulds. And after nine years in Canada, he owned property and equipment worth more than $300,000.

Much was changing in his life, but his fidelity to his Italian origins and the icons of his past would never diminish. No matter where he went — to work, to the Goulds', to night classes — he carried in the left pocket of his trousers a ten dollar gold piece that his father had presented him with the day he sailed from Naples. His father had made him vow that he would never spend the gold piece except to cable home for a return ticket if he had no other money. Against his parents' hope, Franceschini was bound to stay in Canada.

One day leaving his boardinghouse, he was overcome with joy to meet his father, who had come unannounced, not only to see his son's growing success, but to remind him that he should be planning to return to Italy. James heard him out, but was adamant. He was in Canada for good.

In the early spring of 1917, when James Franceschini was twenty-seven years old — a broad shouldered man with a huge chest and hands so large they made him appear bigger than he was — he got word of an excavation job about to be opened to tender in the town of Oshawa, about sixty miles east of Toronto. The Robson Leather Company, which had been founded in 1876, and whose leather was sold to shoe manufacturers in Ontario and Quebec, was about to build a power plant to replace its aged water-driven paddle wheel. A foundation would have to be dug, about sixty by a hundred feet.

The company was housed in a rambling building with many additions, and lay in the town's southern neighborhood. From nearby Oshawa Creek, a small dam provided water power and to the south, the forest eventually gave way to open land and the shoreline of Lake Ontario. The owner was Charles Robson, then in his early thirties, a man of gentle manner and deep courtesy, whose sturdy build was testimony to his early years as a Montreal lacrosse player. Robson had just bought his company from his father for a reported $100,000; he was one of Oshawa's men of means, a lover of thoroughbreds and a confidant of Sam MacLaughlin, the legendary car manufacturer whose sprawling plant was within walking distance of Robson's.[13]

On a warm morning in the middle of April, 1917, James Franceschini took time off his job as a factory foreman in Toronto, hitched up his finest horses, and headed toward Oshawa for a meeting with Charles Robson. They met in Robson's small office, in a corner of the first floor of the tannery, where the smells of tanning oil and warm machinery drifted through the narrow doorway. Robson was impeccable in dress and manner. Franceschini wore a bulky, dark suit, the best he could afford; he spoke in English that was clear but forceful and broken. His sentences were accented by the gestures of his large, thick hands. Robson was taken with this man, not that much younger than he, who was fueled by barely contained energy. In two hours he made a decision that would set James Franceschini on his way to the future.

"Tell me, Mr. Franceschini," he said, "How long will it take your men, with their horses, to do the job?"

Franceschini smiled. He explained to Robson that unlike virtually every other excavator, he worked not with horses, but with a steam shovel. Robson's friendliness deepened to respect. There would be no need for tenders, for no other candidate had a steam shovel. The job was Franceschini's.

He dug the foundation. Then, that summer, Robson took Franceschini to the office of his old friend, Sam MacLaughlin, then about to build a sprawling new automobile plant. Franceschini and his men dug the foundation. MacLaughlin, impressed with Franceschini's efficiency and price, called him later that autumn, told him he was about to build a new home — to be known as Parkwoods — and wondered if he and his men might do the excavation. When it was finished, James Franceschini had a new confidence in his voice and his bearing. He began to talk not as a laborer, but as a businessman. He felt more buoyant than he had ever felt since he arrived in Canada. "I have enough money to pay off every debt I owe," he told a friend. "And I have $15,000 left in the bank. All that from this single summer."

The following spring, he began an association with Charles Johnston, who, like Jack Gould and Charles Robson, would become both friend and benefactor. Johnston, a university-educated engineer, became a business partner to Franceschini, and gave the young Italian with one year of schooling the technical understanding and professional counsel he needed. The two were a study in stark contrasts, Franceschini rough-hewn and rough-spoken, Johnston a reserved Presbyterian of quiet personality.

Johnston was at his friend's side when, in the summer of 1918, Franceschini formed Dufferin Construction, the company that carried him to national prominence and unhoped-for wealth. That autumn, it received the first highway job ever given to a private firm by the government of Ontario: the Rouge River Highway, twenty miles east of Toronto on the road to Kingston.

For Dufferin Construction and James Franceschini, the next two decades were breathtakingly successful. Within a few years, the company established itself as road-builder to the province of Ontario, a relationship that endured regardless of the party in power. Throughout all the regimes, and as he matured, Franceschini strode along highways all over Ontario at the side of Charles Johnston. Johnston had a lasting respect for Franceschini's drive, but even more for his natural business intellect. Without the finishing of secondary education, Franceschini could submit a tender, correct an engineer, or sort out a financial tangle. As one of the hundreds of men working for him by the middle of the twenties put it, "He is a wizard." By then, Dufferin Construction had built part of the highway to Hamilton, the CNR yards in Leaside, and a suburb of Toronto, getting job after job because no other builder could meet Franceschini's low bids and high quality. Moreover, as friends and critics agreed, he was fanatical about keeping costs down, and cutting them whenever he could.

A few years later, the Ontario government called for bids to construct part of what it called The Dundas Highway (also known as Route 5), running west of Toronto through the community of Cooksville and on to Clappison's Corners, for a distance of thirty miles. It was a major project; Franceschini's competitors felt it was too big for him. Nevertheless, he won the contract, and over three years, built the highway, from rock foundation to ditching to grading and paving. It was worth ten million dollars. James Franceschini became the name to contend with in Canadian highway construction.

He was now a multimillionaire, and believed in living like one. In 1925 he bought the Ormsby Estate on the edge of Toronto: fourteen acres on the south side of Lakeshore Road in the community of Mimico. There he lived with his wife and daughter Myrtle, amid greenhouses, gardens, lawns, stables, a twelve-car garage and a baronial twenty-five rooms. The dining room could seat over twenty people, served by staff impeccably attired to the tips of their white-gloved fingers. At the head of the table sat James Franceschini, wearing one of his many pinstriped suits and a rose in his lapel, and taking pride when he was told by one of his butlers — who had once worked for royalty — that indeed, his table was as tasteful as a prince's. Those who sat at it over the years, or strolled the magnificent grounds, were apt to feel that Franceschini was less a man of

ostentation than he was a man of taste; his Mediterranean
ancestry emerged in his love of line and color, whether of the
design of his Italian table, or the splashes of color in his beautiful
gardens.

Franceschini began insisting to his managers Charlie Johnston, Leonard Franceschini, a brother who was a fiercely loyal
right-hand man, and any others who were within earshot, that
Dufferin Construction should find a way around paying the
heavy cost of subcontractors — the gravel suppliers, the rock
crushers, the asphalt producers, the fuel dealers, even the vehi-
cle firms who rented trucks. Shortly after getting a major contract in 1924, he went to New York to talk business with the top
men at Mack Trucks, from whom he had rented vehicles, huge,
lumbering haulers with enormous tires. The rental rate was
$5.00 an hour; he needed ten trucks. Instead of a rental agree-
ment, Franceschini came away from Mack with an arrangement in which he would act as Mack's Canadian agent. He was
able to buy, at wholesale cost, ten trucks which, when they were
not on the road for Dufferin, would be rented out. In this way, he
cut his costs from $5.00 an hour to $1.75. And he was in the
trucking business — just as he would soon be in the sand
business, the gravel business, the asphalt business, even the fuel
business, all with one aim: to supply himself with the materials
at less cost.

In a business that was as rough-hewn as he was, Franceschini
made enemies. He was highly competitive, was somewhat gruff,
and in the Ontario of the twenties and thirties, he was not only
an outsider but an Italian, daring to rise above the menial level
where, according to some, he more naturally belonged. By
1934, after he had been awarded over fifty road contracts by
Ontario governments, he and Leonard expected it all to end.

In July of that year, the Conservatives were ousted by the
flamboyant Liberal leader, Mitch Hepburn. Once again, just as
in the past when new governments came to office, the contracts
awarded to Franceschini were opened and investigated in the
hope that some whiff of scandal might drift from their pages to
sully the character of the departing government. But there was
nothing; from the Liberals, as from the United Farmers and

Conservatives, the contracts continued to come to Dufferin Construction, the lowest bidder and the most dependable. By the end of the thirties, James Franceschini had brought to highway construction a new era of cost control and quality building. He had also amassed a fortune.

His daughter Myrtle was at Havergal College. His dining room was a meeting place for many — though not nearly all — of the well-placed members of Toronto's business and political communities. He had also clearly established himself as the leading patron of the Italian-Canadian community of the day so that when social events of a special nature — garden parties, and receptions for visiting heads of state — were held, they were held at the Franceschini estate.

Franceschini spent all his energies between his three deeply felt commitments — his work, his family, and his hackney thoroughbreds. (Franceschini once made a gift of two thoroughbreds to a visiting Italian cabinet minister.) His business expanded far beyond Ontario, and far beyond road building, so that by 1939, he was not only the country's largest road contractor, but its biggest producer of crushed stone and ready-mix concrete. He owned countless gravel pits, several asphalt plants, and with the exception of cement, every material used in the building of a modern highway. Franceschini's stable of over fifty hackneys not only fulfilled his childhood love of horses, but, as they won awards throughout Canada and the United States, they introduced him to circles of society from which he would otherwise have been excluded. And, of course, there was his home and family; Sundays, he, his wife, and his daughter, home from school, strolled the green and sprawling grounds, Franceschini checking the details of his gardener's work, and cutting a rose for the evening table. To those close to him, he appeared a man who had found himself. Already he had reached milestones far beyond the immigrant's dream.

On June 8, 1940, he left his Fleet Street office and took the train to Halifax for a meeting with Premier Angus L. Macdonald. They met on June 10, in Macdonald's large, sun-filled office in Nova Scotia's legislative building, a few minutes' walk from the Halifax harbor. The slender, slow-speaking premier talked to Franceschini not just of his road building in Nova Scotia, but of Franceschini's great assistance to the federal government in the war effort.

"You are doing so much for us, Franceschini," said Macdonald. "You are building the roads of Canada and now the airports. But with all that, you have gone into building warships. How do you manage it all?"

Franceschini shrugged. His English was still unpolished. But there was in his bearing as in his voice, clear pride in his accomplishment.

At the outbreak of the war the previous year, Franceschini had placed his entire company at the service of the federal government. On September 6, 1939, he had called his senior men together in Toronto, and produced a telegram he had prepared the previous evening and now proposed to send to Ottawa. No one, including his brother Leonard beside him, was surprised as he read: "In order to assist in the present national emergency, I wish to place at the government's disposal the entire resources in plants, equipment and personnel of Dufferin Construction and its associated companies. The services of the organization, including executive officers and technical staff are available immediately. My personal services in any capacity in which I can be of use are at the government's call without remuneration."

On that June day in 1940, Angus L. Macdonald, a Liberal premier, who had already been given word that Prime Minister Mackenzie King wanted him as minister of defence for naval services, knew very well of Jim Franceschini's commitment and, even more, his importance to Canada's wartime activity. He looked across his desk at the man, stocky, barrel-chested, with that practical respect politicians reserve for men who have moved from the street to the executive suite, proving themselves along the way. This man who was not only road builder to four provinces, but was now constructing airports, and indeed, after his telegram to Ottawa, had at Ottawa's own request, gone into shipbuilding, turning out warships and doing so not at his own price, but at the price set for him by Ottawa.

As the late sun began to fall beyond Macdonald's window,

and the streets began to fill with commuters for the ferryboat, Macdonald asked Franceschini about his Nova Scotia work, which was underway at three separate locations. He was in the middle of a question, when a secretary quietly slipped into the office and placed a slip of paper on the large oak desk. Macdonald stared at it, as if wondering how to tell the man across from him what it said. He looked up: "It's from Ottawa, Mr. Franceschini. They are telling me that, this morning, Italy has entered the war — on the side of the Axis. We are at war with Italy."

If James Franceschini felt any ambivalence at Macdonald's words, his face did not reveal it. He was as calm as he was when he entered the room. Italy's entry into the war on the side of Germany was a matter to be regretted, but not one to inspire uncertainty. He had work to do for Canada and Dufferin Construction was committed to it.

He left Macdonald, checked out of the Lord Nelson Hotel, and went by car to Truro, a small community of tree-shaded streets set among the stretching, fertile fields of central Nova Scotia. He settled in a hotel on the main street, and before heading beyond the town to see his men building a stretch of highway, he phoned home. After a few words, his wife Annie told him that there had been a couple of men at the house that morning to see him. She said they were from the RCMP. Franceschini thought a moment of all the war work he had under way for the government, and concluded that they had come to advise him on a matter of national security — perhaps about personal precautions he should now be taking. He went about his business, drove to Moncton, caught the late train, connected with a sleeper in Montreal, and was back in Toronto on the morning of June 13. His driver met him at Union Station and took him to Mimico, where he showered, had breakfast, and then left for the office building on Fleet Street. He was behind his desk by 9:30 a.m., and about to write a note to Ottawa when the receptionist entered to say that the two RCMP officers were in the waiting room. As they came through his office door, Franceschini extended his hand in greeting and gestured for them to take a chair. They did not. Instead in a barely audible voice, one of them spoke: "You are James Franceschini?"

There was a confused silence. Franceschini looked at one man, then the other.

"Of course."

"You were born in Italy . . ."

"Yes."

"Get your coat and hat please. Come with us . . ."

James Franceschini was in custody.

CHAPTER FOUR

DAYS OF DARKNESS, DAYS OF DESPAIR

The events of June 1940 would change forever the life of James Franceschini and almost the entire Italian community in Canada. On the night of Monday, June 10, shortly after 9:30, Prime Minister William Lyon Mackenzie King, then sixty-six years old, entered the lobby of the Château Laurier Hotel in Ottawa. He was, as usual, alone. He took the elevator to the seventh floor, then walked nimbly through the doorway to the offices of the Canadian Broadcasting Corporation and was shown to its main studio. He sat as if imprisoned in silence, while a technician adjusted his microphone. An announcer shook his hand, then slipped into a tiny adjoining studio. At precisely ten o'clock he read the familiar introduction: "Ladies and Gentlemen, from Ottawa, we present a special broadcast by the Prime Minister of Canada, the Right Honourable W. L. Mackenzie King."

King began with the crisis at hand: "Fellow Canadians, the news reached Ottawa a few minutes after one o'clock today that Signor Mussolini, in a speech delivered at Rome, had announced that Italy was entering the war on the side of Germany."[1] He said that during the afternoon sitting of the House of Commons, he had introduced a resolution putting Canada at the side of Britain against Italy. The Leader of the Opposition,

R. B. Hanson, had seconded his motion and it received wide support on all sides. By four o'clock the Senate had passed a similar resolution. Early that evening the cabinet passed an order-in-council to advise King George VI that Canada was at war with Italy. The Prime Minister continued:

> The Minister of Justice has authorized the Royal Canadian Mounted Police to take steps to intern all residents of Italian origin whose activities have given ground for the belief or reasonable suspicion that they might in time of war endanger the safety of the state or engage in activities prejudicial to the prosecution of the war.

The RCMP had already begun the roundup. The plans had been in official documents ever since the previous September, when one of the most influential civil servants of the era, Norman Robertson — a highly gifted man then chairing a federal committee overseeing potential internal threats to Canada during the war — had sent a memorandum marked "secret" to the head of the RCMP's intelligence section, Superintendent E. W. Bavin. With his note, he attached an equally secret report from his committee to Minister of Justice Ernest Lapointe. It included a list of several hundred names of Italian Canadians suspected of being threats to the country and therefore eligible for arrest and detention should war break out with Italy.

Robertson, a man of shrewd intelligence and humane principle, was genuinely torn by what he had been called upon to do. He said in his report to the minister of justice that while some Italian Canadians were zealous members of the Italian Fascist Party, and had taken its oath of allegiance, most were not. "The committee," Robertson wrote to Lapointe, "believing that a large majority of the naturalized Canadians, members of the Fascio, are not at heart disloyal to this country, do not feel it would be in the public interest to recommend their immediate arrest on the outbreak of war on the grounds of their membership of the Fascio unless this *prima facie* evidence of disloyalty is reinforced by corroborative proof from his past conduct that the persons in question are likely to act in a manner prejudicial to the public safety."[2]

Robertson's qualifications gave, of course, wide latitude to the RCMP, a latitude made wider still by one of his final para-graphs to Lapointe: "The Committee believes that the forego-ing recommendations constitute a minimum list — which may have to be lengthened in the light of investigations now in progress."

Given the scope offered the RCMP in Robertson's memo, it was not surprising that on May 2, 1940, a secret directive was issued from the office of RCMP Commissioner S. G. Wood to the force's various divisions across Canada, containing one instruction that was both decisive and sweeping: "The inter-de-partmental committee appointed by the minister of justice for the purpose of reviewing the evidence available against Enemy Aliens and persons considered dangerous have now under con-sideration the Italian question and you are requested to submit any names of Italians whom you would consider a menace in case Italy enters the war on the side of Germany."

It concluded with an even more explicit instruction: "Kindly submit the names of Italians who may prove dangerous or whose activities during the past would warrant internment, together with a brief summary of what is known of their activi-ties, associations. . . ."[3]

About a month after Commissioner Wood's directive, and on the day of Mackenzie King's resolution in the House of Com-mons, a slight, immaculately dressed physician of dignified bearing named Luigi Pancaro entered his clinic which was attached to his home on Morris Street in Sudbury, Ontario. It was just after one o'clock in the afternoon.[4]

Pancaro, then in his early forties, was in his fifteenth year of practice. He had begun medicine here after following in his father's path in the province of Cozenza, Italy, and earning an honours degree in medicine in 1926 at the University of Rome. While a student, he had sometimes gone to the university library to read articles about Canada, its geography, its people and its growing Italian population. He decided, much to the sadness of his parents, that he would go to Canada where, as a devout Catholic, he would carry out his vocation among his own people. On the day he had left Cozenza in late September,

1926, the stores closed and horse-drawn carriages followed him
to his train as if in a funeral cortège. He arrived in Halifax in
early October, and though he spoke no English, was able to buy
a train ticket to a place called North Bay, Ontario, where he had
been told a colony of Italians had begun to settle. He arrived in a
few days and became the first Italian-born medical doctor in
Canada's North. For four years he remained in North Bay until,
in 1930, after studying surgical technique at the Mayo Clinic in
Minnesota, he moved to Sudbury, to a larger community of
Italian Canadians.

He had just entered his office on that historic afternoon in
1940 and was talking to a patient and his wife when, without
knocking, four uniformed officers walked in. The elderly Italian
couple fled in terror at the sight of the four policemen. Pancaro
remained calm and, as always, deeply courteous.

"Unlock the files," one policeman said. Pancaro did as he
was told, slowly realizing why they were there. Two officers went
through his patient records. They appeared to find nothing.
Then one of the officers strolled to the wall that faced Pancaro's
desk. He looked for a moment at a print, a likeness of the Virgin
Mary. Slowly, the officer removed it and tore it up.

The man in charge, an RCMP corporal, turned to the doctor
and said tersely, "Dr. Pancaro, you are to come with us." They
put the physician in the back of a police van and took him to
Sudbury's local jail on Elm Street where he met a dozen other
Italian-born men, most of them his patients, locked in a cell.
The next night, with no word of their destination, the police put
them in vans and drove to the CPR station. The platform was
empty. It was beginning to rain. Out of the dark and drizzle a
single figure emerged. It was a friend of Pancaro's, a local
pharmacist, carrying the doctor's topcoat over his arm. He
handed Pancaro his coat and in indignation yelled at the police,
"This man is a gentleman. This is a terrible, terrible mistake."
The police said nothing. They herded Pancaro and the others
aboard and at 10 p.m. sharp, as Sudbury's Italian physician
waved through the window to his pharmacist friend, the train
pulled into a driving rain.

That evening in Dominion, a small town in Nova Scotia

about a half-hour's drive from Sydney, a woman named Camella Scattalon looked out the window of her house. Her husband, Luigi, had come from the north Italian community of Treviso in 1927 to work in the coal mines of Cape Breton, and had settled in this established Italian community.

For the first time in her life she felt the terrible fear of impending violence. The sidewalks and streets seemed to stream with hundreds of people, mostly local miners swearing vengeance against Italy and against Italians, including the two hundred living in their town. Hours before, at dusk, a handful had gathered at the small house and store of Camella's brother-in-law, Romano, for whom the police had come that afternoon.[5] They smashed windows and then surged on toward the house of Camella and Luigi Scattalon.

Camella fled to a neighbor's home but Luigi, a big man with a hot temper, stood in the doorway and faced the insults, many hurled from drunks. He held a huge knife. The men left. But late that night when the crowds had dwindled, he and his wife slipped silently away to spend the night elsewhere. Luigi's brother, Romano Scattalon, was taken to the city of Sydney, seven miles from Dominion. There, along with a handful of other Italian immigrants from the surrounding towns he was placed in the local lock-up. The following day just past noon, Romano Scattalon, shoemaker Domenic Nardoccio, miner Comelli Giobatta, and baker Frank Martinello were placed aboard a train that left for Moncton, New Brunswick, and a connecting coach to Ontario. Their wives and children were not told why they were taken into custody or where they were heading. Late in the day the mood in Cape Breton, especially among the miners, turned ugly.

The next morning the radio carried the news: the coal miners of Cape Breton, members of Local 26 of the United Mine Workers of America, had decided to refuse to work alongside any Italian-born miners. At the pitheads, crowds of idle men milled about cursing, swearing, vowing vengeance on any Italian who came near the mine. No one knew it then, but the mines would be idle for six weeks, depriving the country of badly needed coal, until the Dominion Coal Company gave in, agreeing to ban the Italians from entering any of its Cape Breton mines for a full nine months.

In another part of Canada: eight-year-old Nellida Pattaracchia left Sacred Heart School in Hamilton, Ontario at about 3:45 on Tuesday afternoon, and began her walk home. The house of her Italian-born parents, Nello and Ida Pattaracchia, was on tree-shaded Park Street North. At about 4:10, she rounded a corner and was in sight of her house when she saw policemen at the back and front. Others were inside the house. Nellida, whose parents were strict and religious people, could not understand why the police were around her home. She stood terrified, biting her lip, trying desperately to hold back the scream rising in her throat. The officer on the sidewalk took her inside, and told her to sit quietly in the living room while her house was being searched.

She watched, unbelieving, with her mother as her adored father was escorted from his house and bundled into a police car. At the same time, Francesco Zaffiro, a slight man with bright eyes, was bending over the last in his shoe repair shop on James Street in the heart of the city. He was thinking idly of what he might do that evening; perhaps he and his wife would go to Casa d'Italia, the club he had helped to build, for a couple of hours with friends, talking, and playing cards. The door opened; the police were brief. "You are Francisco Zaffiro? Come with us."

In the forty-eight hours that began shortly after noon on June 10, the RCMP, joined by provincial and local forces, rounded up about five hundred Italian-born men, mostly in Ontario, Quebec, and Nova Scotia. Their captives were men active in one or all of three Italian community organizations: the Sons of Italy, a lodge and mutual benefit society; the Dopolavaro, (meaning "after work"), a club for recreation and study; or the Fascio, a political party which gave those who saw in Mussolini a unifier and reformer of their homeland a chance to express their support of him.

When Francesco Zaffiro and Nello Pattaracchia arrived at the city jail on Barton Street in Hamilton surrounded by policemen, they met over a dozen of their friends, including Berlino

Colangelo, a gentle man who played the guitar and sang at Casa
d'Italia. He was, like Zaffiro, an active member of the Sons of
Italy, and amid the confusion at the jail he told Zaffiro what had
happened to him that afternoon. He had been at work in the
clothing factory where he was a tailor, turning out military
uniforms, when two RCMP officers approached him. One
asked for the foreman. Colangelo said he would go find him; the
other officer asked him his name. When Colangelo replied, the
officer said simply: "Never mind the foreman. We were just
going to ask him for you. Come with us." Colangelo asked why,
but there was no explanation. Would he be gone long? "Oh no,
it won't be very long."[7]

The trains that rolled into the night on June 10 and 11 filled
with RCMP officers and large numbers of Italian-born men with
their belongings in brown paper bags, were the expression of a
new law in Canada. The Defense of Canada Regulations had
been proclaimed the preceding September, 1939, under the
authority of the *War Measures Act*, enacted back in 1914. There
were sixty-four regulations, giving the government of Prime
Minister Mackenzie King almost unlimited powers, one of
which was the right to internment without trial. Nowhere in the
original act or the new regulations was there provision for public
or legal scrutiny of the policy or of specific cases. As R.A.
Farquharson of the *Globe and Mail* wrote on June 11: "The
police on any borderline cases arrest first and investigate later."[8]
There were, of course, a few, mostly academics and clergymen,
who questioned the fairness of the regulations, but they were
quickly, often angrily dismissed. "I know," thundered R.B.
Hanson, Leader of the Opposition, "there are a certain type of
intelligentsia, we call them pinks in the street, who object to
these regulations . . . . I am not going to make an attack on the
professors of our universities but I have often thought that if they
had a little more work to do they would not give so much
consideration to these abstract and academic questions."[9]

The RCMP's deep convictions concerning dangerous elements among Canada's Italian-born citizens had been outlined
three years before the outbreak of the Second World War. On
March 23, 1936, a senior officer, Assistant Commissioner G.L.

Jennings, wrote a memorandum marked "secret" to Dr. O.K. Skelton, the under-secretary of state for external affairs. Jennings said that in view of the rising tide of fascist activity in the country, he felt it would be a good idea to advise External Affairs, in writing, of the RCMP's concern and its opinion as to what needed to be done.

The memorandum attached to his note was five pages long; it claimed that Italian-inspired fascist propaganda was first observed in Canada in 1923, and was now penetrating the Sons of Italy, which the RCMP recognized as made up of devout Roman Catholics. The main worry, however, was the establishment of clearly defined fascist organizations, directed from Rome by the secretary general of Italy's National Fascist Party. "Definite evidence of the existence of the *Fascisti* in Canada was obtained in 1931," Jennings reported in his memo. "We were informed that Signor Luigi Trono, Manager of the Cascade Hotel at Banff, Alberta, received a package of membership cards from the Secretariat of the Fascists Abroad, Postal Box 350, Rome. The cards bore the Fascist oath in Italian: 'I swear to follow without discretion the order of Il Duce and to serve him with all my strength and if it is necessary my blood . . . .' "[10]

The RCMP document did not point out that, as both Norman Robertson and O.D. Skelton well knew, many of the men who joined the Fascist party did so out of naïveté and idealism, and harboured no treasonous attitude toward Canada. To them, the *Fascisti* was little more than one more lodge to join, a club for the perpetuation of nostalgia and loyalties. These meant a great deal to men who hoped that in the land they left, Mussolini would be able to bring about the humane improvements so desperately needed. Perhaps such distinctions as these are impossible to consider in the forming of national policies during wartime. But they were clear to Robertson and to Skelton.

In the late summer of 1939, Robertson wrote to his mentor Skelton that he was "appalled by the programme contemplated [by the RCMP] and that it involved a great deal of bitter interracial resentment and the prospect of endless labor troubles throughout industrial and mining areas, as well as the alienation of the sympathy and support of great blocks of opinion which, if properly handled, could be led to support any efforts the government was making rather than to oppose them."[11]

But Robertson's struggle to apply the new Defense of Canada Regulations wisely and humanely, was doomed. Ernest Lapointe, under heavy pressure from the RCMP, was proving deeply sympathetic to their argument that the federal government had to strike hard against alien propagandists, shutting down their press, their organizations, and anyone linked to them. If some quite innocent Italians were made victims by these harsh measures, Lapointe was heard to say, that was simply the cost of acting firmly. Even the Prime Minister's own reservations about the RCMP attitude — "I told Lapointe," he wrote in his diary that November, "that I did not trust the judgment of the Mounted Police on these matters" — was of little influence.[12] The tides of opinion were strong; both the police, and those such as Opposition leader R.B. Hanson, who thought as they did, had their way.

By June 12, the police had rounded up and taken into custody more than five hundred Italian men, with more to be included all summer long — including virtually every Italian-born physician in Canada, two professors from the University of Toronto, a Catholic priest, a twenty-five year veteran of the Toronto police force and countless tailors, shoemakers, and day laborers.[13] In Toronto, Alino Astri, who ran a small shoe-repair shop in the city's west end, was stunned on June 10 when six policemen, three with guns drawn, entered his home, and after ascertaining his name began searching his papers, which contained minutes of meetings of the Sons of Italy. Astri was a branch secretary there. He administered the benevolent fund of fifteen dollars a month to members who took ill and couldn't work. He was chagrined that such duties would label him a threat to anyone.

Yet he was not surprised. Five weeks earlier, on a May evening, he had been approached by two members of Toronto's Italian community who told him that if he gave them a list of possibly treasonous key members of the Sons of Italy, he himself would be protected. He refused. One of the men to approach Astri was a former clergyman among Italians in Montreal and Toronto[14] who would always be widely suspected as an informer.

In Montreal, where the roundup was described as the biggest in the city's history, police sealed off bridges in order to search all approaching cars. In Ontario, from Sudbury and North Bay to Hamilton and Windsor, citizens volunteered to assist the police, acting as drivers for cars that took the men to the police stations. Here and there a few rocks were thrown and windows smashed, but for the most part, small crowds gathered and contented themselves with shouts of : "Give it to him" or "Take him away for good." In Toronto, the city's chief of police, D.C. Draper, a former army officer, had already said that in his view there were many hundreds who had to be interned. And on June 11 Mayor Ralph Day told the *Globe and Mail* that the city had immediately moved to prevent the men's families receiving relief. "This country is at war with Italy," said Mayor Day, "and Italians cannot very well expect us to spend money required for war purposes for the purpose of maintaining alien enemies."[15] For its part, the RCMP was pleased. "There were no difficulties," said Lieut. Col. S. Stethem, Assistant Director of internment operations. "Plans were carried out without a hitch."[16]

The week of June 10 was one of strange surroundings and new anxieties for the men who had been picked up. They were given only vague explanations — they were being held for questioning, they would be detained for a few weeks, they were being sent to a training centre. Those who were living in Quebec and Nova Scotia made their way to Ontario by train; those living in Ontario arrived by train or truck on June 12 and 13 at the grounds of the Canadian National Exhibition in Toronto. There they were taken by soldiers and veterans to the Automotive Building, a huge, vaulting edifice, where they would be classified and organized for their later trip to internment.

For some, in particular James Franceschini and Luigi Pancaro, the days in the Automotive Building sleeping on the floor were difficult. At times, the soldiers cursed them or said the answer was to take them out and shoot them. Once, on their way to the showers, some of the men looked up to a mezzanine, and felt the fresh embarrassment of being treated as objects of both contempt and curiosity; spectators, including women, were staring at them from above.

On Saturday and Sunday, they were put on the train that made its way through the towns of southeastern Ontario, Peterborough and Marmora and Smiths Falls. No one knew its destination. Finally, in the early evening it headed into a lush green forest. Berlino Colangelo leaned over and said to Francesco Zaffiro, "Where, oh where are we going? We are so far from anywhere. Where are they taking us?" It was nearing midnight when the train arrived in Pembroke, Ontario. They were loaded onto trucks and within an hour they arrived at their lonely destiny, a compound of a dozen huts and a few other buildings, surrounded by two high barbed-wire fences. This was Camp Petawawa.[17]

By the end of June, as summer came to full bloom in the fields and forest around the camp, there were several hundred Italians in the barracks — the leaders of Canada's Italian community, along with many Germans and members of a few political parties that politicians, but mostly the RCMP, felt were dangerous to security. The numbers of Italians changed from time to time, as some had their cases reviewed and were released. Others under more recent suspicion arrived in the back of the police trucks, vainly trying to maintain their dignity. They became numbers, exchanging their clothing for overalls and a jacket with a large red circle on the back, for the guards in the towers to shoot at should its wearer attempt escape.[18]

Not all interned Italians were sent to Petawawa. One afternoon in early July, Luisa Guagnelli, who had come from Pezaro, Italy, in 1925 in her early twenties, and married and settled in Niagara Falls, Ontario, was tending her garden and her five-year-old son, Eugene. A few years earlier, she had joined the Sons of Italy, grateful that the lodge had extended its social activities to women. In 1940, she became president. That was why, on that sunny July afternoon, the RCMP came for her and told her to pack her clothes and come quickly. She asked what for, and was told: "That's the law." She asked if she could dress her son, who was in the bath. They said no.

Antonio Cordasco, the flamboyant *padrone* of turn-of-the-century Montreal.
NATIONAL ARCHIVES OF CANADA PA122612.

(Below) D'Angelo's labour exchange, Toronto, 1915. MULTICULTURAL HISTORY SOCI-
ETY OF ONTARIO.

Italians working on the railway, Thunder Bay, 1927. Long hours and onerous working conditions didn't prevent them from hamming it up for a snapshot to send home. MULTICULTURAL HISTORY SOCIETY OF ONTARIO

(Above) At the other side of the continent, railway workers in British Columbia relax at the rockface. MULTICULTURAL HISTORY SOCIETY OF ONTARIO. (Below) Italian volunteers for service in the First World War muster behind mayor Tommy Church in Toronto, 1915. NATIONAL ARCHIVES OF CANADA PA91106.

(Left) The Reverend J.M. Shaver, a Methodist minister, worked selflessly with Italians of the Lakehead as their friend. THE UNITED CHURCH ARCHIVES, TORONTO (Below) Within sight of the cupolas of a neighboring people and religion, Italians celebrate in a Madonna procession in front of St. Joseph's Church, Fort William, 1920s. MULTICULTURAL HISTORY SOCIETY OF ONTARIO.

(Opposite) Typical of the slum dwellings in Toronto's Ward district, this building was evacuated when the family crowded into the basement was discovered to have tuberculosis. The stalls at the right housed animals. CITY OF TORONTO ARCHIVES DPW 32-191. Below the city, Italians labored to build sewers, water lines and later subways. Note the candles affixed to the walls for light. CITY OF TORONTO ARCHIVES DPW 59-42

(Far left) Storm overflow sewer in Toronto. For years, Italians worked without safety equipment or proper ventilation. CITY OF TORONTO ARCHIVES, Salmon 47. (Left) Emilio Galardo established the first commercial photography studio in Sudbury, and posed with his family in 1932. (Below) Employees' picnic at Inco's smelter town, Copper Cliff, 1920. MULTICULTURAL HISTORY SOCIETY OF ONTARIO.

(Above) Aboard the vessel *Argentina*, March 1952, a group of young men from northern Italy head for Canada. Front row, second from the right, is Lino Magagna, Toronto, who spoke not a word of English. He would become one of the most influential and respected Italian-Canadians of the country.

(Right) Lino Magagna today — a doctoral degree from the University of Toronto, an official of Ontario Hydro, founder of the National Congress of Italian-Canadians, and member of the Order of Canada. KENNETH BAGNELL

Luisa Guagnelli was taken to Welland, placed in jail overnight and then transported to the Don Jail in Toronto, where she spent seven weeks among the coarsest women of Toronto's streets. Though terrified, she maintained a firm dignity, weeping only when alone. Then she was taken to the Women's Penitentiary at Kingston, Ontario where she became one of the three Italian women in Canada to be interned.[19]

While in Kingston, she wrote letters not just to her husband, but to Libero and Clementina Sauro, two friends she had come to know in Niagara Falls in the late twenties and early thirties, when Mr. Sauro was minister to the small Italian United Church congregation. The Reverend Libero Sauro replied to Luisa Guagnelli that he knew she was innocent of treachery and that he would do all he could to work for her release. He was active in the Sons of Italy himself, not only because he saw it as an opportunity for working among Italians, but because he wanted to help prevent it from falling under the influence of Fascist propaganda. Sauro was by then a minister to Italian Protestants in Toronto. He was in his study on Millwood Road on September 7, 1940, when the police arrived at his door to take him into custody.

Libero Sauro was given no reason for what happened on that day in September — other than the assertion that he was in violation of the Defense of Canada Regulations. The RCMP placed him in a form of temporary internment, in the barracks of the Veteran's Home Guard, a rickety set of buildings in Toronto near the intersection of College and Lansdowne. There, he was to await removal, when there were enough men to make a trip to Petawawa worthwhile. He became not only an internee but a prisoner of bureaucracy.

"The fact of the matter is," wrote his wife Clementina in a letter to their member of parliament, "an interned person may file notice of objection to his internment only when properly interned at Petawawa and they are not taken to Petawawa until there are fifty prisoners. If it takes a whole year for them to pick up that many prisoners, my husband will have to remain there all that time without a hearing . . . . I leave it to you to judge how this procedure compares to the Rights of Man of which all British peoples are proud and which I had the privilege of learning as well as teaching in the public schools of this province."

There was never to be a specific charge laid against Libero Sauro. His incarceration, while it got no attention in the press, did initiate a large number of letters to Minister of Justice Ernest Lapointe. Parishioners, fellow ministers, and leaders of the United Church attested to Sauro's character. Still others, dedicated civil libertarians, were baffled that Sauro was left month after month with no opportunity to find out why he was incarcerated, or to offer evidence that he should be released. "As a member of the committee charged with the revision of the Defense of Canada Regulations," wrote the CCF Member of Parliament M.J. Coldwell to Mrs. Sauro in November that year, "I can say that all members of the committee were of the opinion that persons detained ought to be given an early opportunity of making an appeal against charges laid against them. There was no division of opinion on this matter." Nonetheless, three weeks later, the Reverend Libero Sauro was transported under guard to Camp Petawawa.[20]

The camp on the dark Petawawa River was founded in 1904 as a training ground for the Canadian artillery. In the ensuing decades it broadened in size and purpose, to become during the First World War the training ground for over 10,000 soldiers, and the concentration camp for over 1,000 German and Austrian prisoners of war. Given its size of 55,000 acres, and its location (deep in the bush, yet within a couple of hours of Ottawa) it was obvious in 1940 that Camp Petawawa was ideal for the internment of those the department of justice, on the advice of the RCMP, deemed dangerous. An army officer, Lieutenant Colonel H.E. Pense, was made commandant. He took his job seriously but never forgot the fact that the men in his camp were not imprisoned for misdeeds, but interned for reasons of security. They were therefore to be treated with respect and courtesy, though of course if any tried to escape his guards were to fire a warning shot first and then aim at the red circle on their backs.

Each day that first fall, the men would rise to the 6 a.m. bugle and after trooping to the mess hall for a full breakfast of meat, eggs, toast, and coffee, they began the various tasks for which each was paid twenty cents a day. Their families were provided with a few dollars a month. Most men boarded army trucks which carried them several miles from the camp for work on the roads, or deep in the woods where they cleared brush and cut timber to be used to fire the camp's furnaces and stoves. Men of slighter build such as Alino Astri and Domenic Nardoccio, were assigned lighter work; mending the shoes of their colleagues and the soldiers who supervised them.

Luigi Pancaro was made senior medical doctor. He smiled when Lieutenant Colonel Pense took him to his office to announce his appointment, and said it would be a pleasure since he had such a large staff, over a dozen Italian-born doctors. A Toronto man, Nicholas Scandiffio, a graduate in law, helped some men plan their appeals to the tribunals before which they could appear in a dingy building in the nearby town of Pembroke. A chef at the Château Laurier in Ottawa used his talent in the camp kitchen, to the pleasure not only of the Italians but the Germans. Often when the day was over and the fires were lit, all would assemble in the mess hall and there the camp orchestra, with Frank Ferri directing and Berlino Colangelo singing, would play; from the deep Canadian forest, the words and music of Italian opera would rise.

Although they were agreeable companions, the men were lonely, worried and, at times, desolate. After all, they were guilty of no crime. They had been given no length of sentence — some would stay for only a few months and suddenly be freed, while others would remain for years. In the mornings, men who had been known for optimism climbed aboard the trucks with grave, lined faces, and spoke in low, private voices. In the bush, they consoled each other, trying to set aside the endless worry over their businesses, many of which were closed, often never to open again.

All accepted the frustration of their confinement; they no more tried to escape than their wives at home thought of returning to Italy. But they longed for the warmth of the home and the *paesani* of the neighborhood, whether Sudbury or Sydney. That, and worry for their wives and children — how they were managing on the pittance provided by the government. Letters from home were censored, and there were no family visits. With stoic courage, they endured, then tried to forget. (Long after it was over, there was still no effort to seek compensation for the years of deprivation and loss.)

Still, the chief topic of conversation in the huts was their unwavering belief that most of them had been wronged, their only "crime" their membership in social and cultural groups and, in some cases, as with most of the physicians, not even that. Some found their solace in the silence enforced after ten o'clock. Francesco Zaffiro would sit near the window beside his bunk, looking into the swirling snows of December, trying to fathom how he, a shoemaker with a grade-four education from a village school in Italy, had been incarcerated as a dangerous agent. How, he wondered, could he, whose only Italian activities were at his lodge and his church, be a danger to his country?

Zaffiro had never been a member of the Fascio, the political party formed in the mid-thirties in Canada under the influence of the Italian Fascist government through its consulates in Canada. Some of Zaffiro's friends were in the Fascio, though as Norman Robertson told Justice Minister Lapointe in 1939, many joined out of mindless loyalty, signing the oath of allegiance — which assured their internment — convinced that Mussolini, who was making the trains run on time, would also bring schools and hospitals to the barren villages they had known as children. One with whom Zaffiro often conversed in the months of internment was another shoemaker, a soft-spoken, cheerful, and candid man from Montreal named Leonard Frenza.

While in the camp, Frenza explained his membership in the Fascio to another internee. He said that in his own mind, he had made an error, innocent and naïve perhaps, but nonetheless an error. "I was like the rest of us, nostalgic for home, for Italy, for my own people. So I joined every Italian group I could. That was fine. I was in the Sons of Italy and even became secretary of the Grand Lodge in Montreal. And we had over ten lodges. But I also joined the Fascio and really that was a mistake. I was a fool."[21] Other detainees objected strongly to this self-blaming attitude, or even retained lingering sympathies for the Fascio, but for the rest of his life, Frenza would maintain that those who joined the Fascio had no one to blame for their internment but themselves.

Still, of the roughly seven hundred men in the camp, fewer than one hundred had been, like Frenza, active members of the Fascio. The rest were members of the lodges and clubs, while a few were simply well-known in their communities, influential and hence vulnerable to anonymous accusation. This was especially true of the man in Hut Number Five, Prisoner 307, whom his colleagues had chosen to be their spokesman — James Franceschini, Canada's first Italian-born millionaire, owner of Dufferin Construction, Quebec Paving and five associated companies in sand, gravel and road building equipment. In the winter of 1940, he struggled to accept his confinement expecting it to end any moment, so that he could return to the vast responsibilities he had in Toronto and elsewhere. Winter came, and the men turned to him as their natural leader; he accepted the role reluctantly at first, but then with gratitude.

Franceschini was then fifty years old. His face was large and full; his shoulders were as erect as ever, and his arms, thick and strong, gave him the aura of easy strength. They also served him well when he took his place on the road gang, and swung once again the first tools of his early days in Canada. All of the men, among them the physicians and academics who sometimes wondered if he could write much more than his name, marvelled at his native intellect and his rough charm. He became a close friend of Luigi Pancaro, the gentle, courtly physician from Sudbury. Franceschini confided to Pancaro that he had a touch of heart trouble, but urged that it be kept a secret from the camp commandant, lest it prevent him from working on the road gang. "If I can't get out of here to the roads, I'll go crazy," he said, and brooded.

Each week Franceschini went punctually to the camp post office, where invariably among the letters from his wife, there were food parcels from every province where he had built roads, so many that he began handing them out throughout the entire camp. But it was the trickle of letters from his executives that were beginning to unsettle him. His companies were not well. Indeed, they were worse than the letters from his men let on. Dufferin Construction and Dufferin Shipbuilding, then multi-million dollar operations, had been placed under the supervision of a government office called the Custodian of Alien Property. While the newer company, Dufferin Shipbuilding, was to build ships for the Canadian war effort as Franceschini had ordered, it was falling behind. As for Dufferin Construction — the company paving roads and building airports — it, too, was in difficulty. Franceschini would sit up late into the night, a small light above his bed, suspecting that the worst was yet to come. There was no way, in that bleak December before Christmas 1940, that James Franceschini could have realized the extent of it, that the Canadian government would sell much of his business at fire-sale prices and that he was headed for the most serious of all illnesses.[22]

Early in 1941, after he had been in the camp for seven months, he mentioned to Dr. Pancaro that he had a chill that would not leave. He sent a request to Lieutenant Colonel Pense for heavier clothing. "I have a heart complaint," he admitted, "and I am very sensitive to severe cold." The clothing was issued, but it made no difference. He was in the camp infirmary, sometimes for days at a stretch, and then he began to feel moments of numbness and most worrying of all, a choking sensation. The official Petawawa doctors, those in government service, seemed at a loss to determine the problem. Then finally, when he had trouble breathing, two of his interned colleagues, Luigi Pancaro and Donato Sansone, a physician from Toronto, went to his bed in the infirmary. Pancaro put his hand to his throat. He murmured to Sansone who did the same. For a long time they said nothing. Then Pancaro spoke. "Jim, you have throat cancer. You have to have an operation. Soon."

The internment of so many of the leaders of Canada's Italian community did not cause a great stir in the nation. The country's attention and energy were directed at a war in which Italy was a new and dangerous enemy. Here and there, a journalist, a clergyman, an academic, questioned it. So did a lonely handful of civil libertarians in Winnipeg, in a letter to Mackenzie King: "You cannot escape a grave responsibility. It would be a very sorry epitaph for a great Liberal prime minister that he was the man who opened the way for the extinction of Canadian liberty."[23]

The most important criticism of the internment — and especially that of James Franceschini — came from Toronto, from Bernard Keble Sandwell. Sandwell had been born in Britain, taught economics at McGill and English at Queen's and was, by 1940, the editor of the magazine *Saturday Night*, for which he wrote an editorial addressing itself, in very moderate language, to the internment.

He did not, he said, oppose it, at least in principle. The government, he conceded, had the right to intern those it suspected of subversive activity:

> Internment is, in the majority of cases, neither a punishment for a proven crime, nor the result of proven misconduct. It is, as Mr. Lapointe claims, a precautionary measure, the result of a suspicion on the part of somebody, shared by an officer of the RCMP, that the interned individual is intending, or is likely, to perform some act detrimental to the war effort. Inability to establish proof, the kind of proof required in a court of law, is the sole reason for setting up the kind of procedure provided for in the Defense of Canada Regulations.

But then Sandwell made his central argument: that the internment then underway in Canada was too severe, too harsh, too punitive.

> I shall not suggest however that in this respect, Mr. Lapointe is out of step with the general opinion of the country which I regard as dangerously apathetic to the whole internment problem, much too willing to aquiesce in the theory that anybody whom the RCMP suspects of subversive intent must necessarily be an enemy of the state. . . .[24]

On most Wednesdays and Fridays, a dull grey 1938 Chevrolet driven by an army corporal left Camp Petawawa for the modest town of Pembroke, and pulled up in a lot beside the magistrate's office. Throughout the dreary winter of 1940, and for the next two years, the rattling old car drove through the seasons, the corporal at the wheel, and beside him and behind, men from the huts of Petawawa. For them, the half-hour ride to Pembroke was a journey of hope. They were on their way to stand before a judge, who would listen as they told him why they should be released.

Francesco Zaffiro, for whom the Petawawa years were terribly lonely, made the trek to Pembroke three times, sitting in the room before the judge, and replying in a low voice and hesitant English, to the questions: What associations did he belong to? What literature did he read? Did he possess fire arms? What was his view of Mussolini? Why did he feel he was not a danger to Canada? Through his replies ran a consistent claim: he took part in Italian activities because he felt at home among his own people, he harbored no disloyalty, and as for Mussolini, he had read that he was a symbol of hope for his homeland, that he would unite its factions and bring its people out of poverty and illiteracy. Each time, Zaffiro returned to Petawawa where three days later he received a brief note in his mail: "The detention is to be continued."

For some, there were rumors of release, then whispers and smiles from an internee who was in the know: "Monday, Berlino. Monday. *You!*" Until Monday, Berlino would not sleep for turning and tossing and praying that it was true. Then he would be called to the commandant's office, asked to sign an oath of allegiance, and given a ride to the station and a train ticket home.

On a windy, spring morning in late May, 1941, Francesco Zaffiro, after a year in internment and those fruitless trips to Pembroke, was in the mess hall, when one of his friends nudged him, whispering that he should be ready for good news. He found it difficult to restrain himself. The next day the call came. He went to the office. He was not told, of course, that the judge had determined he was innocent, for he had not been charged with a crime in the beginning. Nor was he told a mistake had been made, or an apology would be issued. He was told simply that he could sign the oath of allegiance and leave.

Francesco Zaffiro left Camp Petawawa on May 18, 1941. It

was late in the afternoon when his train arrived in Hamilton. He stood for a long time on the station platform, then, with his suitcase in his hand, he walked down Barton Street and along James, beneath the trees and through the neighborhoods he had passed each day for years on the way to his shop. Then he saw his home, his wife in the doorway waiting; somehow, miraculously, she had known he would be coming. Behind her were his children and a few old and good friends. There were hugs and tears and then a long night of food and wine and talk. Francesco Zaffiro was home.

Others, too, left alone and quietly, returning by train to warm reunions. But in the case of James Franceschini in Hut Number Five, now seriously ill, it was not to be that way. He had made the trip to Pembroke to appear before the judge on two occasions and to his great satisfaction Mr. Justice Hyndman of the Ontario Supreme Court, described by the *Globe and Mail* as one of the most brilliant judges in Canada, recommended strongly that he be released. But when Hyndman's recommendation was forwarded to Justice Minister Ernest Lapointe, nothing happened.

Franceschini grew not only despondent, but suspicious that somehow someone was exerting pressure to keep him behind the barbed wire of Petawawa. And though he could not have realized it, he was about to become a victim of one of the most unfair acts ever taken against a Canadian citizen by his own government.

That December in 1940, as his health worsened, officials in the office of the Custodian of Enemy Property, under whose jurisdiction the business interests of the interned men fell, began a very close examination of the corporate properties of James Franceschini. Just before Christmas, they took the machinery and equipment he had purchased to open a new cement plant in Montreal — material estimated by the government's accounting firm as being worth $1,750,000 — and sold it to a Montreal firm which Franceschini, had he not been interned, would have challenged in direct competition in the cement business — at one-tenth its stated value.

Franceschini, when he was told of it, was bereft. He wrote a letter to his lawyer, Dalton McCarthy of Toronto, asking why he was remaining interned while others were leaving. McCarthy's reply confirmed all Franceschini's suspicions: "Apparently, there is some opposition fostered by certain competitors of yours in the Province of Quebec which is holding matters up and there has been a whispering campaign against you which has an influence upon the minister. . . . "

Finally, the Premier of Ontario, Mitchell Hepburn, intervened. Hepburn had been correctly told that Franceschini was dying in Petawawa. Hepburn insisted he be released or else he would disclose things he knew that were better left unsaid. On June 20, 1941, James Franceschini was released from Camp Petawawa on compassionate grounds. He was taken by car, still wearing his prisoner's uniform, to a military hospital in Toronto, from which he was transferred to Toronto General Hospital to be operated on for throat cancer. The surgery, described by the renowned throat specialist Harold Wookey as a matter of life or death in which he could guarantee nothing, took place on June 28. The following day, Franceschini's own doctor told the *Globe and Mail* that he had pulled through, but was in serious condition, partly because his condition had not been promptly treated by the official medical staff at Petawawa.

Nonetheless, within a week, he had his executives — who had remained loyal while the business was run by the Custodian of Alien Property — at his bedside. One of them, his first partner, Charlie Johnston, told him the bad news first: not only had the equipment for the planned cement company in Montreal been sold at fire-sale prices, but the contents of his greenhouses in Mimico had been sold for eighty dollars; and his show horses had been disposed of. Dufferin Construction, however, despite the absence of its owner, had eleven major contracts underway, six of them for airport construction, awarded by the federal government that had interned its owner. Dufferin Shipbuilding, the company he had created and placed at the service of the National Department of Defense, was in need of him — the minesweepers were being built, but schedules were not being met.

The summer of 1941 was, strangely, to be one of his happiest. Returning to his offices on Fleet Street in Toronto renewed him. He strolled the gardens of Mimico and it was as if the events of the year began to fall away. Toward the end of summer, he told Charlie Johnston he was going to leave within a week for a tour of all his airport construction sites, from Nova Scotia to British Columbia.

Then, one morning, in late August, he was at home in Mimico when the phone rang. The caller was a businessman, who at the time was serving the government, advising on matters of finance. Franceschini agreed to a meeting. Within an hour, courtesies were exchanged, and the caller came to the point. "Jim, the government is taking over your shipyard. We'll name the price. If you don't accept the price, we'll acquire it anyway and you can spend the next ten years fighting us in court. What's more, we're taking your property next door — where the construction company stands. We need it. That's the deal, Jim. You're out of shipbuilding. And you're out of Fleet Street."

Franceschini had been put in Petawawa without just cause; while he was there, his business properties had been partly sold off; he had been let out of Petawawa not because his innocence was admitted, but because he was ill, and now he faced the ignominy of having his properties confiscated by the very government that had already heaped injury after injury upon him. Franceschini recalled an incident that had taken place over a year earlier, in May, 1940, in the lobby of the Château Laurier. A man he did not know had approached him and, after identifying himself as a shipbuilder, warned him to stay out of the business, that those already in it deeply resented his plan to build ships for Canada for less than the going rate. "Stay out," the stranger threatened, "or else." Now in the living room of his home on a summer evening in 1941, the full force of what he had been told was clear. The Canadian government meant to wreck him.

He glared at his visitor. Then he exploded. "Get the hell out of my house!" The man left. Within weeks, Dufferin Shipbuilding became a crown corporation, Toronto Shipbuilding, with offices in the former headquarters of Dufferin Construction. James Franceschini would never return to Fleet Street.

By December 1941, almost five hundred Italian-born men were still in the dozen huts of Petawawa, clearing the roads, cutting the timber, and tending to the lighter work in the buildings and on the grounds. Most of them had come to terms with their incarceration, finding their encouragement and hope in the letters that came from their families, though each could receive only three letters of twenty-four lines or less, each month.

By then it was clear to many of them that they would remain interned, if not for the duration of the war, for most of it; they could not foresee that Italy's involvement would cease in November 1943, when they would all be sent home. They were, in the eyes of their supervisors and inspectors, exemplary prisoners, making few complaints, and nurturing their depression — a common experience — in private or in long conversations among themselves. Still, not all prisoners shared this passive acceptance of their lot.

On Christmas Eve, 1941, Frank Ferri and his band from Hamilton, along with a choir he had assembled, gathered in the mess hall to play carols and sing the old songs of Christmas before their fellow prisoners. At nine o'clock sharp they packed their instruments and, along with the hundreds of men in the audience, began to make their way back to their huts and the long silence of the night. At the door, one of the officers stopped Ferri.[25] "Frank," he said, "you and the others have had a good Christmas Eve. The guards haven't. They're out there in the towers alone. It's no way to celebrate Christmas Eve. How about you and the band and choir going outside to give them some Christmas music."

Ferri went back to his group and they gathered in the hard snow of the camp compound — all but two German prisoners who found the idea of singing for their captors repugnant. The crisp, star-lit night carried the voices of Italian tenors and baritones bringing old words of peace on earth to men whose job it was to keep them captive in their adopted land.

On November 26, 1941, Ernest Lapointe, the minister of justice under whom the men had been interned, died in Montreal after

months of declining health. His successor, a Montreal lawyer
invited into the cabinet by Mackenzie King, Louis St. Laurent,
was moved by humane impulses toward the men in Petawawa,
embarassed by several of the internments, and seriously tried to
see to the release of many of the men. Ever more frequently,
Colonel Pense, the camp commandant, would receive a terse
note from Ottawa: "Vincenzo Martinello had been determined
to be no longer a threat to national security. He may be
released." In the Italian communities of the country, the winter
of 1942 was a time of family reunions as men returned to their
homes, but often, as well to businesses that had been closed or
jobs that had been filled.

In Europe, and in North Africa, Italy's campaigns had fal-
tered, so that toward the end of 1942 it was clear that Italy
would soon withdraw. In June, 1943, Mussolini resigned and in
early September the country offered its unconditional surrender
to the allied forces. In Toronto, bonfires were lit in the streets of
The Ward. Men and women danced and sang.

In Petawawa, the huts were silent, the last remaining prisoners having been sent a few months earlier to spend their final
days in the cold damp of primitive, hard Gagetown, near the
city of Fredericton, New Brunswick. There, many dreamt not
only of home, but of the comparative luxury they left behind in
Petawawa.

When it was all over, many found a welcome in their own
Italian communities, but vague alienation in the towns and
cities they had come from. A few moved to new parts of the
country, to begin again. Luisa Guagnelli of Niagara Falls was
released from Kingston Women's Penitentiary and returned to
her home in Niagara Falls, to her husband and small son, but
found that even in her church, where she had spent so many
years in the Catholic Women's League, there were reservations
toward her that would hurt deeply and for many years. Her son
Eugene was seven when she came home. "We will go to Italy,"
he said to his mother the first day she was back. "And there will
be no trouble anymore." His mother took him in her arms and
said, "This is our country. This is where we will stay."

For a few, the new friends of Petawawa were forgotten, as if it had been such a dreary and difficult time, that in shedding its memories, they shed its friendships. Others were to remain steadfast by letters and visits the remainder of their lives. After he had been free for almost a decade, Frank Ferri fulfilled a long-held promise to one of the physicians who had been in his hut — Ignatius Scozzafave of Welland, Ontario. He had promised the doctor, who had spent three full years in Petawawa and who liked the music of big bands, that one day, he would come to Welland with his band and play for him.[26] One very late spring night, when the town was wrapped in pre-dawn silence, five automobiles, filled with Italian musicians from Hamilton — on their way home after a concert in Fort Erie, Ontario — pulled up beside a stately three-storey house in an affluent Welland neighborhood. Over a dozen men got out, assembling on the lawn with saxophones, trumpets, cornets, drums, guitars, and a bass fiddle. Then softly, but with growing confidence, the band filled the still, dark air with the tune "A String of Pearls." Light appeared in a top floor window, then throughout the house. A police car arrived, then another, and another. The officers got out, smiled, and shook their heads. And then, from the wide door of his home, Dr. Scozzafave appeared, a tray of brandy glasses in hand, to serve his old friend Frank Ferri from Hut Number Five, his band, and the members of Welland's police department who would never know what it all meant, except that the music was unforgettable.

In every part of Canada, the Italian community knew the internment as a historic tragedy; it would not recover for two decades. Italians had been on the verge of finding a sense of pride and a feeling of place in Canada. Then suddenly, the community had been decimated, its leaders interned, its presses silent, its organizations dormant. Even worse, it was rife with confusion, discouragement and even resentment, as young Italians, feeling fresh stigmas because of the labels placed upon their elders, began to shy away from any assertion of their culture. Some, who might have assumed leadership in the years immediately after the war, avoided doing so in favor of simply getting by, making a living, forgetting the past. Some of the institutions of the day, out of misguided judgment or a vague indifference, helped them lose their pride and place. When the Reverend Libero Sauro, minister of Toronto's Italian United Church, St. Paul's, was released from internment, he found that his congregation had almost been rejected by the United Church; that their church was no longer available, and that they had to worship in the basement of another congregation. It was a blow which the tiny congregation of two hundred families — a minority within a minority — would never fully forget. In that experience, they symbolized Italians in Canada in the 1940s — leaderless, rejected, and dejected.

For Luigi Pancaro, the physician who had served as head of the interned medical men, the road back to his practice among the Italian men and women of Sudbury was not easy. He had been away for a full two years. But by 1944, he appeared to be a man fully restored in spirit. His gifts as a surgeon seemed to grow and gain wide respect. On certain days of the week, after he had been back home for over two years, he would assist a fellow surgeon on nearby Manitoulin Island: it was a chance to help another physician in his more complicated cases in the operating room. One morning, in the spring of 1944, he went to the small island hospital at Little Current. The other surgeon told him the first case was a patient brought in with a burst appendix. Examining the anaesthetized patient, he murmured, "Louis, it is bad. Very bad. It's a serious case of peritonitis. I'm not touching it. This is for you."

Pancaro moved quickly to the table. He saw there the officer who on June 11, 1940, had entered his clinic in Sudbury, removed the print of the Virgin Mary from his wall, gone through his patient files, and taken him into custody. He said nothing, and proceeded; the operation was a routine success. Many years later, a friend reading some of his private papers found a reference to that day and to how he felt.

"I proceeded with the operation very calmly," he wrote, "and asked God to guide my hand. The physician's prayer came to my assistance: 'Dear Lord, Thou Great Physician, I kneel before Thee. Since every good and perfect gift must come from Thee, I pray, give skill to my hand, clear vision to my mind, kindness and sympathy to my heart.'"

PART TWO

CHAPTER FIVE

THE LONG JOURNEY FROM VALLELONGA TO LORETTO

On the day World War II ended, May 7, 1945, there were fewer than 100,000 people living in Canada who regarded themselves as Italian: immigrants who had settled in about twenty Italian communities across the country — from large Little Italies in Toronto and Montreal to small neighborhoods in Trail, British Columbia, and Dominion, Nova Scotia — and the children who had been born to them. No matter where they were situated, they were a discouraged people.[1]

In Nova Scotia, as the summer of victory drifted into autumn, the Italian immigrants of Cape Breton, a couple of hundred people in Dominion, Glace Bay, and Sydney, seemed the most injured of all, a small, nervous group of laborers who had barely begun to feel their acceptance when the sudden fury of war and internment had descended. Their leaders were taken from them, their fellow workers refused to enter the mines with them, and many of their neighbors, through organizations like the Canadian Legion, had urged that virtually every last one of them should be interned. It was an injury which in a few cases was never to heal — some of the Cape Breton families left for new lives in Ontario. In Dominion, the most hostile town, several decided to leave the coal mines and retreat to the quiet, almost empty countryside of Cape Breton, where they took up farming, and raised their children in sight of the peaceful, winding Mira river.

In Montreal that September, Leonard Frenza, who was released from Petawawa before the end of the war, and had left shoemaking for a more agreeable life at tailoring, decided he would make some effort to revive the dormant organization he had done so much for, the Sons of Italy. He got in touch with the RCMP. "Do you think," he asked an official one autumn afternoon, "it might be okay to have the records that were taken from me returned? They were the minutes of meetings held in chapters of the lodge all over Montreal." Nothing was ever returned.

But Frenza faced another, more telling disappointment. There was little interest in reviving the Sons of Italy. In Montreal, the largest Italian community in Canada, the vast majority of Italians were not interested in the sentiments of men such as Leonard Frenza who wanted to maintain the old language and culture or to provide help to the ill and the bereaved. Not now; not after he and the others had gotten the entire community into trouble by celebrating their Italian heritage. For the generation to which men like Frenza were fathers, the years after the war were a time to forget the things that were Italian. After all, they reasoned, the best way to get along is to become invisible on the streets of Canada. It was the same everywhere, even in Winnipeg and Saskatoon, where the communities were so small and so passive that very few prairie Italians had been interned. The young, begrudging their elders for the hostility they endured in the war years, tended not to blame the people they might have — the politicians and the police — but their own community leaders instead.

In Toronto, where the same divisions marred even the strongest groups — the Sons of Italy and the Dopolavaro — scores of Italians changed their names: men who had been Rossini became Ross, Riccioni became Richards, Ciccomo became Jackman and others, going back beyond even the memory of their Italian past, became Smith and Jones. A few remained bitter for many years, their bitterness taking on the complex psychology of continual self-abasement. It was the leaders, the litany went, who led to the troubles, they who did not know what they were doing, they who caused the stereotype of Italians as disloyal, they who brought on the smashed windows, the loss of customers, the loss of jobs. In Montreal, in Toronto, in Vancouver, as well as in the northern towns of Ontario, the mood was almost the same: speak English, act Canadian. "We don't want to be too prominent," one Italian in Toronto told a friend from Calabria, in 1948, "and we don't want to be too quickly identified as being Italian." It was clear: *italianità* was to be shunned. At the ports where thousands of Italians had walked down gangplanks to Canada, the lines were mere trickles. It was as if, in the eyes of Canada, they who had built so much were now, more than ever, undesirables. In 1946, more than 71,000 immigrants landed in Canada. Only 146 were from Italy.[2]

In the autumn of 1942, fifty-two-year-old James Franceschini, was still muscular in his shoulders and brisk in his stride, but was somewhat frail from three major operations for cancer at Toronto General Hospital. Worse, he nursed an inner despair over what had happened to him at the hands of his own government. "I have been cut to pieces," he would say to friends with a sardonic smile, referring to his spirit as well as his body. After the assaults made on his property by the government of Mackenzie King, he was virtually a ruined man, so full of hurt that at the suggestion of friends, he left Toronto and moved to the peace and serenity of land he bought in Mont Tremblant, Quebec, about ninety miles from Montreal. The land was high on a hill, in sight of a wide, silent lake; it seemed to bring serenity to his troubled mind.

In that first year at Mont Tremblant he roamed the land alone, brooding over his misfortunes from the day of his internment, to the day, when, after his release, the government confiscated his property and sold his equipment against all the dictates of fairness and due process. Moreover, he felt hurt that so many of his former friends in Toronto had remained silent as he was destroyed. Only the *Globe and Mail*, the leading editorial voice of the day, spoke clearly on his behalf, arguing that he had been unjustly interned and was owed an apology. For himself, he left matters with his Toronto lawyer, but expected little. The *Globe* persisted. Finally, in the summer of 1943, a year after Franceschini had moved to Quebec, Louis St. Laurent, then minister of justice, admitted, if obliquely, that indeed it had probably all been a mistake. "In the case of James Franceschini," he said in a letter to Toronto lawyer George Campbell, "I have no objection to state to you now that Mr. Justice Hyndman, after full inquiry into all the circumstances which had prompted the internment of this man and careful consideration of the case as a whole, had reported he was satisfied and convinced that he (Franceschini) was not disloyal to Canada." St. Laurent avoided saying what ought to have been said: that the internment itself was wrong, that the release on grounds of compassion was an unworthy pretext for a government unwilling to admit its own error.

A few days later, in the King Street offices of the *Globe and Mail*, A.A. MacIntosh, the paper's editor, sat for an hour with a couple of his writers reviewing the Franceschini case and their own past comments on it. One of the writers slipped into a tiny, paper-strewn office and, with a pile of clippings beside him, wrote the editorial that appeared the following morning, June 17, 1943:

> The Minister of Justice has at long last made public his conviction that Mr. James Franceschini, the well known contractor, had not been disloyal to his Canadian citizenship when he was seized and sent to an internment camp in June 1940. . . .
>
> The case has been the most notorious in the annals of Canada's secret internment procedure, attracting wide attention on account of the prominence and wealth of the contractor, and the doubtful circumstances which seemed to surround it, including alleged political persecution . . .
>
> When it became common knowledge that Mr. Justice Hyndman [who had been appointed to conduct an inquiry] reported himself unable to find any proof of subversive conduct on the part of Mr. Franceschini and recommended his release, we argued that in all fairness, this report should be acted upon and made public to justify the release. But ... the department stubbornly refused either to release Mr. Franceschini or give its

reasons for disregarding the report. Now, Mr. St. Laurent has needed a further eighteen months before he could decide that Mr. Franceschini is entitled to a clean bill of health.

But several pertinent questions can fairly be asked. First, why did the late Minister of Justice, having appointed an experienced judge to examine the case, not accept his report at once and act on it? Secondly, why did the present Minister of Justice need such a long time to be persuaded that Mr. Justice Hyndman was right? The real reasons for this extraordinary procedure will probably never be disclosed, but its consequence was that for three years a Canadian citizen was allowed to lie under a serious stigma of disloyalty for which there was no justification. He should not have been arrested at all; but the much greater offence against him was the failure to release him as soon as Mr. Justice Hyndman had reported . . .[3]

For the next two years — while James Franceschini rallied his strength and his friends began a historic business recovery — the *Globe* kept up its campaign insisting that the wrongs be righted. It was not until the end of 1945 that St. Laurent admitted the flimsy reasoning behind the internment: "From the information that Mr. Lapointe had," he told the House of Commons late that year, "he was convinced that this man had done nothing wrong, but he was fearful he might do something which would be injurious to the safety of the state." Little wonder that the *Globe and Mail* bristled with suspicion: "Mr. Lapointe stubbornly refused to produce an explanation and thereby created a suspicion that James Franceschini had been interned to gratify the spite of political or personal enemies . . . Was there ever such a flimsy and contemptible excuse for the internment of an innocent Canadian citizen?"

While the battle raged between the Liberal government and the *Globe and Mail*, James Franceschini was making long strides in the rebuilding of his empire. The hills of Mont Tremblant were a balm to his spirit, and once his recovery was complete, his energies burst forth, fueled by his discovery that there were men of influence all over Canada ready to stand by him and his reputation.

In cooperation with Canada, the United States announced early in 1942 a plan to begin one of history's biggest and most romantic road-building ventures: a highway to Alaska. Once he heard of it, Franceschini wrote to an official of the United States Army engineers, with a request for an opportunity to bid on three parts of the gigantic highway to the north — the road from Dawson Creek to Fort St. John in British Columbia, from Fort Nelson, B.C. to Watson Lake in the Yukon, and, finally, the substructure of the bridge over the Peace River at Fort St. John. The Americans appeared to be quite familiar with his history, and were at least willing to have him submit references. He was astonished at the words men wrote on behalf of himself and his company.

"The Dufferin Company did a large mileage of work in Nova Scotia," wrote the province's deputy minister of highways, "and the mileage they did was as great as, if not greater, than any other contractor.... Their work was of the highest quality and I, personally, found them a splendid company with which to do business."[4] Similar praise suffused the letters from deputy ministers of highways in every province; they were all he needed. He became himself again, traveling and overseeing the work that would leave his imprint on a chapter of North American contracting history.

In the winter and spring of 1947, three events of historic influence on hundreds of thousands of Italians and on the future of Canada, took place in Ottawa, but went almost unreported by the press and unnoticed by the country. On February 10, 1947, Prime Minister Mackenzie King, signed a peace treaty with Italy. Shortly afterwards, Italians were removed from the distasteful wartime category of enemy aliens and Italians abroad with no relatives in Canada were permitted to apply for immigration. Then, early in April that year, the government withdrew its restriction — placed there because of the practices of men such as Antonio Cordasco — prohibiting the importing of contract laborers, men ready to come in groups to Canada with the simple promise that once here, they would find a place in the old army of the pick and shovel. Finally, almost unremarked by anyone, on a January day in 1948, when the weather in Rome was unseasonably warm, the Canadian government opened a small immigration office not far from St. Peter's Square. By the end of 1948, 3,202 Italians had been admitted to Canada; by the end of the next year, 7,742 more had come.

Late that year, on December 9, 1949, a Liberal member of Parliament named David Croll, then forty-nine years old, slight but vigorous, and with a life-long reputation for standing by progressive and humane causes, rose in the House of Commons. In his soft voice he delivered a speech on immigration which was to stand for many years as a reflection of the attitude towards immigration of the Liberal government of the day, and its leader Mackenzie King. Croll was at least indirectly commending his own party, but no member of the Opposition saw fit to challenge what he said, which was reasoned in tone and factual in content. He paid tribute to the recent announcement that a new Department of Citizenship and Immigration was to be formed. He noted not only the significance of the new department but the fact that the previous Friday, the Prime Minister had taken a positive position on the question of admitting more immigrants to the country.

When he had diplomatically paid his acknowledgement to the Prime Minister's earlier statement, Croll outlined the reasoning behind what would become, in two short years, the opening of the doors of Canada to an ever-widening stream of new citizens from Europe, notably Italians. Britain, he said, was no longer able to send the numbers it once had. "Faced with that situation," argued Croll, looking out upon a half-empty House in the late afternoon, "we must revise our standards considerably if we want to retain our present healthy level of immigration. If the flow is dwindling we must open the sluice wider. People," he said, "have always been our most valuable import."

On that quiet December afternoon, David Croll — former cabinet minister in the Ontario government of Mitchell Hepburn and now Member of Parliament for Spadina — proposed that the regulations governing immigration be revised and made more liberal. The present categories were both restrictive and unfair. In his view, the test of admissibility should be twofold: "First, is the immigrant a useful citizen, and second, is there someone in Canada who will accept responsibility for him, who will guarantee accommodation and maintenance until he becomes self-supporting? Then, providing they are in good health, they should be encouraged to come to Canada to build new lives here. A second solution is to attract settlers from countries which, in the past, have sent us many fine Canadians."

As David Croll paused, a lone voice from one of the back benches — as if from the fading recess of history — shouted "Scotchmen!" Croll, as adroit as he was generous, smiled and replied that there were none better. Then he went on to the point he had in mind when he rose a half-hour earlier. "I was thinking," he said quietly, "particularly of Italy. Today Italy is a great reservoir of manpower .... Italy is a country that has always been overcrowded, lacking resources. Her economy is reduced to a point where she must export people, if she wishes to achieve any kind of stability. This is a great opportunity for us and we cannot afford to miss it."

David Croll continued for another fifteen minutes. The afternoon was nearly over; members began slipping away quietly, to offices, to meals, to trains. Croll launched into his conclusion. He said that Italians were ideal immigrants, hard working people who would fit in, who would come to stay, who would bring enormous benefits to Canada. "I should like," he said, "to see this government mount a full-scale immigration scheme, designed to draw us the best type of settlers from Italy ...." The applause was scattered and light.

But Croll's proposal, left unreported by the press and unheard by the majority of MPs, was a landmark in Canadian immigration history.[5] Within a year, the Italian stream would be under way, as the country recruited men for the backbreaking work still to be done, and as relatives already here sponsored the applications of others. Almost 20,000 applicants were already in the line to come by 1950. Each year in the fifties, at least 20,000, sometimes as many as 30,000, would arrive on the ships and, soon, the planes, in Montreal and Toronto, in a river whose current would grow stronger and stronger.[6]

In many ways, they were destined to relive the pains of their emigrant forbears. They did hard work in harsh places, bound under contract to remain there at least for a year in climates they had never imagined. They were, as Franca Iacovetta (a child of one of them who many years later became a historian of her people) would write, ordered in bulk and treated that way — not as men with high hopes and personal dreams, but as commodities — bodies to dig the land and turn the wheel of progress.[7]

The stream began slowly and at first, almost entirely from the north of Italy. Canada's prejudices were still alive, and expressed in its immigration bureaucracy's preference for the sturdy men of the industrialized north over the peasant men of the south. In villages of brown streets and stone houses resting among the mountains of Trentino, and low, quiet villages sleeping in the lush greenery of Friuli, men left, just as their grandfathers did, for Argentina, for the United States, and for Canada. They were leaving a land rich in everything but opportunity. Italy in 1950 was not, as generations of Canadians believed, full of desperate men and women with starvation in their eyes. It was a beautiful, agrarian land, but with too many people to live from agriculture. And, more profoundly, it was a land in which boys became men believing their destiny lay elsewhere. Emigration was in their history and in their hearts.

In the early spring of 1950, the year of the first wave of the new emigration, a priest in a small church of a few hundred families, on the edge of the old town of Azzano Decimo in Friuli, the Reverend Enrico Battiston noticed he was saying good-bye to many, many members of his poor parish. His four hundred-year-old church, St. Lawrence the Martyr, stood just beyond the town, on a stretch of flat land swept by the wind that left the trees bent and leafless. Father Battiston had come to the church in 1943, and stayed the rest of his life. The population of the town was about ten thousand, of which only a few who owned large tracts of land were able to prosper. The saddest years of Father Battiston's ministry came in the early 1950s, when day after day, he bade farewell to young men, usually his best, who would visit him, often very unsure of themselves, to ask his blessing. "They do not really want to go," he said to members of his parish and other priests. "Not really. They are going because they have to go. If only the land were better, if only we had industry."[8]

His congregation, like the town, began to dwindle. The men went first, then their families. He lost more than fifty. Letters came with money for the church, from Toronto, from Windsor, from Fort William. One family — the husband a factory worker in Windsor — sent enough to put a much-needed furnace in the old building. But in time, the number of letters and the gifts dwindled, and ceased. "They have helped us as they could when they could," the priest said sadly. "But now they are people of another land. Their loyalty is there."

In the town of Azzano Decimo, a businessman named Rodolfo Hoffer — a sturdy, confident young man with a firm, decisive style — saw many of his boyhood and army friends leave. He, too, thought he might go, but for family reasons and out of a personal sense of his own future, he remained in Azzano Decimo to become a prosperous civic leader. He understood, he told them, only too well why they felt compelled to leave — the land was poor, the work, scarce. Thirty years later, Azzano Decimo would grow green from irrigation and prosperous from industrialization, but in 1950, its future seemed as barren as the ground near St. Lawrence the Martyr Church. So hundreds left in 1950, followed by hundreds more, so that by 1970, the stream from Azzano Decimo to Canada had become a river of four thousand people.

From the region of Friuli to the province of Abruzzi is a journey from land that is mostly low and marshy to terrain of rugged, earthen hills and rock-encrusted mountains, where throughout the century too many men have fought a failing battle of farming wheat and growing grapes. In the city of L'Aquila — an ancient Abruzzian city where churches from 700 A.D. still stand, a man named Tulio de Rubeis saw, as Rodolfo Hoffer had in Friuli, the stream of 1950 that became the river to Canada: hundreds of people he knew from childhood, and many more that he did not, leaving the towns and villages for overseas. For Tulio de Rubeis, it was a scene so familiar that it became a routine part of his days in the 1950s, as familiar as the act of eating or sleeping: "I have seen so many leave for Canada for so many years. It is the most common aspect of history that I have observed. I remember them going when I was a boy before the First World War. They had to go. It was an emigration of absolute necessity. They would go to the United States or to Canada and they would return and then go again and return again. Then came the Second World War, and, of course, it was over for a time. In 1950 when it resumed, it was different. Then men would go and stay. And then the families would go — so many. So very many."[9] De Rubeis lived to see almost a hundred thousand leave Abruzzi for Canada in the fifties and sixties. As in Friuli, villages once populous were almost emptied.

Southward from Abruzzi the land grows warm and green, until at last it opens on the foot of the country, the region of Calabria, where narrow, endless roads, turning back upon themselves as they follow the old cattle paths, climb the land, and where sudden hills almost brush the sky, on top of them small towns or villages which have been there from before the time Rome was great.

   Calabria is the deep south of Italy, and it was from the south that the greatest wave of the emigration of the fifties and sixties left for Canada. Like the *Friulani* of the north and the *Abruzzese* of the centre, the *Calabrese* had been emigrants throughout history, but in their case, they had been emigrants within their own country. For generations, back into the 1800s, they had been leaving their beautiful, barren land, fleeing the prison of poverty, for Rome and Milan where they could be found in the most servile of jobs and under the thumb of the discriminating north. The south, they would always feel, was the exploited cousin of their country — not so much taken into the fold of the nation when it was unified, as annexed to it, a source of cheap labor. The claim of Italy's national government, that it was intent on bringing the south, the *Mezzogiorno*, into the modern world and replacing its poverty with prosperity, was either a cheap posture or a sincere but ill-considered program. It found-ered on the shoals of confusion in Rome, ineptitude among politicians, and a bureaucracy that confounds the world with its

strangling red tape. The facts of this dreary truth of Italian life —
that there are really two Italies, the north and the south — was
put clearly by one of the country's most distinguished journalists
and essayists, Luigi Barzini, himself a Liberal deputy in the
Italian parliament:

> To begin with, the immense poverty is too old and too deeply
> rooted really to have disappeared. It has been mostly swept
> under the carpet. Most of the improvements and moderniza-
> tions can be observed around a few chosen cities, a few favoured
> sites, and the most fertile agricultural sections. Everywhere else
> where the casual visitor from the north does not usually go,
> around the corner from a prosperous scene, a stone's throw from
> the resplendent new hotels, factories or workers' housing pro-
> jects, the *miseria* is still supreme . . . Even if it were to disap-
> pear, however, the problem would still not be solved . . . The
> malaise and the restlessness, the feeling of being the victims of
> historical injustice and the prey of other people's greed, the
> desire to revolt and break away from the centralized government
> of Rome would go on.[10]

Calabria is at the foot of Italy — the familiar "toe" of the
Italian boot which seems almost to touch the island of Sicily.
There, the deep south actually unfolds upon what some histori-
ans call the most "Italian" part of Italy. In 1950, just over two
million people lived in Calabria, in provinces with such lyrical
names as Catanzaro and Cosenza. In a thousand towns set upon
the grey-green mountains, peasant men and women raised
sheep and goats, figs, olives, and a few grapes for themselves. In
Cosenza, which is toward the north of Calabria, farmers worked
the small parcels of soil with the hoes their great grandfathers
used to break the slopes of the mountain ranges.

The road beyond the capital city of Cosenza — itself called
Cosenza — winds upward, apparently aimless and unending,
spiralling through hills to a melancholy sky, until at last it comes
upon the village of its destiny, Vallelonga. It is an old place, its
origin lost in the past, but rumored among the old people to
date from the sixth century, when men built high on the side of
the mountain to give themselves protection against the inevitable Vandals.

Vallelonga in 1950 was a town of about 2,700 people, who scraped the most modest living from the land which sloped from the village's edge. There was a small main street, a tiny town hall — for the mayor, the clerk, the two *carabinieri* — an old church, and a maze of narrow, cobbled streets lined with wood frame houses whose tiny windows looked out on the distant fringe of the Ilex forest, and beyond the grey groves of olive trees. There were few sounds, only the jangle of the goat bells upon the almost Sabbath silence.

There was, of course, a *piazza*; on its benches sat the old, the village children before them, listening to the talk of men who had worked in Canada in the twenties and thirties, and came home with a gold watch and a hundred stories. Beyond the *piazza*, in the bar — a small room where the sun flickered upon the walnut-dark wood — on a morning in the spring of 1950, a group of men in their early thirties sat talking. The talk was about a city they had never visited but whose name was as familiar as the street where they lived: Toronto. The conversation, drifting across tables upon which glasses sat empty, was laden with nostalgia, almost as if Toronto was a known place. From time to time, the name of the city was spoken in the slow Calabrian dialect — *Torr—on—to* — as if it were part of their own memories. Of course, it was not. They did not know Toronto. But their fathers had. Some had lived there and died there. Others had been sojourners, returning to Vallelonga and passing to their sons the names of people and places, so that for years the very streets were part of the daily vocabulary of young men in Vallelonga: Clinton and Manning, Euclid and Grace. Toronto seemed as much a part of their youth as the very square beyond the bar.

One man's name was spoken more than any other on that day in early 1950: Joe Pilleggi. *Mister* Joseph Pilleggi. They spoke his name with that measured respect that *Calabrese*, for centuries, accorded an elder. And, of course, Joseph Pilleggi was all of that. He had gone to Canada when the century was young, before the first of the wars, a bright man with his eye on his future. He was in Toronto in 1912. He dressed well, he spoke well, and he became, in St. Agnes Church and in the old Little

Italy, a leader. He also became, in the thirties, the good friend of a politician named George Drew, later the premier of Ontario. Joe Pilleggi was a Drew man, the representative of the Tory Premier among the Italians of Toronto and all Ontario.

In the bar in Vallelonga that afternoon, his name was spoken with respect because he had twice come home in recent years and offered men jobs in Canada, in the lumber woods of Ontario. He was, like the men who went before him in the commerce of emigration, a *padrone*. Unlike many of them, he kept his promises. For three hundred dollars, payable later once a man was on his feet, he could leave the poverty of Vallelonga, guided by a man from his own village, Joseph Pilleggi, and receive guaranteed work in the country he had dreamt of.

Within a week, the face of Vallelonga began to change in ways that would never be reversed. In the mornings, usually on Wednesdays, with the mist of dawn hanging upon the slopes, groups of men gathered in the *piazza*. Most wore dark wool suits, shirts, ties, and heavy black shoes. Each carried a battered suitcase that looked as if it were about to break open. Dozens of women and children crowded about them, kissing them, weeping for them, and pressing into their arms paper bags filled with bread and fruit and pickles. Sometimes it seemed as if the men could not bring themselves to leave. Then, suddenly, they piled into the old car, the doors slammed, the crowd surged forward as if to touch a departing hearse, and they were gone. Over the square the towering silence fell.

For months the morning ritual took place. The men of Vallelonga were leaving. They would make their way by car — rarely by mule train — over the hills to the town of Pizzo, forty miles away, and there board a train to Naples, then the ship to the port of Halifax in Canada. One day, toward the end of 1951, when the sun began to lose its warmth and the first hint of the Calabrian fall crept over Vallelonga, a boy whose father had gone to Toronto was heard telling his friends that it was as if his father had died and with him many other men of Vallelonga. So many men were leaving, day after day, that it was, the boy said, as if there were six funerals every afternoon.

The mayor of the village consoled his community, and told

the women and children that it was for the best, that there was no other way, but that some day the women and children would join them. There was no way, in the early fifties, that the mayor could realize that in time so many of the people of Vallelonga would go to Canada that it would become a special footnote in the history of Italian emigration of the twentieth century: Vallelonga gave a larger percentage of its people to Canada than any city, town, or village in all of Italy. Its population of 2,700 would dwindle to 800, mostly the very old. The greying, small houses on the jumble of twisting streets emptied; the wood dried and cracked in the sun; the windows fell in. One day, a young man, Mimmo Garisto, who had left for Canada and then come back to his home, took a friend for a walk through the town, to the silent houses. Garisto pointed to house after house and in the whisper of a man at a wake, said, "*They* went to Toronto. And here too — *they* went to Toronto. They are in Toronto."

John Zucchi, who grew up in Toronto's Italia and later became a member of the history department of McGill University, explained it in more scholarly terminology: "The peasants who emigrated to Toronto from many villages in Italy left their country not as Italian *nationals* but as people of their *hometowns*." Their families, both immediate and extended, were large and the links extended to neighboring villages because of the proximity of one *comune* to another, or because of intermarriage between men and women from neighboring *comuni*. Thus, virtually an entire *comune* would sometimes come, over the course of a decade or two, from Italy to a new home in Canada.

This phenomenon, known as chain migration, while not unique to Italians — groups of people from Finland, the Ukraine, and Asia also adopted the kinship route — was more pronounced and visible among Italians. An interested observer strolling in the great hall of Union Station in Toronto during the 1950s would have seen handfuls of volunteers from the Italian Immigrant Aid Society (IIAS), there to meet arriving men and women from villages they might never have visited, but which were, in truth, part of the *mentalità* of Toronto Italia — Campobasso, Cosenza, Pisticci. Almost always, the newcomer, if not met by a relative, would pull a slip of paper from an inside pocket, hand it to a volunteer who would read it and direct him to the address, usually that of a friend from the village who was expecting him. Always, it was in a neighborhood of fellow citizens of the *comune*, no matter if it was in the remnants of the city's first Little Italy near College Street, the newer Little Italy emerging to the northwest, or, in the case of many from Sicily, in the eastern part of Toronto.

The newcomers would, in time, consider themselves Canadians; yet many of the same ties that had bound them as *Calabrese* or as *Friulani* would continue to link them later as *Canadese*.

One early November morning in 1952, Antonio Galati, born in Vallelonga thirty-two years before, and a cabinet-maker by trade, sat on the thin hard cushions of an immigrant train he had boarded in Halifax four days earlier. He was silent, imprisoned not only by language but by bewilderment. He stared out the window: the western edges of Toronto, its backyards, scrapheaps, warehouses, and low trees, swept past him as the train entered the city he had heard about from childhood. He had been a soldier in World War II and had seen the great cities — Rome, Vienna, Berlin — and he thought that Toronto, also a city, would be large, with broad boulevards lined with sweeping greenery and grand buildings. He was not sure, even when the conductor said Toronto was next, that he understood. It seemed small, like a town. Only when the train stopped and everyone left it, did he know for sure. He gathered his bag, walked out of Union Station and stood for a moment alone, looking across at the Royal York Hotel, as if he needed such a building to confirm that he was, indeed, in a city called Toronto.

He reached in his pocket and removed a crumpled slip of paper. The address scribbled upon it was 23 Scully Crescent, near College and Clinton. It was the home of his sister and his brother-in-law who had signed the paper — as thousands of other Italians had for their brothers or friends — assuring that they would be responsible for the first year of Antonio Galati's life in Canada. He hailed a cab and within minutes he was there.

That night, at dinner among relatives and many friends from

Vallelonga, someone asked Antonio what his first impression of Toronto was. He replied in only two words: "I like." A couple of the men at the table, each of them working in construction, murmured that he should wait, that he would find the winters cold, the work hard, the hours long. Galati shrugged and repeated what he had already said: "I like." On Monday, his brother-in-law, a bricklayer, was about to leave for work — on a house being built in the city's northwestern section, near Jane and Wilson — when he told Antonio that, really, he could take a few days before looking around for work. But Antonio said he would like to go along that day, just to see the site, to help if he could. They gave him a pair of old work boots, a tattered pair of work pants and a heavy shirt. Then they got in the truck and drove to a vast cluster of half-built houses. Antonio jumped down and began clearing away debris. Then a truck pulled up. A man said he had building materials to be unloaded; he would pay two dollars. Antonio Galati borrowed a pair of work gloves and earned his first wages unloading blocks from a supply truck. In time he became a highly skilled carpenter, then a cabinet-maker, then an artist in wood.

Galati became one of Canada's finest wood carvers; his work graced public buildings from Osgoode Hall in Toronto to the St. Lawrence Seaway at Cornwall, Ontario. When he was in his middle sixties and beginning to think of retiring, he would still say that his most satisfying day in Canada was that Monday in 1952, when he discovered that far from home, with no word of English, he could arrive on one day and begin work on the next.

On Sundays, in 1952, the men and women from Vallelonga, about 100 in all, including a handful who arrived in the 1920s in Toronto's original Little Italy near College and Clinton, sauntered up Grace Street to the cool sanctuary of St. Agnes Catholic Church, near the corner of Dundas and Grace. There, when the Mass was over, they would remain on the steps and lawns for an hour or more, exchanging news of the community — they referred to each other as *Vallelonghesi* — and reading aloud letters and clippings from the village six thousand miles away.

A few had plans, dreams shared by tens of thousands of other Italians from other towns. They would form a club for the people of Vallelonga. It would have two main purposes. First, to maintain the town traditions in the midst of the new land. For example, the club would hold, on the feast day of Vallelonga, the *feste*, an outdoor Mass and picnic, to commemorate the patron saint of Vallelonga, the Madonna of Montserrat — regularly, on the second Sunday of July. But the club would do more than maintain the past in a new culture. It would encourage adults to improve their lot in life by participating in organizations other than Italian ones: and it would encourage children, through an active scholarship program for teenagers in high school and university. The Club of Vallelonga was to become a mirror image of the ambitions of the Italian Canadian: to maintain Italian-ness within Canada, and to move ahead, by improving himself, and even more, the future of his children. There would be the usual club rooms — in this case, in a modest storefront building on Dufferin Street — where the men of the village can be found most evenings, drinking espresso, smoking cigarettes and playing cards deep into the night.

In time, the club boasted over 270 active families, and another 250 who, while less involved, were still within its care and concern. When the second Sunday of July arrives, thousands of people, most born in Vallelonga, but others who are their Canadian-born children and grandchildren, find their way to a farm in the Italianate-sounding village of Loretto, north of Toronto, owned by a man from Vallelonga. There are fields encircled by a wall of spruce and pine and birch, which seem to enclose the farm as the sanctuary in a cathedral. There is a small ornate altar, and a statue of the patron saint. And in a corner of the field, where the wind never seems to blow and where only the morning birds break the silence, there is a large oak tree. For every man and woman from Vallelonga, the tree has a historic meaning. It is the symbol of another tree in another place — in a park, at home in Vallelonga. There, also on the second Sunday of July, the people still in Vallelonga will gather at the old tree.

On the feast day at Loretto, there is an outdoor Mass celebrated sometimes by a priest born in Vallelonga, and a ritual procession. Hundreds upon hundreds of men, women and children begin the slow walk past the oak tree. There is no sound, only the rustle of feet upon the grass and the whisper of children, as they near the tree. Now and then, a woman weeps, placing the photo of her late husband upon the tree and with it a gift to good causes of the town and the needy. The procession goes on for hours and as it does beneath the bright blue sky of the new land, the old ways are for a day as new as the morning and as real as they are in Vallelonga. Their religious duty fulfilled, the *Vallelonghesi* gather at the tables, the wines are opened, the food is shared, and for a long Sunday afternoon, they know that the town is more than memory.

One *feste*, when the sun was high and strong, Bruno Suppa, the man who became the first president of the Vallelonga Club and has been the leader in many of its causes and the mediator of its occasional dispute, sat at a picnic table alongside his wife, his three daughters and his many, many relatives and friends. He is a sturdy, friendly man, who came to Canada as a teenager just as the tide of immigration was beginning to form in 1947. He grew up in an old Little Italy, and studied sociology and then social work, becoming, in time, a judge of the federal immigration appeal board and one of the leaders of the national Italian-Canadian community.

He was in a reflective mood on that feast day at Loretto:

My feeling for Vallelonga has deepened as I have grown older. There is the longing for the place where I began. It is partly a matter of maintaining identity in a new land; and it is partly nostalgia for the town of my fathers. I go back often. ... And in Canada, of course, we have done what we could to maintain a sense of the community we all came from. I think we are better Canadians for that — we offer a heritage that is alive, a tradition that we do our best to keep. And we work hard. The first priority for a Vallelonghese is to own his home. In part that is the equivalent of owning a bit of land back in Vallelonga. And the Vallelonghesi will work extremely hard to pay off that mortgage in two or three years. Why? Because he fears poverty. And debt is a whisper of possible poverty. There must be no debt. And, of course, there is the garden with the house. There he can stroll in the evening, pick a tomato and a pepper for dinner. And in his dream he is back in an older garden in an older town in Italy — the garden of the world.

For many years now, Suppa has served his townspeople, not only as their leader and counsellor, but as editor of their quarterly newsletter, sent not only to all the *Vallelonghesi* in Canada, but to those still in the old town and to about two hundred other *Vallelonghesi* who went many years ago to Argentina. Often, on winter evenings, he leaves his home in one of Toronto's western suburbs and drives to the small club rooms where amid the aroma of espresso and the clouds of smoke he will pass the evening with the barbers, carpenters and, increasingly, the wealthy businessmen, who come to nurture a past which will never leave them.

Once, a few years after the club was formed, several of its leaders thought it would be interesting to organize a visit to Canada by the mayor of the town of Vallelonga. He came, a tall, immaculate school teacher named Francesco Costantino, forty years old with short black hair, a trim mustache, and a dignified, serious manner. They held banquets in his honor attended by many hundreds of people from Vallelonga as well as mayors, cabinet ministers and members of Parliament. Then, on the second Sunday of July, the feast day, four thousand people — five times the number living in Vallelonga today — made their way to the *feste* in Loretto to mark the day and also to see the mayor, who was only a child when they left in the early fifties.

He told them that. But he said that despite his having been a boy when they left, the events of their leaving were so deeply remembered that the days are still vivid in the memories of the entire town. Now, at last, he knew that indeed, as he was told as a boy, it was all for the best. The people of Vallelonga had not only done well, but, in some cases, exceedingly well. "There were," he told a few friends at the Vallelonga Club one morning, "ninety children born in Vallelonga in 1947. Today only three remain. The rest are in Canada."[12]

The children of Vallelonga became men and women in Canada in the fifties and sixties. They helped to make the new land newer still. They saw their old die here, and many of them were the harbingers of a new generation of Italian Canadians. They helped to found the powerful national councils of Italian-Canadian life. They began to move into Canada's mainstream social and political culture. They would clearly never forget the land of their beginnings, especially the town of their birth. Yet, in some way we might never fully understand, they became some of the most passionate Canadian people of the generation.

One day, when he was leaving the courtroom in Toronto where he hears men and women speak of why they want to remain in Canada, someone asked Bruno Suppa about the passion of his fellow *Vallelonghesi* for the land they left, and their loyalty to the land in which they would live. He meditated for a moment. "Put it this way. Today, with the new affluence of the *Vallelonghesi*, you will find many of them in January on a beach in Acapulco. [But] ask any one of them where he comes from, where he belongs, and he will say he is from Canada. Canada is home."

CHAPTER SIX

THE SECOND WAVE: MEETING THE UNKNOWN BROTHERS

November 5, 1955. At about ten minutes before noon, a number of Toronto's leading businessmen checked their coats in the corridor of a downtown office building, then moved to the large, plain dining room of the Toronto Board of Trade. Many were real-estate men — executives and realtors with companies such as A.E. LePage, Canada Permanent, W.H. Bosley & Company — but a large number were from the city's financial and construction communities, come to hear one of the most influential politicians in Canada, Frederick G. Gardiner, Q.C., chairman of the Municipality of Metropolitan Toronto, who was scheduled to speak on Toronto's progress. Gardiner, at fifty-five, was a man of stout build and serious style, often referred to in the newspapers as "Big Daddy," an affectionate appellation which nonetheless seemed at odds with his character. Far from being a mediocre local politician, he held the gold medal from Osgoode Hall Law School and was the most incisive mind in municipal affairs in Canada at the time.

As Fred Gardiner rose to speak that day, he did so as the leading figure of a city which was viewed across Canada as dull, selfish — and very much on the move. It had a booming population, then over 680,000, but in the eyes of a large number of Canadians, including many Torontonians, it was a place

121

of wall-to-wall monotony. "This is Toronto the Good," wrote its most distinguished journalist, Pierre Berton, "smug, solid, respectable. This is Hogtown where money talks. This is where the Dullest Sunday in the World was invented."[1]

Nonetheless, in Gardiner's mind, Toronto was on the edge of a new maturity. In fact, its new life had already begun, written not just in the rows of new houses that spread from its edges, but in certain almost imperceptible changes in its makeup and personality. Gardiner knew, for he had the statistics on his desk, that the arrival of the Italian immigrants encouraged by David Croll seven years earlier was the beginning of a tide. Whereas in 1950 about 5,000 Italians had come to the city, in 1954 the numbers had swollen to almost 20,000.[2] Even as Gardiner rose to speak to the real-estate board that day, thousands upon thousands of the men who had arrived a year earlier were at work in Don Mills, Scarborough, Etobicoke, and deep in the underground of the city, digging sewers, laying pipes, carrying bricks, raising scaffolds, doing everything a man could do in the physical act of building.

"At the beginning of this century," Gardiner began, "Toronto was a city of about 280,000. It was as proud of being called 'Toronto the Good' as it was of its British traditions. It had grown and prospered during the last fifty years and was bursting at the seams." Slowly Gardiner led up to his main message: the fact that once again, Toronto was bursting its seams and this time its growth would be phenomenal.

He revealed a building program which was so stunning in its scale that it was not readily grasped. "We have laid out," he said, as the realtors warmed with expectancy, "a capital program for the next ten years. It involves $750 million. If in addition we decide to add an east and west subway to our north and south subway, which is already operating at near capacity, the capital program will be increased by another $150 million, which would make a ten-year capital program of $900 million."

He spoke of expressways, one of which (later to be named after him), was already begun, the other, the Don Valley Parkway, about to start. He expanded on his vision.

Canada is on the march. It is the land of opportunity. As
Canada prospers so will Ontario and so will Metropolitan
Toronto . . . . Within a radius of a hundred miles of Toronto is
located one third of the purchasing power of Canada and by far
the most lucrative market in the nation. Our destiny is that by
1970, we will have a population of two million people. We will
be the tenth largest city on the North American continent and
with some courage, some foresight and with the will to do the
job, not only will we be the tenth or twelfth largest city on the
continent, but there is no reason why we cannot be one of the
best.[3]

Frederick Gardiner's vision — so charged with supreme and
infectious confidence — was like a signal to men in several parts
of Toronto's business life. Some were in the quiet offices of
banking, still occupied by the city's Protestant Anglo-Saxon
leaders. But there were others who, like James Franceschini,
had come from Italy years before and, beginning with raw
hands and a couple of wheelbarrows, had built companies,
almost always in construction.

One who had already taken part in the earlier Toronto growth
and heard Gardiner's words with ever deepening interest was a
sixty-year-old man of medium build, a broad, open face, and
large eyes, named Sebastian Ruscica. He was known everywhere in Toronto — and in government offices in Ottawa — as
the presiding figure of Ruscica Brothers Construction Limited,
whose offices were in a small, unpretentious building on Industrial Street in Leaside, but whose work — underground water
mains, sewers, piping — lay beneath virtually every street in
Toronto. It was the country's largest underground construction
company.

The Ruscica family — his wife and eight children — lived in
the 1950s in a large, decorative house in north Toronto, on
DeVere Gardens, a world away from the rooming house in
which Sam Ruscica first lived when he came to Canada as an
illiterate teenager in 1910. On Sundays in the early fifties, he
presided over family dinner with quiet grace. He was impeccably attired and his children, who revered him, did not sit at the

table until their father sat. No one raised a fork until Father did. No one left before him. Often, on those Sunday evenings, the doorbell would ring. It would be an Italian laborer, a man Sam Ruscica would know well, come to borrow a little money. Ruscica, a devout Catholic, always gave. Once, his son Frank, then 15, annoyed at one man who came back time and again, spoke up, admonishing his father for being generous to someone who had no thought of repaying. Sam Ruscica looked at the boy and put down his fork. "Frank," he said, "I want to tell you something. I have made a fair amount of money. God gave me the gift to make it. That man did not receive the gift. Be grateful that I can give him a little money. And be grateful for something more. That he comes to me, that I need never go to him."[4]

His children knew their father's struggle well. While they were growing up, they wondered about the town he had left — Pachino, a town of about 20,000 in the most southerly part of Italy, Sicily. He told them — so often that they could almost sense the reason for his leaving — that he could never remember an evening as a child when he was not hungry. In 1910, unable to read or write, add or subtract, he left, along with nine other teenagers from Pachino, for Canada and the city of Toronto.

He lived, as did all the men from Sicily in those years, not in the familiar Little Italy of Toronto's College Street, but in a small neighborhood in the east end, in a rooming house on Ontario Street run by a woman from Pachino. In the November cold, he worked with pick and shovel, for a company called Godson Construction, digging a ditch along the shoreline of Lake Ontario. Since there was no other way to learn, he spent the evenings teaching himself to read. In a couple of years, after he had learned the most elementary reading and arithmetic, he got to know a man at City Hall who handed out contracts and materials for companies who supplied laborers. Ruscica persuaded several of the men who had come with him to form their own company and since Sam Ruscica was the only one who could read or write, it was natural that he should run the company. "You always want to be a big shot," one complained. But they all came.

In 1913, he brought his brother Joseph from Pachino, making him a partner for life, sharing half of every dollar with him, even though Joseph would never really be fully able to read or write. The company struggled through the twenties, the men rising at three in the morning, walking a mile or two to the work site on the fringes of the city, working the entire day, and arriving home so weary that often they fell into deep sleep without eating. Sometimes Ruscica had barely enough money to pay his men. Once, during the fierce heat of an August day, when he was swinging a pick in the trenches along with the others, an Italian fruit peddlar came by offering watermelon for five cents apiece. Ruscica put down his pick and stared at the watermelon. He could already taste it. But he hadn't a nickel. He turned to one of his men. "Have you got a nickel?" The other man dug deeply and handed one over. Ruscica bought a watermelon, split it ten ways and passed it out.

"There you go Sam," taunted one of the men. "You're a big shot like we said, but you haven't even a nickel to your name." Ruscica, never a man to raise his voice, shrugged but did not let the opportunity pass. He mopped his brow, a signal to all his men that the boss was about to speak. He sat on the edge of the trench, his chest walnut-brown, his work pants soaked and sticking in the terrible heat. "Listen to me," he said. "And listen carefully. A few years ago we came here with nothing. Now we have enough to eat, a bed to sleep in, and some money to send home. We are doing work which will always be needed. We have a future. Stick with me and someday it will all be well."

He built his company through the twenties and thirties, not just with brawn and peasant wisdom, but with a rock-ribbed reputation for fair price, good value, and finishing the job on time. In 1940, when World War II began and discrimination against Italians kept him from getting contracts, he worried for months that, like too many other Italians, he might be bankrupted. One evening he announced at dinner that the next day he was getting in the car and driving to Ottawa to see why he was being refused even the right to tender. Two days later he was back. The phone rang that morning in his office in Leaside; it was a federal purchasing officer. "We are letting a contract for servicing land in Brampton for an army base," he said. "The tenders close at 4:00 p.m. Can you put together a bid in that time?"

He did. When the bids were opened, his was the lowest. But whereas other firms, MacNamara Construction and J.P. Porter, had stipulated a completion time of six months, he made his four.

"Sam," the government man said skeptically, "how can you handle this in four months?"

Ruscica's eyes narrowed. "If I can't," he replied, "I'm broke."

He called his men together. "Listen to me," he began as usual. "Listen carefully. We have a job at last. But this time it is different. You will not work for wages. This time you are partners. If we finish the job faster than the contract says, you will all share in the profit." It was finished, not in four months, but three.

Middle-aged and wealthy by 1955, Ruscica heard of Gardiner's expansionary dream with both expectation and enthusiasm. He had, after all, been part of the growth that had already taken place.

In the early fifties, beyond the northern boundaries of Toronto near where Leslie Street met Lawrence Avenue, people would see dozens of sturdy Italian men carrying pipe or riding backhoes, and beside them an agile, well-groomed man in a dark business suit. Sometimes, when the men in the trench struck trouble, he would roll up his trousers, stride to his car and put on a pair of boots to get into the trench beside them. The young businessmen in the Pontiacs and Chevrolets, passing by each morning on their way downtown, had no way of knowing it, but the man in the business suit was Sam Ruscica, head of Ruscica Brothers Construction, in charge of laying every length of sewer pipe and roadway in the famous new community of Don Mills then being developed by E.P. Taylor.

The boom was only beginning. It was written boldly in the spirit of Fred Gardiner: "The Metropolis is an irresistible magnet. It is where big business is located, where big money, big decisions and big reputations are made." And to Gardiner, along with the politicians, businessmen and labor bosses who looked up to him, bigness meant building and building meant profit for everyone, from the man in the ditch to the man in the boardroom. The speed at which Toronto was being catapulted into its future in the fifties was evident in one statistic from the Toronto suburb of Don Mills. In 1950 Don Mills did not exist; in 1955, when Gardiner laid out his grand design, it had already become a community of 15,000. In a decade it would triple. It was clear that where cattle grazed, a forest of subdivisions would rise and with them mile upon mile of sewers and side-walks. By 1955 Ruscica needed more troops to help his army of the pick and shovel, fast becoming an army of the trenching machine and backhoe.

All through the late fifties, the phone would ring during the middle of the evening at the home of a Toronto immigration official who lived on Avenue Road, and whose office was in the Meighen Building on St. Clair Avenue East. The caller would be Sam Ruscica who had, years earlier, established a relationship with the official that was as personal as it was professional.

"John," he would begin, "I have a man working for me who has a brother-in-law back in the old town in Italy, Pachino. He would like to come out. Can I come to see you? Tomorrow? Fine."

Ruscica would slip down to the immigration office, present the man's name, sign papers and give formal assurance that he, Sebastian Ruscica, contractor of 41 Industrial Street, Toronto, would assume responsibility for the man for one year, assuring him of work and keep, so that he would not be a burden to anyone. Ruscica's son Frank, then a young man of twenty-three and working for his father, would drive a panel truck to the neighborhood where the men from Pachino were living, to pick some up for the drive to work. Every Monday without fail there would be two new faces, perhaps four — a brother-in-law of one man, the cousin of another, the friend of still another, as the chain lengthened. In the history of chain migration there is no equal to the altruistic effort of Sam Ruscica, who sponsored 400 men, all from Pachino, the town he'd come from years before.

Every Christmas, he would host a party for them all, and

before the evening ended at The King Edward Hotel, he would speak with each one and hand him an envelope: a Christmas bonus, a cheque based on a percentage of the man's annual salary. Ruscica would speak to him:

"Tony, this is my gift to you. I do not owe it to you. The company does not owe it. But we give it. Now I have a request for you to give. I would like you to give some of it back to Pachino — to the church and to the orphans." Each year, he raised several thousand dollars and then, though the men did not know it, he matched it, and so did his quiet brother Joseph. Thus, every January, over $10,000 went to the charitable works of the church in Pachino.

He was surprised one evening, when he was just past his sixtieth birthday, to receive a call from the office of the Roman Catholic archdiocese of Toronto. The office of the Cardinal, Archbishop J.R. MacGuigan, was phoning to advise him of a decision taken that week in Rome by Pope Pius XII. He had advised the archbishops of Toronto and Sicily that he was investing Sebastian Ruscica as a Knight of the Holy Sepulchre of Jerusalem, the highest honor that can be conferred on a Catholic layman, one rare among Canadians.

When, some weeks later, Cardinal MacGuigan, on behalf of Pius XII, spoke at the gathering of church leaders, businessmen and family friends who witnessed Sam Ruscica's investiture, he made a point of stressing not just all that Sam Ruscica had done for Italians in Sicily and in Canada, but that he had done so — in keeping with the spirit of the knighthood — quietly, modestly, and with no search for personal recognition. When it came time for him to reply, Ruscica did so warmly but briefly: "What little I have done, you also have done. Even more you have done, for without that, this would not have been possible."

Years later, on a quiet street in the old Sicilian town of Pachino, a visitor came upon a modest bust of Sebastian Ruscica. It stood not far from the centre of the town, warmed by the sun that fell through a sheltering oak tree, a memorial few knew existed, to the man and the hundreds of his fellow citizens from Pachino who shared anonymously but decisively in the shaping of Canada's largest city.

The men from Pachino, like those from Vallelonga, represented an enormous exodus from their hometowns, but in the even larger stream of men and women flowing to Canada after World War II, they were almost an unnoticed handful. Every year, tens of thousands moved through the ports of Halifax and Montreal, and then began to descend from the jets of Canadian Pacific Airlines, and in time, Alitalia. Once the landmark vision of Frederick Gardiner had been translated into concrete plans and the awesome need for labor made clear, the river from Italy became a Niagara. In the following year, 1956, 30,000 Italians arrived, almost 20,000 of whom were bound for Toronto. In 1958, 30,000 more arrived. While several thousand would go each year to the established colonies of Sault Ste. Marie and Thunder Bay in Ontario, and Montreal and Vancouver, the vast majority headed for the expanding community of Toronto, where chain migration had established almost a daily shuttle service from Rome to Malton (now Pearson International Airport). It was the most dramatic influx of newcomers in the history of Canada, continuing in large scale for decades, and making Italians the largest ethnic group in the nation after the English, the French, and the Germans. In the city of Montreal, there would in time be a community of 160,000 people of Italian origin. In Toronto, where in 1940 Italians numbered 18,000, the population would boom for decades until, by the end of the 1970s, they would constitute a full ten percent of Toronto's population, making it one of the largest settlements of Italians outside of Italy.

Their coming would change the character of Canada. But even before that, it would change the character of Canada's existing Italian community, as the old Italians and the new met in a land each claimed for their own. There were subtle differences between those who came in the 1920s and those who came in the 1950s. The first, in many cases, had had no schooling at home and had received little in Canada. One of them, Joseph Gennaro, who came to Toronto when he was eight years old in the early years of the century, spoke no English, had no schooling and took only four years of it in Toronto before he had to go to work at twelve in a factory. In time, after working for his fellow Sicilian, Sam Ruscica, he went into business for himself, running a fruit store. Even there, the experience was harsh with episodes of cruel discrimination.[5] In 1940, when the roundup of Italians got underway, dozens and dozens of Toronto people who had been Joe Gennaro's customers on Queen Street East simply stayed away. Some would cross the street when he approached. A few remained loyal, one woman phoning to ask that he deliver groceries only when her husband was not home to see an Italian arriving at the door.

In contrast, the Italians of 1950 and later, a large number of whom were helped to come by Gennaro and his family, entered a land with a widely established Italian community, a country needing their work, albeit in menial jobs, and a government at least poised to offer programs, some effective, some not, in everything from English language studies to occupational development. There were natural differences and sometimes conflicts between the generations. As Robert Harney, a Toronto academic and a noted scholar of Italian emigration put it: "The historical and cultural distance between the two groups was immense. To the newcomers, Italo-Canadians were more like Canadians than Italians or they were 'umbertine' that is, fossils of the Age of King Umberto (roughly the equivalent of 'Victorian'). Their sense of probity and even of Italy was remote from that of immigrants who had lived through Fascism and the Allied occupation. The Italo-Canadians, in turn, found the greenhorns blatantly Italian, obtuse and ungrateful."[6]

It was the same in Montreal, where from its pathetic origin in the years of Cordasco's reign at the turn of the century, the community had grown at the end of the war to almost 100,000 people living quietly in very modest houses, mostly in sight of railyards and stockyards in districts such as Mile End, St. Joseph and St. Henri. They were mostly from the south — a large number from the province of Campobasso — and they were poor. The internment, the Depression, and the War had defeated them. But to the new immigrants of the 1950s, they were misunderstood and perhaps misrepresented as indolent. A student of the community, Jeremy Boissevain, noted: "Many of those who have arrived since the war criticize the prewar immigrants for lack of ambition and failure to make the most of their opportunities. But they overlook the smothering effect the Depression had on those who had just begun to establish themselves in their new country."

In the late 1950s, roughly 40,000 Italians had settled in British Columbia, in old and small neighborhoods in places such as Trail, Kelowna, and Prince Rupert and in the largest settlement of all, Vancouver, where more than 20,000 lived, most of them in the heart of the city on streets bounded by Main and Broadway, and along the meandering shoreline of Burrard Inlet. They were for the most part a defined if somewhat divided community, with roots that went back to the turn of the century and even beyond. One of their better-known compatriots, a large-framed man named Cap-Pasquale Capozzi came in 1919, settled in Kelowna, and built a large and renowned winery that would carry his name into contemporary history.

The Italians of British Columbia, in particular the leaders, had come mostly from the Italian north country — from regions such as Trentino, Friuli and Veneto. They were, by the fifties, a strong community with men at work in lumbering, mining, fishing and farming, and in Vancouver itself, businesses of every kind, including, of course, construction. They had formed, like Italians everywhere, a variety of associations, The Sons of Italy Mutual Aid Society, for example, and supported two newspapers. And they had dozens of smaller clubs, fraternities, societies, and groups, all formed around the regions from which they came. They were, by their own proud admission, the most highly individualistic of Canada's Italian communities, many of them celebrating their unique understanding of what it meant to be an Italian in Canada. Only one thing united them until the middle of the 1950s — their leader, the brilliant criminal lawyer renowned in every courtroom in Canada, Angelo Branca.[9]

Branca was not born in Italy but in Canada, in British Columbia, the third child of Filippo and Teresa Branca, who had emigrated from near the northern city of Milan, and arrived in Canada just before the turn of the century. Filippo Branca went north in the Klondike gold rush, did well, and opened a store in a B.C. mining community which soon became one of the West's

many ghost towns. The Brancas moved to Vancouver where
Filippo went into business, founded one of the earliest Italian
benefit societies (Società Veneto, for the help of northerners)
and saw his four children through school.

Angelo, a personable boy with a casual attitude to studies,
entered a legal office in 1921, where, after articling with a
lawyer who stressed that he must work harder because he was
the son of alien immigrants, he developed an early social con-
science, a skepticism about wealth, and a passion for the courtroom. He began his own practice in 1926; he was twenty-three
years old.

By the time he was in his middle forties, Angelo Branca,
square-jawed, greying, with a demeanor some compared to the
actor Spencer Tracy, was admired and revered in British Columbia. He was unsurpassed as a criminal lawyer, representing
people with power and privilege one day and men on legal aid
the next, with equal zeal and intellectual vigor. His style of
presentation was clear, direct, and persuasive. His approach to
criminal law was thoroughly pragmatic: "I never gave a damn,"
he would later say, "whether my client was innocent or guilty. I
gave him the best defense I could under the law." He was a man
of many parts, who in his early thirties took up amateur boxing,
fighting in rings in British Columbia and Oregon, and once,
before a crowd of seven thousand at the Vancouver Forum,
knocked out the country's top amateur middleweight to claim
the Canadian championship.

During those years and after, Branca often retreated to the
sanctuary of his Italian garden, a showpiece spread over two
acres beside his house on Cambridge Street, where he strolled
amid the daffodils, and invited neighbors to help themselves to
the beans, lettuce, and peppers. He was, though not a native-
born Italian, committed to the heritage of his father; he maintained his fluency in the language and, like his father before
him, founded an organization to further Italian welfare, an
umbrella federation called Confratellanza Italo-Canadese, in
time called by its critics "the Branca group."

In 1940, during the infamous months of the internment,
Angelo Branca put his hand firmly on the leadership of Italians

in British Columbia. For several years before the outbreak of the World War II, he had traveled the province, speaking in church basements and tiny Italian halls, his clear voice warning his people against the rise of fascism in Italy and against Mussolini's program to use Italian diplomats in Canada as instruments to subvert groups such as the Sons of Italy. In May, 1940, sensing that Italy's alliance with Hitler was imminent, Branca formed a committee to have every Italian in British Columbia sign a pledge of loyalty to Canada.

He sent out thousands of fliers inviting Italians to a mass meeting in Vancouver on the evening of June 10. Ironically, that afternoon Mussolini sided with the Axis — the national roundup of Italians was underway by dusk. Still, the meeting went ahead; the dynamic lawyer rose before four hundred frightened Italian men, and said: "The world has been shocked by an act of perfidious cowardice. This declaration of war by Mussolini will be recorded by history as one of the most cowardly and traitorous acts since the beginning of time." The four hundred agreed to form an association, led by Branca, to back the Canadian war effort. It spread throughout British Columbia (and was one reason why the number of men taken into custody and sent to Camp Petawawa was, in proportion to population, smaller than those from Ontario and Quebec). For months, Branca's Vancouver office was the centre of frantic phone calls. He worked long evening vigils studying letters from aggrieved families and arguing with Ottawa for the release of husbands and fathers who had been interned.

In the forties and fifties, and into the sixties, no Italian leader in Canada was held in more esteem than he. In 1963 he fulfilled his ambition to become a judge of the province's Supreme Court, and then of its appeal division, where, in the words of the chief justice, he presided with an integrity unsurpassed by any judge who ever sat. But during these crowning years of his career, Branca was at the centre of a conflict within Vancouver's Italian community. It would sadden all who observed it, and become a key symptom of the change sweeping Canada and its Italian communities as the new Italians of the fifties met the Italians of early Canada.

Angelo Branca took life-long pride in the heritage of the land his father left in the 1890s. He was among the most articulate of men in English, but he remained fluent in Italian, speaking it at home in his youth, and using it with ease in his role as the leader of British Columbia's Italian community. During the fifties, hundreds of Italian men and women found their way to the city's Arbutus Club to sit silently, captivated by the power of Branca's personality.

He basked in their adulation, just as they basked in the renown he had achieved and had, to some degree, conferred upon his community. But as the change-filled sixties dawned, Angelo Branca sensed that he would no longer remain the unchallenged father of Italian culture and society in British Columbia. Thousands of new people were swelling the Vancouver community. They brought fresh views on what it meant to be Italian in Canada. Many new associations ranging from the Associazione Nationali Alpini to the Circulo Abruzzese and the Famee Furlane, were to become strong and vocal.

By the late 1960s, with Vancouver's Italian population growing steadily, the members of such groups were finding fresh confidence in their numbers and fresh convictions about retaining their culture in a new society. They also sensed that the umbrella federation that Branca had formed and nurtured was not in touch with the rising aspirations of the post-war immigrants for a stronger Italian identity in their Canadianism.

To them, Branca and his Confratellanza Italo-Canadese echoed a passing generation in which Italians gathered for banquets or bingo, but not for the deeper aspects of the Italian heritage. Further, Branca's people were more inclined to adapt to Anglo-Saxon custom than to retain their own culture; the new generation sought to make its own culture an enriching contribution to the multicultural mosaic of the country.

In 1972, a young, well-educated foreign officer from Rome named Giovanni Germano arrived in Vancouver to fill the post of Italian consul to Western Canada.[10] He was energetic, charming, and, most of all, ambitious. One morning in the spring of 1974, Germano strolled into the office of Premier David Barrett. He was on very friendly territory. Barrett, of the New

Democratic Party, looked upon the Italian community with favor, and on its people as supporters, or potential supporters, of his government. The meeting went well. Barrett suggested Germano take the lead in encouraging Italians throughout British Columbia to build a community centre where their language would be taught, their culture enhanced, and their community made stronger.

Furthermore, added Barrett expansively, his government would subsidize the building of the centre with a grant of $333,333. Germano could only smile: just before he had left Rome, his government had passed a new law providing funds for its foreign affairs representatives to promote Italian language and culture among emigrants abroad. It did so after millions of Italian emigrants had severely criticized it for the incompetence that had led them to emigrate in the first place, and the indifference with which Rome treated them once they had settled in other countries. Now Giovanni Germano was in the best of positions, not only to further his government's desire, but to do so with British Columbia's help.

At that point Germano might have thanked Barrett, left his office and handed the opportunity over to local leaders of the Italian community. He then could have stepped aside and maintained the discreet distance of the diplomat. Instead, he took it on himself to found the centre. Thus he inspired the wrath of some Italians who saw him as a representative of a foreign government interfering in the affairs of a Canadian community. The years ahead were dark with anger and division.

Angelo Branca was incensed. He saw that while the building of the cultural centre was the focus of Germano's ambition, the ramifications were wide. His leadership was ignored; it was therefore endangered. But more than his personal feelings were at issue. Germano's involvement summoned up Branca's oldest convictions about the role of Italian consuls in Canadian affairs. He had seen, he told his friends, what that meant back in the 1930s when, from one end of the country to the other, Italian foreign affairs people were intruding in Canadian life on behalf of fascism. Now, again, his province was feeling the ominous hand of an Italian outsider.

For days, in that spring and summer of 1974, Branca, then in his early seventies and still an imposing man with a brisk youthful stride, left the court building shortly after dusk, and drove to a downtown restaurant where, with a few members of the Confratellanza, he would talk about why he opposed Germano and what all of them ought to do about it. It was the beginning of a spectacle that would go on for a decade, and raise certain side issues: the fact of Germano, a representative of a foreign government, plunging headlong into a local political controversy; and of Branca, a justice of the Supreme Court (he was to remain on the court from 1971 to 1978), rallying the opposition, and becoming a spokesman for one group of citizens against another.

In weeks the hostility burst over Vancouver. Germano had solidified his position in forming a federation called The Italian Folk Society of British Columbia. It included some fifty groups, all dedicated to his vision of the cultural centre. One group was absent: Angelo Branca's Confrattelanza. Soon the Italian weekly paper *L'Eco d'Italia*, a longtime supporter of Branca, attacked the idea of the centre, Germano, and his backers. The attacks continued for months, founded on the views of an older generation of Italians who were secure in their material well-being, and annoyed not just at an intrusion by an outsider, but by the willingness of the intruder and his main supporters to go deep into debt to fulfill their vision. The views might have been *L'Eco d'Italia's* but they were also those of Angelo Branco. "The Italians," he said to his friends, "are being led by a consul who should stay out of their affairs. Now they are going to be faced with over a million dollars worth of debt. They and their children will have to pay off the banks. Not the consul; he'll be gone while the debt is still deep."

Meanwhile, elsewhere in the city and in nearby Burnaby, Germano and a handful of members of the new federation spent hours in meetings, worried over the opposition and what it could mean not just to their conviction that a centre was needed, but to themselves and their careers. They respected Branca — some even feared him — but their differences from him, in terms of understanding the Italians of the new generation were profound. One of them explained to a friend, "He does not realize that this generation of Italians does not simply want a hall to go to have a banquet on Christopher Columbus Day. That is past." Moreover, they argued, he did not realize — perhaps because he was not born and raised in Italy — that Italians are highly individualistic, that they are not prepared simply to fall in line collectively behind one leader. Branca and his supporters in the Confratellanza saw this individualism as divisive and anarchic. But to the group around Germano it was not. It was pluralism: the Italian way. As one of them put it: "We are not monolithic. We are a very diverse people. And the centre, with its openness to variety and diversity, will accommodate that and strengthen all."

L'Eco d'Italia did not agree. In almost every issue from that spring and even after the erection of the gleaming centre, the paper railed against the plan and the people — their motives, actions, activities, and financing. In his own column, Angelo Branca took aim at the centre's idea of teaching Italian to children, through federal and provincial funding, and a subsidy from Italy's national government. Who, he asked again and again, would direct it? Why was it necessary? Soon, in order to counter the power of *L'Eco d'Italia*, another paper, *Il Marco Polo*, appeared, spearheaded by a bright, young Italian of enormous energies, Anna Terrana of Burnaby.

Terrana, a self-confident woman who came to Vancouver from near Milan in 1966, had become a member of the British Columbia Police Commission, working at the paper by night. She tried, while supporting the need for the centre, to moderate the conflict. *Il Marco Polo*, reaching about five thousand homes with each issue, appealed for civility: "In particular," ran a petition signed by many Vancouver Italians, "we ask the weekly newspaper *L'Eco d'Italia* not to abuse the freedom of the press which is granted in this country, in order to launch insinuations, defamations and insults against the Italian consular and diplomatic authorities."[12] *Il Marco Polo* asked the government to step in to stop the attacks. The mood, as one of the centre's supporters told a friend outside the Italian community, was that of open war. It was to remain the clearest example in this century that Canada's Italian community is less a single community than it is many communities, with many points of view, and the readiness to put them to vigorous debate.

There was more lurking in the background than Branca's conviction that the Italian consul was an intruder, whose high-flown ideas were going to land the Italian community deeply in debt. Branca had, at the same time, a profound philosophic opposition to the way the centre was being financed, in which belief he reflected the opinion of many men of his generation, Italians who had risen in their communities and careers largely by their own efforts. Branca was opposed to government help for the centre because he opposed government assistance to ethnic communities generally. He was against multiculturalism.

In Branca's opposition to government support of his community Branca's opponents saw at least a paradox, if not disloyalty. But Branca was not alone. The revered Hubert Badani, three times mayor of Thunder Bay, Ontario and long-time member of Parliament, feared that federal and provincial funding would foster first distinctiveness and then divisiveness. But unlike Badani, who kept his views largely private, Branca was extraordinarily blunt:

> I think the Canadian theory of multiculturalism is quite out of place. I believe the traditions, customs and culture of an ethnic group are important to that group, and that its people should be encouraged to keep them. By doing so the cultural life of that group will be enriched and these things in turn will enrich Canadian life. But I am strongly opposed to multiculturalism as it is developing in Canada, both on the federal and provincial scene. While ethnic groups should be encouraged to keep their languages and their customs, they should be told that the cost of maintaining these things must be borne by the group. If they cannot be so maintained, then they are not worth keeping. I learned to speak my parents' language at my mother's knee. And this I have always believed: that foreigners who make Canada their home have a duty to become Canadians and to conform with the culture of Canada while maintaining their own if it is worthy of survival.

Branca's passion was obvious, as was his integrity. Nonetheless, for a man of his experience and standing, his views were founded on a surprisingly flimsy understanding of Canada's history and practice. In Canada, unlike the United States, government funding of culture (as in numerous other aspects of life, including immigration) is a deeply embedded tradition. Out of that tradition flows multiculturalism. Canada has a vastly different view of the relationship between state and culture than does the United States.

But, apparently, Branca preferred the American way: "Then came the multiculture movement, federally and provincially supported — to try it was said, to counter the melting pot tendency seen in the United States. In the States immigrants have become good American citizens I think." Perhaps because he had not visited any of them, Branca did not realize that Italo-American communities are significantly different than Italian-Canadian communities. Once in the melting pot, the Italian character is inevitably altered, usually dramatically.

Branca's view of multiculturalism could be baffling in view, too, of his considerable legal intelligence. He once hinted that he felt governments were simply pandering to Italians and others through multiculturalism, then added: "Why don't we teach ethnic groups to speak and think Canadian?" Branca's time as a leader of Italians — a deeply dedicated and selfless leader — had passed. He did not realize that in the new Canada, to "think" Canadian could well mean to treasure a mother culture, to celebrate a mother heritage and to speak a mother tongue all in the name of being Canadian.

The centre he fought was built. It opened in the fall of 1977: The Italian Cultural and Recreational Centre, a gleaming, low, white building with numerous arches and open spaces, and inside, conference rooms, classrooms, a ballroom, a gallery, a library, a day-care centre, and, in time, a complex for senior citizens. Each year hundreds of thousands of visitors came to the centre, Italian children for language classes, teenagers for lessons in fitness and culture, adults for concerts of Italian music, and others attending meetings of one of dozens of regional Italian clubs which convened in its conference rooms.

It would have critics. They would claim that it was elitist, too common, too distant, a divisive symbol. But most found it a doorway that led out of the ghetto mentality of the past, and a sign that the various segments of Vancouver's Italian community could find a common goal. As Mario Pastro, a man who came from near Venice to Vancouver in the late fifties and became a director of the centre put it, "The past differences are just that: past. We are many, but when it is time to act as one, we are one."[13]

One element was sadly missing. The name Angelo Branca did not appear on any stone, plaque, or memento of the centre. Its absence was a poignant reminder of the ways in which Canada and its Italian communities changed, as the tides from Italy flowed west to alter forever the character of British Columbia's Italian life.

CHAPTER SEVEN

THE TRAGIC TOMB AT HOGG'S HOLLOW

On the western fringe of downtown Toronto, not far from the corner of Bathurst and Bloor, where the garish lights of Honest Ed's discount emporium light the sidewalks, lies a street called Palmerston. It runs parallel to Bathurst, and like the streets around it — Manning, Clinton, Grace, Montrose — it was, in the late 1950s, still the heartland of Little Italy, which by then was poised for its great expansion northward in Toronto. In the late fifties, Palmerston, especially south of College Street, with its tiny front gardens and knee-high picket fences, was a street of laborers living in narrow houses left for them by the generation of fruit peddlers, knife sharpeners and street musicians who, decades earlier, had helped to begin the neighborhood. But whereas the Italians of the early part of the century lived and worked in the same neighborhood, the men of the fifties moved all over Metropolitan Toronto, fulfilling the grand design of Fred Gardiner, digging, tunneling, hammering, plastering, and painting.

The men from Palmerston stood in small knots, just before dawn, at the corner of Bathurst and College, talking cheerfully, then climbing aboard open trucks that took them to one site for one week, to another for another week. The pay was low — usually $1.65 an hour — and the conditions harsh and unsafe.[1]

There were more than 10,000 men, almost all non-unionized, the raw rank and file of the city's growing Italian community, now developing its old and new cultures wherein the laboring newcomers found themselves strangers to all but their own families and fellow workers.

The trade unions of the day — the bricklayers, carpenters, plasterers, and others — were led for the most part by men of British and Irish background, raised with the outlook of the British Labor Movement, in which quotas were unwritten but strictly observed. Throughout the fifties they had looked warily upon the tides of Italian laborers, hesitant to recruit them either as tradesmen or apprentices, lest they swell the ranks beyond the number of prized downtown Toronto jobs the market offered. The Italians were left to the suburbs, where in the boom of the late fifties and early sixties, construction companies were created overnight, and hired and fired every day, with no time to consider anything other than the basement to be dug, the cement to be poured, the frame to rise in the unending suburban sprawl. The new Italians of the growing neighborhoods in the western part of Toronto were uneducated, unskilled and unwilling to pass up a job. But there was also — some of the older Italians of Toronto noticed — a certain passive quality to many of the laborers, as if deep within, they were dependent, and therefore vulnerable to exploitation.

In the evenings, after the shifts were over in the suburbs, they would be given a ride to the intersection of Bloor and Bathurst, and make their way home on foot, many of them arriving on Palmerston at dusk, where their nonchalant stroll, and their pauses along the street to speak to neighbors on front steps, presented a contented exterior. Beneath it, too often, were feelings of anxiety, bewilderment, and despair.

In the early spring of 1960, two brothers were staying with distant relatives on the second floor of a neat, narrow house on Palmerston Avenue, with a small garden in the back and a postage-stamp lawn in the front. One was Allesandro Mantella, a stocky, muscular youth of twenty-five, the other, his younger brother Guido, lighter, slighter, and twenty-three. They had left a hill village in southern Italy the year before and had lived on

Palmerston since their arrival, spending their days in the army
of the pick and shovel, their evenings — when they were not
working — strolling along College Street, where they often
stood listening to the music drifting from the doors of small
espresso cafés, and joining in the street-corner conversations.
They talked about home, where they dutifully sent their money,
moved by the same diligence they applied to their religious
devotions every Sunday at St. Agnes Church.

On Thursday afternoon, March 17, just after four o'clock, the
brothers hopped aboard a pickup truck with several other men
and drove up Bathurst, then east to Yonge Street, just beyond
the city limits of Toronto, in a district called Hogg's Hollow.[2]
They walked a couple of hundred yards northeast of Yonge,
where the ground opened to form a shaft, about ten feet square
and thirty-five feet deep. It descended to a tunnel about six feet
high, in which men could work if they crouched and crawled.
The tunnel ran west beneath Yonge Street, and carried a water-
main the men were laying. The pipe, at thirty-six inches in
diameter, left, in places, only ten inches of crawlspace. Allesandro and Guido Mantella would squeeze by, hooking up a section of pipe, then move westward to do another. They were
called "sandhogs," a term for the often highly skilled men who
did the tunnel work of North America. But the Mantellas were
new to the job. They climbed down the shaft to begin the night
shift at about 5:15 p.m. With them were Pasquale Allegrezza
and Giovanni Fusillo, both in their twenties, and Giovanni
Correglio, in his forties.

There was some doubt that the project — begun a year
earlier to provide water to the Borough of North York — was
entirely safe. Two foremen had quit in the winter expressing
concern about safety. One went so far as to list his reservations to
the contractor who, after dismissing him, went into receivership,
so that a bonding company, with headquarters somewhere in
the United States, was overseeing completion. The foreman had
insisted that the shaft was not secure, the tunnel was inade-
quately shored against quicksand, the timber supports were
weak, and that there were no fire extinguishers underground,
just as there were no resuscitators or telephones connected to

the surface. He felt it was the worst project he had ever been asked to supervise. Still, in strict terms, the site met the safety standards of the day.

In March 1960, it was unlikely that Allesandro Mantella and his brother Guido knew what a resuscitator was, or for that matter, what a safe tunnel looked like. As they climbed down the ladder of the shaft, they wore no hard hats, and carried only their work tools. They had no flashlights.

Once they reached the tunnel, the men inched their way westward, squeezing past the huge pipe, until they arrived at a point about three hundred feet west of the shaft. They began to work, the roof of the tunnel almost touching their heads.

At about ten minutes to six, a dispatcher in a North York Fire Department hall took a call from a construction foreman who said some rubbish had apparently caught fire near Yonge Street and York Mills, in Hogg's Hollow. A pumper and crew were sent to the scene by the district chief, John Boddy, who reasoned that a rubbish fire could be quite adequately handled without his attendance. When the firemen arrived, they found wisps of smoke rising from the shaft into which the Mantella brothers and their fellow workers had descended an hour earlier. Quickly, they began searching for an alternate entryway; and called for their chief.

When John Boddy arrived he asked the foreman the obvious question: "Are there any men underground?" The foreman said he did not know. Boddy, surprised, crossed Yonge Street where three of his men were about to enter the tunnel through a shaft they had located closer to the tunnel's west end. Just as they began the climb, the foreman came back with word that, indeed, there were men below, though he had no idea who they were, how many there were, or where they were working. He thought they were Italians.

Once they reached the tunnel, the three firemen worked their way about forty feet eastward, all the while shouting to the Mantella brothers and the others in the hope of a response. They heard nothing. Worse, the thick, heavy smoke, from smoldering welding cables that had been accidentally ignited near the bottom of the main shaft, made it impossible to go further eastward. They got out, then went down a third, most westerly shaft. One of them, Alex Baird, duck-walked his way east until, to his surprise, he came up against a cement wall installed to help support the tunnel roof. The Italians were trapped: on the east, by the smoldering cables near the foot of the shaft they had entered; on the west, by the cement abutment. It was now 7:30 p.m., an hour and a half since the arrival of the firemen, the police, the ambulances, and the Ontario Hydro trucks, mounted with huge lights that played over the shaft and the gathering crowd.

Confusion reigned. None of the men trying to rescue the workers knew tunneling; the project supervisor, it turned out, was not a professional engineer; there was a difference of opinion among company officials and others over one crucial suggestion: that the compressors forcing air into the tunnel be shut down, the shafts cleared, and the smoke allowed to escape so that rescuers might be able to reach the laborers. At first the company men refused on the grounds that stopping the forced air would remove the pressure necessary to keep the tunnel from collapsing. For awhile their arguments prevailed. But by eight o'clock someone — it was never established who — shut down the compressors so that much of the tunnel caved in, including the section west of Yonge Street where Allesandro and Guido Mantella were working.

It was three days before experienced sandhogs, brought in from working on the extension of Toronto's subway line, were able to dig and scrape their way to the bodies. They had been told by the only man to escape, an older Belgian tunnel-worker named Walter Andruschuk (who fought through the smoke to the eastern shaft) that the inexperienced Italians were frozen in panic. But when the sandhogs reached the bodies of the five men, encased in slime and sand, they noted something else, something unforgettable: the bodies of Allesandro and Guido Mantella were kneeling beside each other in the posture of prayer.

On the evening of Wednesday, March 23, a week after the accident, a large crowd streamed through the doorway of The Cardinal Funeral Home at 366 Bathurst Street, just above

College and only a few minutes' walk from the house on Palmerston where the Mantellas had lived. Inside the Home, the men and women overflowed the small entrance and hallway, waiting to enter the room where, against a wall blanketed with flowers, two open caskets stood, with mourners kneeling before them. Just after nine o'clock, a fair-complexioned man in a trenchcoat made his way among the sea of black suits and dresses, shook hands with a few cousins of the brothers, and knelt to make the sign of the cross. He was in his early thirties, of medium build, with thick, dark hair and a strong jaw. His name was Frank Drea; he was a reporter from the *Telegram.*

Drea was in the prime of his career as a reporter with a special interest in labor matters. He had contacts with the unions, the companies, the government, at every level, and his stories were often dramatic, written not in the cold language of economics, but in moving prose, about human suffering. He was the son of an Irishman, and while not a socialist, his underlying sympathy and passion were with the rank and file, with immigrant tradesmen like his father. Over his desk on the fourth floor of the Telegram building on Bay Street, he argued passionately with editors over union issues, declaring time after time that tradesmen and laborers, so many of them Italian, were mistreated in Toronto as a matter of course — from the unsafety of their working conditions, to the integrity of their paycheques.

Some of his stories of abuse ran in the *Telegram*; others did not, often, he suspected, because editors on his paper, as on others, did not want to offend large developers, the old Anglo-Saxon firms, whose advertisements were the foundation of important new real-estate sections. But Drea, whose view of life encompassed the necessity of compromise, accepted the killing of some of his stories with equanimity, sure that the truth would prevail as long as he stayed persistent.

On the night of March 23, as he pushed through the door of the funeral home and headed back to the *Telegram*, he felt that the Hogg's Hollow tragedy was a portent of change for Italians in Toronto. He elaborated to a fellow journalist:

> For years they've been dying in ones and twos in Don Mills and Scarborough, falling off rickety scaffolds with no safety hats, no

work boots, not even gloves. Guys are climbing ten stories like that — with big squares of plywood in their hands. They get blown away in the wind and do you know what the bosses say? 'Guess he went sailing.' That's a fact. The safety regulations in this province are just terrible. And even then they aren't enforced. The only thing different about this one at Hogg's Hollow is that five guys died in a hellhole underground.

But there was another factor that even Drea could not have foreseen. In the final days of March, one of the *Telegram*'s editors, who was filling in for an absent managing editor, approached Drea's desk in the newsroom. He knew of Drea's interest in Italian workers, and he believed that a newspaper should not simply report a disaster, but follow it up, if for no other reason than to hold public interest. "Frank," he said. "Let's keep this one alive a few days. Give us something for tomorrow on Italian laborers."

On the morning of March 25, the *Telegram*'s front page carried a headline saying that Italian laborers in Toronto were being "treated like animals". Drea wrote that many of them were lined up like livestock, their muscles examined before hiring. Few received vacation pay, a great number were forced to work weekends without pay, and, most damning of all, too many found that their paycheques were worthless. Moreover, the conditions under which they labored were unsafe and the climate was of abject fear. He quoted a report, then three years old, by the Ontario Federation of Labour: "Wages are pitifully low — when the worker can collect them. Men daily work in fear of deportation. Half have never heard of Unemployment Insurance or Workmen's Compensation."[3]

On the morning the story was published, Frank Drea appeared in the newsroom as usual shortly after ten o'clock, picked up a copy of the paper, propped his feet up on his desk and began reading. Suddenly, he looked up to see the editor who had requested his Italian story, a pleasant, gentle man now standing over him, his face ashen, his voice almost quavering:

"Frank, we have a problem. It's big. Real big." The editor, in some distress, explained that minutes earlier he had arrived at work to hear his phone ringing. It was the *Telegram*'s publisher,

John Bassett. "He read your piece, Frank. And he wants to know who assigned it and wants us both in his office. Right now, Frank. This is it, Frank. What now?"

Quickly, Drea got to his feet, put on his jacket, and headed through the newsroom to the stairway leading to the floor below and the large paneled office of the publisher. He was worried, not only about what might await him, but for the older editor at his side. When they arrived at the outer office of John Bassett, Drea turned to the other man and tried to calm his nerves: "Listen to me. When we go in there, I'll take all the blame." The editor seemed to calm down. "Oh, thank God," he said. They went in.

Bassett, a tall, rangy man with long arms and a gravelly voice, was on his feet behind his desk, looking as though he were about to bound over it. He barked one word: "Tremendous." Drea sank into the large chair to the left, his editor smiled, and they listened as John Bassett explained how, as a young man, growing up in Sherbrooke, Quebec, he had heard his father recounting the ordeal of Italians in Montreal at the turn of the century, when the notorious Antonio Cordasco and the railways had exploited so many of them. Now, he said, he was amazed that in Toronto in 1960, something like that was still able to happen. He looked at Drea: "Frank, the paper is yours. The story is yours. I want you in the paper every day with it. If you need help, we'll give it to you. But I want this covered from start to finish. I want to see the *Telegram* lead in putting a stop to it."

In the hallway, the editor asked Drea if he needed other reporters, photographers, whatever. Drea said no, he would like to be left alone, free to write what he knew had to be written. For the next several weeks, no issue of the *Telegram* appeared without one of his articles detailing the mistreatment of thousands of Italian men and women in Toronto — from the dangers of seamstresses working at sewing machines with faulty wiring, to the cheating of the men who were putting the plaster in the apartments of Don Mills. Drea was to win The Heywoud Broun Award, an international award from the Newspaper Guild of America, for his series, but his greatest impact was in the offices of the Premier of Ontario, Leslie Frost. Week after week, Frost read what Drea wrote and within days he began to change Ontario's labor laws to give the first promise of a decent life to the men from Italy who were building Toronto.

When Leslie Frost read the first reports of the Hogg's Hollow disaster, he was in his eleventh year as Premier — a white-haired lawyer shaped by the virtues of Methodism in rural Ontario and the culture of the town of Lindsay where he had practiced law until 1937, when he was first elected as a Progressive Conservative Member of the Legislature. He was, despite his carefully nurtured public reputation as a country lawyer, a calculating, even cunning politician who absorbed the socialist ideas of his opponents like cells envelop an invading organism, instead of fighting it head to head, and who knew, above everything else, that when the tides of history changed, it was time to go with them.

He was, as well, a quiet advocate of immigration, and had once said: "Our creed is that more people leads to more industry, more jobs, more wages and more opportunity. . . ."[4] Frost knew that given the existence of an Italian community of more than 200,000 in Toronto — 30,000 of them in construction — and the possibility of tens of thousands yet to come, the Hogg's Hollow disaster was not to be discreetly handled or left to underlings. It could not be downplayed. But that was the most elemental aspect. For a politician of Frost's style — for whom timing was always crucial — Hogg's Hollow provided the necessary opportunity to begin bringing Ontario into the modern era in its labor codes, compensation laws, and safety regulations. Ontario was many years behind progressive jurisdictions — mostly in the United States — in terms of worker compensation, worker safety, and worker health. Finally, the incident so galvanizing to the Italian community (which not only set up a relief program but appointed lawyers to attend the inquest with a view to suing negligent parties) could be turned to political opportunity. It could be used to send a strong message to Toronto's booming Italian population that the Progressive Conservative government, generally suspect to Italians, was its strong advocate.

In the third week of March, Frost discussed Hogg's Hollow, construction industry practices and the province's outdated labor legislation with a handful of trusted confidants — most of them either political advisors or senior civil servants, rather than members of his very conservative cabinet. He called his attorney general, Kelso Roberts, and instructed him to see to it that in the case of the Hogg's Hollow inquiry, the panel of jurors should be more than the usual cross section of citizens. It should be weighted with specialists and community leaders. When it convened on the first day of April in the council chambers in North York, its members included a mining expert, a geologist, a contractor, a vice-president of one of the large international oil companies, the president of a large ratepayers association and the secretary-treasurer of the Ontario Federation of Labour.

Frost then swiftly but quietly instructed the Department of Labour to pass an immediate regulation requiring all pay-cheques to be itemized, thus ensuring their integrity and pre-venting fly-by-night contractors from working hundreds of men at breakneck speed for seven days but only paying them for five, or telling them they were being paid for vacation time when they weren't and, most scandalous of all, giving them unemploy-ment stamps which were worthless since no remittance had been made to the unemployment offices.[5]

The Hogg's Hollow inquiry proved that the disaster had been preordained through carelessness. The testimonies of witness after witness was a litany of negligence that would leave an imprint of shame on the history of Ontario's treatment of labor-ing men. The man operating the compressor at the site had never run one before and was not there when it was shut off; he had no idea who turned the switch. A workman running an excavation car carrying earth to the surface was often so drunk he would fall into a stupor. The tunnel workers wore no helmets, no protective clothing, no safety boots. The underground tele-phone didn't work, nor did the underground lights. The men carried no flashlights or headlamps and there were no fire extinguishers underground. There was much more. Less than three days after the inquiry opened, the jury filed its report, castigating callous management, incompetent foremen and a slipshod Provincial Department of Labour.

"According to the evidence presented," said coroner Dr. D.K. McAteer, "almost all the safety regulations governing the tunnel project were violated at one time or another, and many of the regulations were violated continuously. The attitude of the management towards the safety of the individual worker can be described as no less than callous. Many of the workmen both on the surface and underground were inexperienced, untrained, or unqualified for the work to which they were assigned. Several of the foremen were not sufficiently competent to be entrusted with the instruction or direction of the workmen. . . ." The jury's first recommendation was aimed at the safety regulations of the Department of Labour, calling for their revision and improvement — a restrained way of asking that various acts dealing with construction, some unexamined since they were drawn up in 1907, be replaced. The damning verdict of the report made further systematic changes imperative. Premier Frost announced the formation of a Royal Commission, before the end of the week, to begin hearings to improve safety standards in Ontario. A half-century of neglect would, he swore, be remedied.[6]

Frost, now in the final year of his leadership, had inherited a government which, if it did not despise labor, held it in disdain. The years of Tory rule under George Drew — who boasted of "stopping socialism" and fought unions as a matter of course — had left their strongest legacy in the province's Department of Labour, where benign neglect had been a guiding principle. Safety legislation scarcely existed, there was only a grudging acceptance of the Workmen's Compensation Act, and a minimum wage for men had not even been enacted.

Frost's cabinet, with rare exception, was made up of men he himself often thought reactionary in their attitude to government's responsibility to intervene to protect the welfare of citizens. But probably no man who sat around the cabinet table in Ontario in the fifties was as conservative as Charles Daley, the Minister of Labour. Daley had been a carpenter and later Mayor of St. Catharines before being elected to the legislature in 1943. He became Minister of Labour shortly afterward, presiding over a department with some of the weakest labor legislation in Canada. He was virtually committed to keeping it that way. Once, Leslie Frost sent a young career civil servant to see Daley, asking that he speak on behalf of amending a small piece of social legislation on human rights. Daley drew in his breath and looking straight at the young man replied: "I'll resign first." The civil servant was a former journalist from the *Toronto Star* named Tom Eberlee, a bright, progressive man, who was to become Ontario's deputy minister of labor, presiding over the modernization of labor law in the province. "He is an extremely conservative man," Eberlee later said of Daley. "He believes the world has been perfect since about 1928. He suggests nothing; he resists everything."

But Daley alone could not be held responsible for the lack of labor legislation. His cabinet colleagues argued simply that as long as industry kept pouring into the province, nothing need be changed. "Is industry dissatisfied with our regulations? Is labor, which is pouring in from other provinces?" When the tragedy of Hogg's Hollow struck, Daley rose to the occasion by insisting that the site was acceptable. But by the spring of 1960, in the aftermath of Hogg's Hollow, it was clear that new laws were needed to keep pace with new machinery, new procedures, new dangers, on the job site. The combination of tragic accidents of the late fifties, articles by journalists such as Frank Drea, and the crusading advice of advocates such as Tom Eberlee, then assistant secretary to the cabinet, would close one era of history, and usher in a new one. But it would not take place without two massive strikes in the summer of 1960 and the spring of 1961, confrontations on the streets, and Premier Frost's connivance to get around the resistance of men in his own cabinet.[7]

The Italian laborers who poured into Canada from Italy in the fifties, who were unable to find work in downtown Toronto and were shunned by the established unions of the day, were a boon to the emerging residence-building industry putting up houses and high-rise apartments in the city suburbs — Don Mills,

Willowdale, and Scarborough. The industry was in turbulence for one basic reason: tremendous demand was being met by inexperienced people, whose overnight construction companies had no stability.

"If we want a suit," said one housing expert of the day, "we go to a tailor; if we want legal advice we go to a lawyer; if we want medical attention, we go to a doctor. But if we want a house, we go to an ex-grocer who has found there is more money in slicing up property than slicing up ham. . . ." Or, as an observer of Italian immigration later described it: "Many of the subcontractors themselves were not formally qualified. They established their own businesses in carpentry, masonry, plastering, painting, and concrete work, without having gone through a formal apprentice-to-journeyman-to-master classification within their occupations. In such a climate, Italian laborers sought a place and most found it — working for a myriad of subcontractors who struck a deal to supply laborers for someone named 'Joe' who was putting up houses in the suburbs of Toronto for a developer, financed by someone nobody really knew in an office tower in the downtown of the city."[8]

The men from Calabria and Sicily were often nameless as well. Naturally, they were exploited by shady companies — sometimes run by their countrymen — but they were also manipulated by laborers of their own rank who, often for ambivalent reasons, sought to lead them.

In the late fifties, Bruno Zanini was one such man. A slight man in his late thirties with red hair and a roman nose, Zanini had been born in Italy, in a town called Variano, and had come to Toronto as a child. Despite a later return to Italy to study to become an opera singer, he eventually followed his father into bricklaying.

He was angered by what he discovered in both the conditions of the meager work he got and the cold shoulder he sensed from the established unions of the day. Zanini was not without a gift of charisma or a passion for justice for his people. On many Sunday afternoons in 1959, his tenor voice, rising and falling in dramatic tones, had brought hundreds of laborers to their feet cheering in dingy meeting halls in Toronto. But his ambitions seemed somehow doomed, partly through his lack of trade-union understanding, partly, some felt, because of a certain self-centredness. Once, in the mid-fifties, he had managed to form a makeshift union for Italian tradesmen in the suburbs, under the umbrella of the international union for bricklayers. But the Toronto bricklayers' local, worried Zanni would raid it for members and dollars, complained to union headquarters in the United States, so that in a year or so Zanini's local was absorbed by the downtown local working on the city skyscrapers. The residential builders of the suburbs ignored the unionization; they used non-union workers of which there were plenty. Zanini was powerless.

The efforts of Zanini and his unionist partners were flamboyant, exciting, but in the end chaotic and unsuccessful. The huge crowds came, the papers ran favorable articles, but their ambitions were doomed by the complexities of their endeavor and the disinclination of the men to tend to the less glamorous side of trade unionism — the day-to-day task of administration without which organizing a union is hopeless.

Almost always in the audiences for Zanini and those he shared the limelight with was a tall, black-haired teenager with brooding eyes. He sat almost alone and silent, a bit apart from the boisterous, chattering men from Calabria and Sicily. His name was John Stefanini; he was nineteen. He had come to Toronto the year before, in August, 1959, from Rome, where his father had once run a restaurant in the heart of the city and where, in his spare time, the boy had spent hours in museums and churches, nurturing a fascination for the history of Italian architecture and statuary. But his dream since the age of sixteen was to come to Canada to join his brother, his sister and his uncle. When he arrived, his relatives saw to it that he went to school, taking mostly English classes.[9]

In the early spring of 1960, John Stefanini's uncle, a union worker with the plasterers, helped get him work. Although he dreamed of university, Stefanini felt he'd better take what he could; conditions were so bad that his older brother Sergio — who had started a small bricklaying business with only three men — had had to move to North Bay. Prices in bricklaying were low and getting lower, so much so that Sergio was forced to forego his own salary to keep paying his men. As well, builders often simply withheld payment, complaining and needing no proof that work was substandard.

John began his work as a hod carrier, hopping aboard a pickup truck at dawn that took him to a high-rise building on the northwest edge of Toronto, where he helped plasterers by putting mortar in a wooden carrier, and carrying it up six floors on his shoulder. Within weeks his life changed forever.

On a Sunday afternoon in early August 1960, Stefanini went with several of his working relatives to the Italian Recreational Hall on Brandon Avenue for a meeting to organize an umbrella union for Italian laborers. Bruno Zanini was on stage.[10] Stefanini knew him as the man who had taught bricklaying to his brother Sergio. He listened with about two thousand others as Zanini said that enough was enough — their pay was disgraceful, their cheques unsound, their working conditions unsafe. He waved a fistful of worthless cheques given to Italian workers. They must organize; they must strike, and make sure every Italian on every housing site from one suburb to the other struck as well. He played the crowd like an actor. Once, he paused, and pointing to the vast crowd, asked how many men had never received a dollar of vacation pay. John Stefanini, still in his teens and a laborer in Canada for only a few months, could not believe what happened around him. Virtually every man in the hall arose, shouting.

Two weeks later — almost overnight, as such things go — they formed a union, The Brandon Group, so named because the Italian Hall was on Brandon Street. Three thousand men voted to strike, with no provision for strike pay and no guarantee of bettering their condition.

Next morning, John Stefanini was among a dozen volunteer organizers racing across the city in battered cars, rushing up to half-built houses and telling men — plasterers, carpenters, bricklayers — to put down their tools, walk off the job, and sign their names to the union list. He had begun a career that would occupy him for life. He saw what he did in those days of 1960 not as a job but as a cause. "Some people call it a strike," he told a relative. "It is not. It is a peaceful revolution by men who have been treated with disgrace."

There was the occasional act of violence. Charles Irvine, an intelligent, confident unionist with thirty years' experience in the plasterers' union, met with hundreds of subcontractors — the men, often Italian themselves, who supplied the crews of carpenters, lathers, and common laborers to do the work for the builders. They talked of a new deal — for injury compensation, hours, and vacations. A collective agreement was put forward by Irvine, but the contractors, while assenting to it, said they doubted they could afford it. If they took it to the builders, they said, asking for the increases they needed, the builders would simply ignore them and turn to unorganized pickup tradesmen who would do the work for less.

At this point, in the middle of summer, 1960, Zanini and Irvine made the decision that young John Stefanini regarded as a serious tactical mistake: they refused to negotiate with the subcontractors. Irvine, a rigid Scot, and Zanini, an amateur who knew little of the give-and-take of labor-management negotiation, simply told the subcontractors to take it or leave it. Stefanini, not included in the discussions of the union leaders, began to develop a lasting doubt of their skill. "They should sit down again," he told a friend, "and look at amending the collective agreement. Half a loaf is better than no loaf." He watched as within two weeks, hundreds of small contractors began changing their company names in order to avoid dealing with the union with which they had signed an agreement too rich for their meager resources. They then hired non-unionized carpenters, bricklayers, plasterers and laborers. Zanini and Irvine and The Brandon Group were on the sidelines, and the men were out of work for the rest of 1960 and well into the winter of 1961. Stefanini continued to work for the union, getting by on family resources, but his doubt about Zanini, his sense of trade unionism, and his commitment to it, deepened.

When spring began in 1961, Toronto was filled with rumors of another impending construction strike — one that would not just shut down housing, but highways, such as the extension to the Gardiner Expressway, and the extension to the city's subway system. "The housing locals," Wilfred List of the *Globe and Mail* wrote, "affiliates of international unions in the construction field, claim that the contractors who were forced to sign agreements after last summer's organizing drive have violated the contracts and short-changed the workers in pay and working conditions." List predicted the strike would involve up to 15,000 men and tie up projects within a 30-mile radius of Toronto. At Queen's Park, the Premier, brooding with his ministers, feared it was inevitable. His personal sympathy was with the workers who had been so abused they knew no way other than to strike, but it would be serious; it would tie up projects estimated at $150 million.

Charles Irvine announced the strike on May 29, before an array of microphones and popping flashbulbs. It would be long and mean and crippling, he said. The possibility of ugly and spreading violence emerged in the talk of the men organizing the strike, among them John Stefanini. At Queen's Park, Labour Minister Charles Daley, outraged and trying desperately to hold his temper in check, said that as far as he was concerned the whole affair was evil and illegal and employers should feel free to take whatever course they could against the laborers. On June 7, a disconsolate Leslie Frost rose from his desk to stand at his window, peering into a rainswept afternoon. He was frustrated with his department and his labor minister, though never so vexed as to rid himself of the man. But he was also deeply worried. He fretted over the consequences of the massive strike now underway. Late that afternoon he made a decision to call in Zanini and Irvine and brief them on his plan, in return for their effort to get the men back to work. Shortly after eight that same evening, they arrived and were met by one of the Premier's men, who took them to an elevator and into the dark paneled room where Frost rose to greet them.

Frost told the men that the grievances of their members were for the most part justified. As Premier, he would do all he could to rectify them, to begin to set up a Department of Labour that would, step by step, right the historic wrongs. For the next ten minutes, as the lights of Toronto began to glow beyond the south window of his office, Frost outlined, for the first time, the immediate steps he would take on behalf of the immigrant laborers he felt to be the victims of Ontario's labor history.

He would immediately set up a tribunal to hear grievances, in order to get around the encrusted Labour Relations Board of the current department. He would authorize creation of a team of investigators, competent and large enough to police contractors cheating on wages or cutting corners on the existing labor laws, weak though those were. Most crucial of all, he would call for a royal commission, to be headed by Canada's most respected arbitrator, Carl Goldenberg, who would be empowered to look into every aspect of labor-management relations and make the recommendations that would pave the way for a modern labor act in Ontario.

Bruno Zanini and Charles Irvine left Frost's office that evening and returned to union headquarters, but did not urge the men to return to work. The strike was underway, they said at a rally, and while certain vague promises were in the air, the men must stay out until things were in writing.[11] Within two days Frost, his face mirroring the indignation he felt at being let down, agreed with Attorney General Kelso Roberts that violence was imminent, that it should be met firmly by the police, and dealt with swiftly and sternly by the courts. In fact, said Roberts, the first offenders should be given sharp sentences to set an example.

On the morning of June 20, John Stefanini — then twenty years old, a slender youth of six feet and just over 140 pounds — rose at dawn at the home of his sister. Having left Zanini and Irvine's group, he was by then a business agent for a fledgling group with the Toronto Labour Movement called Local 183, the local led by one of the most reputable and legendary labor men of his time, the Irish-born unionist Gerry Gallager. Stefanini had a busy day ahead, trying to persuade men leaving for work in an hour to stay home and to respect the strike.

At six a.m. he got in his old car, drove first to pick up a union colleague and then, his friend beside him in the front seat, headed east on St. Clair Avenue, through the Italian neighborhoods where men gathered in the dim light on corners to await the pickup trucks. At around six-thirty, Stefanini turned north on Dufferin Street where, near Rogers Road, he saw two men in work clothes headed south. He stopped; his friend rolled down the window and asked the men if they knew a strike was on and why were they going to work. One man explained that they were not in residential construction but commercial, and hence members of a downtown union. The other reached in his pocket and produced his union card. While he did, Stefanini got out to inspect it. It was legitimate; the men went on their way and Stefanini stepped back into the car. He was turning the ignition when he looked up to see four police cruisers blocking his car. He glanced immediately in the rear-view mirror. Two cruisers were behind him.

Stefanini was terrified. He had never had a run-in with the police, in Italy or in Canada, although that very morning, he had left St. Clair Avenue fearing that some of the union squads were about to get rough. Within minutes on that June morning, as the crowds gathered to watch, Stefanini was charged with obstructing police, put in a cruiser and taken to the Don Jail.

At his trial just two days later, as the tensions of the strike reached fever pitch in Toronto, the arresting officer testified that when he and his colleagues arrived on the scene, forty laborers — Italians for the most part — were piling out of cars, and, with Stefanini in the lead, were beginning to fight on the sidewalk. When Stefanini's lawyer asked how many cars were there, the officer said there were two. He had no real answer when asked how forty men could pour out of two cars.

The officer said he told the men to disperse and then he accused Stefanini of instructing them to disobey the order. Stefanini's lawyer asked, "Did Stefanini give that instruction in English or in Italian?" The officer said Stefanini had spoken in Italian. Then the lawyer asked the officer if he could speak Italian. He could not. The lawyer asked the obvious question: how, if he could not speak Italian, did the arresting officer know that Stefanini had instructed the men to disobey the order to disperse? The policeman gave no answer. The prosecutor argued that given the danger of more violence, he was asking for a stiff sentence. The presiding judge strongly agreed. Stefanini got six months. Immediately, the prosecutor came over and expressed his regrets. He didn't expect six months, he said; two weeks would have been adequate.

For Stefanini, whose youth was unblemished and whose record was impeccable, prison — first Toronto's Don Jail, later, the Guelph Reformatory — was a horror, not just because he felt he had been wrongly charged, but because he was foreign to the violence and blackmail of prison culture. Once, in Guelph, he was given a fresh uniform. One of the hardest inmates approached him, saying he'd like the jacket. He offered cigarettes. Stefanini didn't smoke. "I want the jacket," the inmate said, "and if you don't give it to me, I'm taking it."

Stefanini's reply reflected his pathos and his ignorance of prison culture. "If you try that," he said, "I'll call the guard." Within minutes he was surrounded by inmates. Three had knives. He was certain he was about to die. He searched the room looking desperately for an escape. Eventually the cons backed off. Stefanini implored the guards to have him moved to a safer section, where he spent the remaining months of his imprisonment. When he was released late that summer and went back to his sister's house, he weighed even less than when he was admitted. "To really appreciate freedom," he told a friend, "you have to lose it, or you'll never really understand how precious it is."

The strike went deep into the hottest weeks of the Toronto summer. Over one hundred men were charged with minor infractions: a special "strikers court" was established to expedite the cases. But once the stiff sentence had been given to Stefanini and widely publicized, the militancy seemed to disappear from the strike; and though it continued, it was, as Stefanini pointed out, always on the verge of collapse. It dragged on for forty-nine days. On July 16, Irvine and Zanini climbed to a stage in front of 2,500 men to announce the end, but the terms were almost the same ones they had been given by Leslie Frost at the very beginning. "This is the day you can become men again," Charles Irvine shouted to the cheering crowd. "You have a place in this country now and you can keep it."

The grateful laborers swarmed to the stage, and lifted Irvine and Zanini to their shoulders. The *Toronto Star* commented the next day: "Exact terms of the strike settlement haven't been made known. The Ontario government finally was forced to step in and has created a special board to speed up arbitration of grievances and contract violations. Investigators of the Provincial Labour Department are going into contractors' books."

To Frank Drea, in the offices of the *Telegram*, his files, like his memory, overflowing with the stories of abuse, the strike meant more still. That evening he sat at his desk talking by phone to the men he knew well in the unions and in politics. Then, loosening his tie and turning to his typewriter, he wrote that the workers had won Canada's greatest labor victory since the steel strike of 1946: "The $150-million residential construction industry is working at full speed for the first time since May 29, as the immigrant workers streamed back to work." Then, with an afterthought of Irish faith, Drea added some words which may, in truth, take a little longer still, to find fulfilment: "Their days of exploitation," he wrote, "are ended forever."

CHAPTER EIGHT

THE HUMBLE VOCATION OF JOHN STEFANINI

Carl Goldenberg, a dapper Montreal lawyer with a trim mustache and dark wavy hair, was one of the leading labor negotiators in North America when he arrived in Toronto in the last week of September to prepare the details for the royal commission of October, 1961. Frost's commitment to correcting the outmoded labor legislation of the province was plain in his choice of Goldenberg, but also in the public servant he made secretary of the commission. He picked the young, promising adviser Tom Eberlee, who had served him in several jobs, the latest as assistant secretary of the cabinet. To Eberlee, the labor act of the province was at best pathetic, at worst an abomination. Its irrelevance was reflected in some of the titles of antiquated acts lying in cobwebbed corners of the department, such as the Factory, Shops and Offices Act, not changed since it had been formed in the 1880s, and as outmoded as its Victorian title.

At ten o'clock on the morning of October 18, in a plain, high-ceilinged room at Queen's Park, Goldenberg nodded to the handful of union men, turned to Eberlee, had him read the terms of the inquiry, and then asked for the first submission.[1]

A lawyer named Irving Freedman spoke first on behalf of The Brandon Group — the collection of local unions of bricklayers, masons and plasterers created by Zanini and Irvine in 1955. He stated that the membership was virtually all Italian, that in August 1960, the men had struck for the first time, and that when contractors failed to live up to contractual agreements, they struck for the second time from May 29 to July 16, 1961. About 22,000 men were employed in residential construction in Toronto; The Brandon Group represented 5,000. When he summed up what his union felt to be the situation the members faced, Freedman was succinct: "Against a background of illiteracy and quiet desperation, workers were being compelled to accept conditions — sometimes under threat of deportation — which were startlingly deplorable."

Freedman said the Brandon people realized that by its very nature, construction work was irregular and unstable, that firms formed and failed overnight. He conceded that the labor movement itself was not without fault, because too many of the craftsmen — plasterers, hod carriers, masons — were negotiating their agreements individually. "This very method," he said, "can create widespread dissatisfaction and unrest. . . . It is conceivable that one craft — albeit a minority — may, by its inability to conclude an agreement even after exhaustive conciliation, create hardship and distress for a majority of construction workers by placing picket lines on various sites." Clearly, as an umbrella for several crafts, The Brandon Group saw itself as part of the answer.

Freedman asked that the minister of labor call a conference of all the parties — the tangle of employer groups and the army of unions — to set up a clear process of negotiation, one that would be able to produce what he called "a master agreement." But his most controversial recommendation, one that released a chill in the offices of the contractors when they read their newspapers the next morning, was still to come. He approached it by repeating the fact everyone in the room already knew — that anyone with a wheelbarrow today could be a contractor tomorrow: "Ironically enough, many incompetent workers who find themselves repeatedly discharged, seek the solution to their problems by becoming subcontractors." The solution was obviously to prevent such incompetent and fly-by-night operators from entering the business: "We recommend enactment of legislation which will make it mandatory for every contractor in the construction industry to be licensed as a condition precedent for performing work in the industry and that such licences be issued by a provincial licensing board . . . ." Thus, argued The Brandon Group, only businesses that were competent in their craft and sound in their finance could be formed, and once formed, they would be subject to stern discipline — for example, the revoking of the licence.

If the men from The Brandon Group gave the most reasoned response to the intricacies the commission raised, the most impassioned came from John C. Pedoni, a soft-spoken social worker, who, as the administrator of the Italian Immigrant Aid Society, knew hundreds of Italian families, and was probably the man closest to their personal grief. Pedoni explained that he had seen a great many Italian workmen and their families endure the abuses of the construction industry. About halfway through his carefully written brief, he read Goldenberg a long, definitive list of the forms the abuse took:

> Employers have many ways of exploiting their employees and these are the most common: (a) Marginal or below marginal wages. (b) Nonpayment of wages. (c) Kickbacks (payroll registers and pay cheques show regular wages, but workers are forced to return part of their wages in cold cash, usually through a foreman or company man). (d) Overtime. Construction workers get straight pay regardless of hours worked in a week. There is no such thing as overtime pay for them, even if they work sixty hours a week. (e) Holiday pay. A survey conducted among Italian bricklayers in 1959 revealed that nearly fifty percent of them did not receive holiday pay, or if someone did in the remaining fifty percent, it was not in the measure of two percent as per existing regulations. (f) Individual and small contracting firms disappearing between jobs. This is the worst kind because towards the end of the working session, workers having the misfortune of being employed by them stand to lose not only their wages but Unemployment Insurance stamps and sometimes even their tools . . . . (g) Phony cheques issued by companies mentioned in point (f).

When he finished reading, Pedoni looked up at Goldenberg. He said the list was based not on impressions but on records kept by the Italian Immigrant Aid Society. Goldenberg, wishing to confirm the list's reliability asked him pointedly: "This information of exploitation that you submit is based on your records?" Pedoni's answer revealed that behind the records, there were thousand of terrified men. Yes, he said, it was based on records, and although he had tried to get men to stand with him at the commission, they were too frightened.

It was the same the year before, he continued, when he appeared before the Royal Commission on Safety, called in the aftermath of the Hogg's Hollow disaster. He had four Italian laborers with shocking revelations about their working conditions, but each was too intimidated even to let his name be known. They were frightened, said Pedoni, not just of losing their jobs, but of their employers' threats to deport them should they speak out. "We must not forget, Mr. Chairman," Pedoni continued, "that people who come to my office are people of very limited education, haven't seen the world, and every little thing may scare them." He ended with his recommendations, the most important of which was that builders and contractors be licensed.

Other small contractors confirmed what was being said by Pedoni and Freedman: there was flagrant cheating in safety, on wages, on hours. The language problem, ignorance of their rights and the laws of the land, and their financial need to hold a steady job, made the Italian laborers a natural target for unscrupulous employers. Only the Ontario Federation of Construction Associations seemed unaware of the litany of mistreatment. In its brief, presented by J. Pigott, it said simply that "labor in general is satisfied with the hours of work, rates of pay and working conditions." The problem, it said, was with unions and union leaders who were agitating. But they made one concession: a minimum wage would help end "the exploitation of unskilled immigrant labor."

The hearings ended early in November, and Goldenberg began to write his report; he re-read not only the submissions but the work of numerous academics in labor and industry throughout North America. Now and then he would call Eberlee or John Crispo, a young University of Toronto academic who was his research director. By the end of the year, the report was complete; it was released in early March, 1962.

The findings of Carl Goldenberg were all that the handful of men wanting to reform the outdated labor department had hoped for. After conceding that there had been widespread exploitation, he called for a wall-to-wall renovation of the labor department, and the creation of legislation that, in most ways, was that asked for by the men who had appeared before him on behalf of labor. The Labour Relations Act, he stipulated, should be radically overhauled to help the unorganized workers form bargaining units. "The minister of labor," he said, "should call a joint conference of employers and trade unions in the construction industry to consider and to formulate plans for multiple bargaining master agreements, . . . and related matters." He called for a board to enforce the upper and lower limits on hours of work and rates of pay. He suggested legislation that would require the prime contractor to be held responsible for the wages of employees should a subcontractor not pay them. He wanted the legislation governing vacation pay amended so that employers could not avoid paying it without stiff penalty.

But his most far-reaching recommendation had to do with an obscure piece of labor law which had been gathering dust in the sleepy corridors of the department for decades. The Industrial Standards Act, wrote Goldenberg, does not protect the unorganized worker and the responsible employer in the sectors of the industry where collective bargaining is weak. He suggested ways in which collective bargaining could be made easier and more effective. However, on the claim that contractors should be licensed as a way of keeping crooked or incompetent firms out of the business, Goldenberg was reluctant. He felt that if other of his recommendations were implemented, simple registration of contractors, not licensing, would suffice.

Goldenberg's report, given wide coverage in newspapers all over Ontario, heralded a true reformation in labor legislation. It insisted irrefutably that the time was past when the most prosperous province in Canada could exist with labor legislation that was fifty years out of date. At Queen's Park, John Robarts, who had become premier in October 1961, confirmed by several decisions the pragmatic approach of Leslie Frost, his predecessor. He removed Charles Daley, less than two weeks after coming to office and gave the job eventually to Leslie Rowntree, who, with Tom Eberlee as his assistant deputy minister, would preside over the most historic change in the labor traditions of Ontario.

Rowntree quickly announced that his department's budget and staff would both be increased by twenty percent and its organization would be renovated from top to bottom. After all, he explained, no other part of the entire government touched the lives of so many people — in their working lives. He said that the idea that labor and management could be left to their own devices was an outmoded one that history had disproved. It was this false doctrine, said Rowntree, that had contributed to much of the labor strife in the recent history of Ontario.[2] Already, Eberlee and Deputy Minister James Metzler had convened a conference of the main antagonists in the recent construction strife to try to bring about a better atmosphere and some specific results. One of these had already been achieved: an agreement that, instead of the jungle of trade-by-trade bargaining, builders would be able to negotiate on an industry-wide basis. All aspects of labor law would be revamped — the Minimum Wages Act, the Industrial Standards Act, the Hours of Work and Vacations with Pay Act — with especial attention to health and safety standards.

It was becoming clear that Tom Eberlee was to be a central architect of a new era in Ontario's labor history. Eberlee was a man of quiet, understated style, whose work would touch the lives of tens of thousands of Italians he would never know. In the winters of the early sixties, as the brief twilight over Toronto was overtaken by darkness, Eberlee and several of his staff — lawyers, academics and various consultants — moved back and forth in a suite of offices at Queen's Park, writing and revising the changes to the speech Leslie Rowntree would give when the session of the Ontario legislature got underway.

A few miles north from Queen's Park, on Caledonia Road, deep in one of the emerging Italian neighborhoods, John Stefanini was spending the winter working as an organizer for the Toronto unit of the Laborers International Union of North America, a group granted a union charter in Toronto in 1952, mainly to bargain for men working for Ontario Hydro. It was called Local 183. Despite his youth and his modest education, Stefanini had read the report and agreed with Goldenberg's observation on the absence of unions among the Italian men. The housing industry was hard to organize, but that fact did not deter Stefanini: his commitment to the right to a union was founded not on economic consideration but on moral conviction.

Each morning, Stefanini climbed into a battered old Ford and drove from site to site, hoping to sign up men in a variety of trades. That January of 1963, his mind wandered to his early months with The Brandon Group, the strikes of 1960 and 1961, and his waning confidence in the leadership of the union leaders of that time. "The long strike of 1961, the many men in court," he said later, "all that was unnecessary. If they had only lived up to their promise to Leslie Frost, to call the men back to work in return for the royal commission. I gave three months of my youth to them, spent in jail, for absolutely nothing."

Stefanini had other practical reasons for leaving Zanini and Irvine and their union to work instead for Local 183 of the Laborers International. He was convinced that both men were indifferent to the day-to-day duties of running a union. "If you build a house, you must tend to it," he said, "or it will fall apart. Tending to it, its finances, its membership, will not make headlines, but it makes the union." History was to prove Stefanini correct in most of his judgements on the future of the union started by Charles Irvine and Bruno Zanini.

Local 183 had been founded by Irish-born unionist Gerry Gallager; its offices were in a set of dusty buildings near the intersection of Dundas and Dufferin in the city's west end. From there, Stefanini worked quickly towards two big objectives: an increase in the membership, then about a thousand and, more important, the creation of social programs for the overwhelmingly Italian members — a dental program, a training centre, a welfare plan. He went to work sites on the frozen northern edge of the city to talk to men twenty or thirty years older than he about the union that failed and the one he worked for now. He was met with the old fears: joining the union would mean trouble, even deportation. Stefanini spoke calmingly about the social programs, the safety inspections, the honest dealings. "If you go by the book," he said over and over, "the union will survive. If you don't, it will not. We go by the book, by the law."[3]

He also spent time with Eberlee and others at the labor ministry and with contractors, and often that summer, with an older trade union man named Ed Boyer. Boyer lived outside Toronto and stayed in Stefanini's Caledonia Road basement apartment when he came to the city in his work as a member of the Ontario Labour Relations Board. An old-time CCF member and a carpenter by trade, Boyer was a father-figure to Stefanini, and over many months he also became his teacher — on the history of trade unionism in Canada, the Ontario Labour Relations Act and how it could be interpreted and, above all, on the need for integrity in a union's internal affairs. "He is the salt of the earth," Stefanini told a friend. "He is what a trade unionist is all about — he lives for the members."

While Stefanini made his way, deliberately, cautiously, into union leadership, the men who planned and promulgated the labor laws of Ontario were also at work, as quietly and almost as cautiously. By early 1964 the ancient Factory, Shops and Offices Act had been completely rewritten and replaced with modern safety regulations. Men could no longer enter tunnels without adequate shoring, proper compressors, and personal equipment. Moreover, Rowntree noted in a contemporary report, the government was intent on policing safety. The field staff, the officers who were directly involved on a day-to-day basis in the enforcement and administration of legislation, had been increased by fifty percent in the past two years.

A reformation was underway. It would transform the world of Italian men on the scaffolds and Italian women in the factories, from one inviting disaster and disability, to one which in the sixties would be livable, providing better safety and in the case of construction, prosperity to countless Italian working people.

In the early sixties, the men who crowded the Italian Hall on Brandon Avenue waving the cheques that so often bounced, could only hope for two dollars an hour when work was available. By the late sixties, their livelihood was improving and the conditions in which they earned it were substantially better, the result of an active Ontario government, the continuance of economic prosperity in Ontario, and above all, a far more sophisticated union representation.

In the mid-sixties, Gerry Gallager appointed Stefanini Secretary-Treasurer. Stefanini was taking courses in labor relations at night, hoping to study trade unionism at Harvard University. He delegated some of his administrative responsibility to others in order to put on a membership drive for Local 183. By the late sixties, the membership had grown from one thousand to eight thousand — ninety percent of it Italian, many of them the men who years earlier had jammed the hall on Brandon Avenue to seek redress for their grievances.

In 1967, Stefanini succeeded Gallager as Business Manager and Secretary-Treasurer of Local 183. For years to come, Stefanini was elected to both offices, almost always by acclamation. He brought about the relocation and re-equipment of the local: in bright new office buildings, its recruiting and administration tracked with sophisticated computers, and its members aided with dozens of programs from language training to citizenship courses. Stefanini ended the old disputes between carpenters, masons, and laborers — over who worked on what and when — by making a number of them the members of a single union, Local 183. In time, the Italian laborers — whose ranks would be swelled by Portuguese newcomers in the seventies — found that while they still faced the harsh realities of a tough occupation, they were no longer the menial army of the pick and shovel; they were members of North America's largest laborers' union, 13,000 strong. That union was considered one of North America's most effective bargaining organizations, trusted by its members and respected by the companies that negotiated with it. Many events permanently changed the life of the Italian laborer for the better, but significant among them was the work of the young man from Rome for whom the labor movement was a true vocation.

The presence and influence of Italians in Canada in the twentieth century was most strongly imprinted on the landscape of the country by men who built. Still, our world is not made of buildings and sidewalks alone. By the 1960s, names with an Italian cadence were sounding in the ears of Canadians like a familiar tune, and influencing national taste in decisive ways — conductor Mario Bernardi at the National Arts Centre orchestra and later the Calgary Philharmonic, actor Bruno Gerussi on the stage and on television, and publisher Daniel Iannuzzi through a large Italian newspaper, *Corriere Canadese* and then multilingual television in Toronto.

One especially interesting and influential Italian Canadian was a man whose name was not apparently Italian at all. He opened a small store on March 10, 1960, in an unpretentious building along Yonge Street in the midst of the season of construction discontent in Toronto. Above the door he placed a replica of the signature that would accompany him to renown in the world of male fashion: "Lou Myles, Disegnatore."

Lou Myles was, in fact, Luigi Cocomile, a compact man of endless energies, who grew up in one of the old neighborhoods near the city's early Little Italy, where his parents, Joseph and Lucetta Cocomile, settled after arriving from Calabria in 1928. Their son showed little interest in school, leaving at fifteen, but by the time he reached his twenties, people noticed that he had not only a fascination with fine clothes, but a desire to design them. For a time, he moved from job to job, selling suits, but by the opening of the sixties, with a shoestring of financial backing, he opened his own store. His decision to change his name was an illustration of the mood of Toronto at the advent of the sixties, one that would change rapidly over the next two decades. "I just felt that my family name, Cocomile," he said later, "would not be that well received in the city of that day. Things would certainly be different later on, so that, in time, being Italian would be an advantage in the clothing field. But back then, Italians had come through a lot of discrimination."

Myles continued to draw and plan, working his way towards what was to become a legend in male fashion: the Lou Myles suit. He knew precisely what he wanted, and in search of it, he took his sketches from factory to factory, until, in a small shop in the drab downtown clothing district, he found Vittorio Romeo, who had spent his entire life in gentlemen's tailoring, first as a boy in Genoa, Italy, later in the United States. Romeo took Myles' designs, translated them into a suit which had precisely the look that Myles sought: masculine, slenderizing, declarative.

Some people might have looked upon Cocomile's excitement as a fascination with the trivial; it was not. If we are what we see, then the world upon which we gaze, from the creation of the architect to the creation of the fashion designer, affects our standards and our destiny.

> I was born with an interest in beautiful and artistic things. That came from my Italian traditions. Male fashion is beautiful. To me it is a matter of creativity, not materialism. I also sensed in those years that men would be looking upon what they wear, not simply as a piece of cloth to cover them, but with a developing pride — a suit would be a symbol of purpose and even success.

Lou Myles became one of the major names in male fashion, not just among the well-to-do across North America, but among those who knew male styling professionally. In the clothing salons of New York or Los Angeles, his name was spoken with the same respect that a musicologist reserves for a fine conductor or a scholar for a celebrated historian. In Toronto, he established a factory which turned out thousands of his suits every year to be sold in the better stores of every leading city in Canada and the United States. They were purchased not just by the celebrities of the stage but by corporate leaders, including, in Canada, Harrison McCain, head of McCain foods, Arden Haynes, Chairman of Imperial Oil Limited, Paul Desmarais, Chief Executive Officer of Power Corporation, in the United States, by such luminaries as Ken Taylor of Nabisco and Lee Iacocca, the corporate hero of the eighties.

In 1988, men such as these and thousand of others spent well over 9 million dollars either in Myles' own stores — he owns several across Canada — or in others that carry his creations everywhere from Halifax to Los Angeles. As Vittorio Romeo, who has been by his side these many years once told a journalist: "When it comes to male styling, male fashion, you'd better listen. You'd better listen because this man was born with something very special. He is unbeatable."

The same year Lou Myles opened his store in the heart of downtown Toronto, a young Italian fluent in English, with a degree from the University of Vienna was trekking from one construction site to another, a shopping bag of books at his side. His name was Charles Caccia. The books, which he had written himself, were called *Industrial English*. They contained the basic English words, expressions and phrases a man would use to get through the day: Caccia handed them out to any workman who wanted one.[5]

He was an idealist who had been raised in Milan and who came to Canada in 1955, wrote the book at night in his boardinghouse, had it printed at his own expense, and distributed it by hand. On Sunday afternoons in the union hall on Brandon Avenue, Caccia was moved by the undeserved plight of the Italian laborer. "I have discovered an Italian community I did not know in Milan," he told a friend. "And it is full of problems of adjustment. These men often have great hearts and fine minds but with grade two education, life is too hard." Charles Caccia's little book — five thousand of which were printed and distributed — was his first gesture in a career which would define him as a benefactor of Italian immigrants to Canada.

His contribution began to take shape in the spring of 1961, in the hall of Saint Helen's Roman Catholic Church, a musty old edifice near the corner of Dundas and Lansdowne in Toronto's west end. Caccia had worked at a variety of jobs — planting trees, translating articles into Italian, laboring in a Quebec copper mine, and finally starting a modest business in midtown Toronto designed to build a bridge between the Italian community and the business community. But by 1961, he was so deeply involved in social work with Italians that he was spending more time on volunteer work than in his office. Often, in the evenings, he would sit in the study of St. Helen's parish priest, Father Joe Carraro, and the two would discuss the needs they both saw for training and teaching Italians, many of whom were suffering because of their lack of skills or from an inadequate education in general.

Carraro saw something more: "Look," he told Caccia one evening that spring, "there are thousands of Italians who come here with a trade and can't practice it. I met a young fellow the other night, an electrician back in the old country, but his qualifications aren't recognized in Canada. We need a program of educational upgrading, to bring the skills of Italians to a level where they can be certified."

Caccia agreed with his friend. The priest's commitment to social action had been fashioned by his boyhood in Treviso, near Venice. He had come to Canada in 1958, and while the bishop who recruited him saw the priesthood as primarily sacramental, Carraro was of another mold. He understood the role of religious vocation, but also believed in using the priesthood to improve the lot of Italians in practical ways, mainly by adult education.

"The need is there," Caccia said. "There will be thousands of students, but what of the teachers? Who?"

Carraro had thought about that. He knew, because he had spoken to them, that there were at least a dozen men in Toronto's west end, now becoming a place of several Italian neighborhoods, who held certificates in the trades — electricians, welders, carpenters, bricklayers. They would contribute their time to teach others, those who needed to upgrade the level of their qualifications, or were looking for a new trade because they'd been injured in construction or were simply untrained.

On a windy Sunday a couple of weeks later, dozens of Italian teenagers stood on the steps of the Italian churches of Toronto handing out leaflets. On each was a simple message: a meeting was being held at St. Helen's a week hence for anyone interested in improving his or her skills through night courses, which would be taught by fellow Italians at no cost. Hundreds turned out. It was the birth of COSTI — Centro Organizzativo Scuole Tecniche Italiane. At St. Helen's, in a tiny room beneath the main stairway, a man named Luciano Cecchini, who had his license in auto mechanics, taught six others who in a year would write their examinations for the Ontario Class A auto mechanic's licence. A muscular young man named Joseph Bellissimo phoned Caccia and offered to leave his career as a cabinet maker to work full-time for COSTI. He became its first instructor in a rehabilitation workshop, helping injured workers begin again.

Caccia was busy. He was not only moving from office to office in Queen's Park talking to politicians, but, along the way, beginning to think of standing for election as an alderman. Carraro was taken up with his parish work. (Sadly, neither the parish nor the archdiocese saw Carraro's COSTI leadership as part of his work as a priest.) They were an effective team: Carraro supervised the day-to-day operation, while Caccia raised money and talked with educational bureaucrats. In time, through the help of the Toronto School Board, COSTI acquired the use of rooms in Central Technical School and the Provincial Institute of Trades, both large, commodious and conveniently located in the city's west end.

COSTI's motto was "Integration through Education"; its success was a revelation of the resourcefulness of hundreds of Italian Canadians ready to help others (many of them non-Italian) find their footing, avoid the soul-destroying dependency on welfare, and achieve their full potential. Carraro and Caccia could not, in their most ambitious vision, have calculated the tremendous reach their organization would one day have — teaching, in any year, thousands of people, many of whom were Portuguese and Asian, in more than seventy courses in centres all over Toronto and its suburbs. Within two decades it would teach and train more than a hundred thousand people. Charles Caccia went on to become Canada's first Italian-Canadian cabinet minister, serving in Pierre Trudeau's government.

One of COSTI's most visionary presidents, Lino Magagna — who came to Canada unable to speak a single word of English in 1952, later earned a PhD in engineering, and became a senior official of Ontario Hydro — said truthfully that COSTI had become a senior institution in the volunteer sector in

Toronto. But more importantly: "COSTI is an expression of deep human feelings in our society. It is a way of reaching out by human beings and saying 'Here I am, don't be afraid, here's how you take the first step, let me help.'"[6]

The men who made their way to COSTI's classes and work-shops in the first years of its life were as varied in style and personality as the land they had left — tall, sturdy northerners with names that sounded Germanic; slim, brisk men with the elegant grace of Romans; and the shy, friendly men from the south, the garden lands of Calabria and Sicily. They were Italian, but to those who knew them or to scholars who studied their coming, they were so individualistic as to defy the collec-tive descriptive of most Canadians — the Italian community. In a strict sense, no such community existed — Italians were too independent, too regional, too free-thinking, to conform to a single, easily defined community. As Lino Magagna, the former COSTI president put it:

> The urge to stereotype any group seems to come from an urge to introduce order of some fashion, to categorize. It is easier to deal with people that way — not as individuals but as a group. Yet Italy is an amalgam of such different groups of peoples, that the stereotype doesn't make any sense. The people I come from in the north are closer in history to the Austrians over the hill than to the people of the south around Florence. And the people of Florence are different again than the Neapolitans. So stereotyp-ing is a fact only because people stereotype. Still, it is disappear-ing, there is much much less than when I came to Canada in the fifties.[7]

One feeling ran as a firm thread through the lives of all those who filled the workshops of COSTI — they knew, as a century of immigrants before them knew, what it was to be regarded as the most inferior of the inferior by almost all who met them, beyond their fellow migrants. For many, whose relatives had come in the early years of the century, the experience was an enactment of the tales of their grandfathers: the smashed win-dows; the racist epithets: dago, gringo, . . . spaghetti-eater; the rejections of the street and of the bureaucrats in the offices.[8]

Even in the early sixties, so many decades after the ignominy of the Cordasco years or the war years, the derision lingered, less coarse or explicit, but fixed and ingrained, as if the description of them in *The Presbyterian Record* of 1910 had somehow found a lingering place in the Canadian psyche: "Low in mentality . . . warm-hearted, kind . . . but also given to fighting and violent crimes. . . . "

Robert Harney, North America's most distinguished scholar of Italian immigration, sees these attitudes — the product of what he termed "Italiophobia" — persisting well beyond the sixties. "Laughing at 'little Tony,' the peanut vendor," he wrote, "endowing him with a simple and sunny soul, little ambition, and childlike ways, describing him in diminutives, is simply the Italophobes' way of rendering him impotent, reducing him the way the term 'boy' reduced slaves and colonials. It is also the obverse of 'big Tony' the strikebreaker or anarchist, the womanizer, the impassioned knife wielder, the habitual law-breaker. . . . Both Tonys are projections made by the English-speaking host society upon the powerless . . . . "

Always, hovering over them all, was the suspicion that organized crime was rooted in their collective character — despite the fact that, as time and study would prove, the vast majority of them were among the more morally upright members of society. But the stigma would weigh upon them, and damage some permanently. When the century-old wounds finally began to heal in the late seventies, they had left a permanent scar beneath the accepting surface of Canadian society. To Robert Harney, the prejudice was a compound of ancient and unfounded fear, ignorance, bigotry, and the less admirable myths that find a home in the imagination of man.

In an essay entitled "Italiophobia: an English-speaking Malady?" Harney recalled a visit made by a British official acting for the Canadian government: "In 1942, reporting on the war-time morale of Canadians of Italian descent, Tracey Phillips, an English official seconded to the Canadian government as an expert on ethnic minorities, chided Britons and Anglo-Americans alike: 'It is significant,' he wrote, 'that it is only in English-speaking countries that the Anglo-Saxon Master Race seemed to try to fix upon Italians the insulting or condescending names of wop or dago.'"

The fifties and the sixties were decades when more than 100,000 Italians flowed into Canada, yet that very flow seemed, for a time, to aggravate prejudice. The public opinion polls were the proof: one in 1946 showed that a full quarter of the population wanted Italians kept out of the country, but a 1955 poll revealed it was worse — only 4.4 percent of Canadians would welcome immigrants from the Mediterranean countries (Italy and Greece mainly) as opposed to a full 30 percent who welcomed immigrants from northern European countries (Britain, Germany, France and so on.)[9]

In the sixties, the prejudice had its most harmful expression in the country's educational system. There, men and women designated as vocational guidance counsellors, whose task was to help students decide on careers, were prone to encourage large numbers of children from Italian homes to enter high schools that led not to university, but to the trades and clerical jobs. It was called "streaming".

One afternoon in the spring of 1961, a boy named Franc — then thirteen years old and in grade eight at Alexander Muir Public School in Toronto's west end — was told that he should prepare for his interview with the guidance counsellor about the high school he would enter the following autumn. Franc, who had come with his mother from near Cosenza in Calabria at the age of three, to join his father, a grocery clerk, had done well in school. Each year he was at, or very near, the top of his class. As he tidied up his desk and prepared for his interview, he was confident he would be told to enter Parkdale Collegiate, the school designated for university-bound students. He was not sure, of course, what he wanted to be — perhaps a social worker, perhaps an arts manager, perhaps a teacher.

He arrived at the guidance counsellor's office in mid afternoon — a cloistered room with a window through which the sun fell upon old walls.

"Sit down Franc," said the man across from him. He scanned the boy's marks. He nodded, removed his glasses and looked at the eager lad. He asked about his plans.

(Left, top) Berlino Colangelo, Hamilton, Ontario, who was taken from his family for the internment of the early 1940s. (Left, bottom) Luigi Pancaro MD, the physician to the Italian community of Sudbury, Ontario, who was suddenly taken from his clinic, and shipped off to internment in June 1940. BARRY DURSLEY PHOTO. (Above right) Francesco Zaffiro, Hamilton, Ontario. "We got the shoemaker," the soldiers shouted, "We got the shoemaker." KENNETH BAGNELL.

The Reverend Enrico Battiston, a parish priest in the Friuli town of Azzano Decimo, who watched hundreds of his people leave for Ontario in the fifties and sixties: "They are leaving because they have to leave." The empty streets of a town in Calabria. "They are all in Toronto." KENNETH BAGNELL.

Anna Terrana, executive director of the Italian Cultural Centre in Vancouver: a dynamic woman seeking unity in diversity. ITALIAN CULTURAL CENTRE

Casa Serena of British Columbia: an Italian presence in ninety apartments for seniors. ITALIAN CULTURAL CENTRE.

Italian women in a garment factory on Spadina Avenue, Toronto, 1974. VINCENZO
PIETROPAOLA/MHSO. From below ground to high above it, Italians have built Toronto.
Here, workers finish cement work on the CN Tower. MULTICULTURAL HISTORY SOCIETY
OF ONTARIO.

Bruno Suppa, who came from Vallelonga as a child, and is now a judge of
the immigration appeal court in
Toronto, at a *feste* for the patron saint of
the Vallelonghesi. Montreal playwright
Marco Micone: portraying on the stage
the pain and loss that was an inevitable
part of the pilgrimage of his Italian
parents. Antonio Galati: carpenter to
carver, his work is a legacy of Vallelonga. All photos KENNETH BAGNELL.

Children in an Italian heritage class. MULTICULTURAL HISTORY SOCIETY OF ONTARIO.

Italian fans flooded St. Clair Avenue, Toronto, after Italy won the World Cup Soccer Championship in 1984. MULTICULTURAL HISTORY SOCIETY OF ONTARIO.

Franca Carella: matters of health and reaching the troubled young.

Joe Carraro: for so many years at the side of his people, as a priest, as a friend.

Saverio Pagliuso: looking deeply within the family, with candor and compassion. (All photos KENNETH BAGNELL.)

Beneto John Rossi went home to Revo, high in the mountains of Trentino. Once he had been a barman at Toronto's old Walker House. Now he relives his Canadian years in memory: "In Toronto, for me, every day was a good day."

Franca Rossi of Revo. She began her childhood in Toronto and then, with her parents, returned to Trentino. What does she miss about Toronto? "Everything.".

Gina Inama, in his native village of Taio, northern Italy. He went home, but sadly, it did not work. He is back in Toronto. All photos KENNETH BAGNELL.

"I hope to go to collegiate sir, to Parkdale," he replied.

The counsellor said nothing. He was a sympathetic man, quiet, well meaning. "Franc," he said, "what does your father do?"

"He is a grocer," Franc replied, still with no misgivings, "He works at the IGA."

The man across from him sighed slightly and began to close the file folder in front of him. "Franc, . . ." he said softly. "You might find that your father cannot help you in university. . . . I think, for you, commercial will be better. Try Central Commerce."

The boy swallowed, thanked the counsellor and left. A lump was rising in his throat, the result of confusion, anger, and fear. He raced back to his home room.

"How did it go Franc?" the teacher asked.

"I am to go to the commercial school," the boy said, shaking in bewilderment.

"Forget him Franc," the teacher said. "You are for academic and you will go to Parkdale."

That autumn Franc Sturino, began his life at Parkdale Collegiate. He led classes, advanced quickly, and was soon on his way to university, where he took degree after degree, finally receiving his Ph.D. in history. He was to become the administrator of the first chair of Italian Canadian studies in a Canadian university — The Mariano A. Elia Chair at York University — through which a new generation of students would examine, often in cooperation with scholars in Italy, the migration of Italians to this country.[10]

During the months of 1961 when the young Sturino faced his unsettling interview, a professor of sociology at Carleton University in Ottawa, John Porter, began a sabbatical devoted to the research and writing of a book which would for the next two decades be the classic of Canadian sociology: *The Vertical Mosaic, an Analysis of Social Class and Power in Canada.* Porter, who had written often on the subject of how certain classes of people achieve power and maintain it, noted that wherever privilege exists, it can be largely traced to educational opportunities which some groups have and others do not:

"Consequently most modern industrial societies have introduced policies to democratize their educational systems, and to help bring about more equality of opportunity. . . ."[11]

For Italian Canadians, it would be decades before this truth was evident. When Porter's landmark book was published a few years later, it revealed that Italian Canadians were far below others in social class, and therefore influence. In a chapter on ethnicity and social class, Porter examined the status of Canadians in the thirties, forties and fifties. Of their level by the fifties, he wrote: "The Italians, with the lowest representation in the professional class and the highest representation in the unskilled and primary class (in both cases with the exception of Indians and Inuit), could be said to have held the lowest position in the class system." In 1961, the same year in which Carl Goldenberg came to Toronto for his landmark one-man commission into the industry where so many of them labored, Porter observed that Italians in Canada were in the same position they had been in since the opening of the century: at the bottom.

CHAPTER NINE

NOSTRA LINGUA: WHAT IS OUR MOTHER TONGUE?

In 1965, the year *The Vertical Mosaic* first appeared, it was widely quoted and highly acclaimed. One eminent critic called it a masterly work that anyone wanting to understand Canada and its people would have to read and heed. For Italian immigrants and their families, Porter's book carried another discouraging message besides the plainest one, that Italians were at the bottom of the ladder of status. His analysis of what was necessary for a group to rise beyond such status — through what he and others called "upward mobility" — clearly implied that Italians were very likely to remain in the basement of the Canadian class system.

The barriers to Italian upward mobility were great: poor education, low income, large families. Porter wrote:

> Education costs money and regardless of how free it may be, lower income families tend to take their children out of school at an early age and put them to work. Lower income families are obviously penalized when it comes to higher education, which in Canada, with the exception of the veterans' schemes, has always been prohibitively expensive. A second social barrier is family size. The larger the family, the more difficult it becomes for parents to keep their children in school. . . . The child, therefore, born into a lower income family has almost automatically a greatly reduced horizon of opportunity. . . . [1]

181

The message to the majority of Italian families was direct: they were not just low in status, but destined to remain that way.

By the middle 1960s there were over 450,000 people in Canada who told the census takers that they were of Italian origin: men, women, and children who had come from Italy or were direct descendants of those who had.[2] Almost a full seventy-five percent came from the overburdened south — the regions of Abruzzi, Calabria, Sicily. And while almost 350,000 flooded into Toronto to join relatives, tens of thousands entered old neighborhoods and spawned new ones in a dozen other areas known for their Italian communities: Montreal — the country's second largest centre of Italian life — Hamilton, Vancouver, Ottawa, St. Catharines, and one of the most vibrant of all Italian-Canadian communities, the city of Sault Ste. Marie, Ontario. There the 10,000 Italians constituted a full twelve percent of the city's population, making it, at the time, proportionally the most sizeable concentration of Italians in the country. More important, they were the most visible challenge to John Porter's gloomy prediction about the future status of Italians in the national mosaic.

In 1965, the mayor and aldermen of Sault Ste. Marie sat under the benign gaze of Francis Hector Clergue, his portrait hung high in the council chamber, placed there in tribute to the man who more than any other was the father of their modernity and prosperity.[3]

Just as the century was opening, Clergue had predicted it all. He had come upon the powerful waters alongside the town of Sault Ste. Marie in 1894, while on his way to Fort William on behalf of American investors, when, on a whim, he stopped in Sault Ste. Marie for a day or two to enjoy the clear, cold spring.

In his evening walks, he saw the two enormous promises of the community: its geography and its geology. Its location on the St. Mary River, the exit waterway from Lake Superior, was a natural transportation route; and the waters of Superior, dropping almost twenty feet to the St. Mary River, were a potential source of power that could be harnessed. Clergue further noted that the hills ringing the town were the rim of the great Canadian Shield, a treasure chest of minerals waiting for the unlocking.

Clergue put Fort William from his mind, and settled in Sault Ste. Marie — a historic decision resulting in a few years in a steel mill, a power company, and a paper mill.

The city contained Algoma, Canada's second largest steel company, a railway holding 900,000 acres of land nation-wide, and an expanding population. All of this the men and women of the city would attribute largely to the bold, optimistic man from Maine who had happened by at the turn of the century. As in the evolution of other industrial towns in the north, the role of the men Clergue enlisted to cut timbers, lay track and build damns, was never recorded. It was remembered only privately among the people who settled in a swampy western part of town, a district pilloried in its early years by the local paper as a community of dangerous elements. Yet, in a few decades, that same section would be the home of much of the community's leadership, and some men and women who would find them-selves on the stage of the nation — in law, business, sports and academe. This was Sault Ste. Marie's Little Italy.

As the 1960s began, Luigi Stortini was living with his wife in a house on Roma Street he had bought many years earlier. It was small, like the lot on which it sat, which was so tiny there was no frontage but the sidewalk itself. Nor was there a back-yard, where Luigi Stortini might have planted his garden; back in the fishing village of Sant'Elpidio on the shores of the Adriatic, his family always had a garden. Stortini's father, a stone mason, had come in the wake of Francis Clergue's vision to help erect the Lake Superior Iron Works.

Like hundreds of others, Luigi Stortini was a sojourner, intending to remain in Sault Ste. Marie only long enough to save money for a head start back home in the village and to provide enough for his son to emigrate to Canada. Luigi came in 1914, hired as one of Clergue's army, to work in the steel mill. There he would spend his life, first as a laborer, but later, by dint of his resourcefulness, as a stationary engineer. "It has been hard," he told his children later, "but the life for the children, it made it right."

One morning in the early months of 1930, Luigi Stortini, in his early forties and the father of three boys, reported to the steel plant to be told, along with hundreds of other men from his neighborhood, that there was no work and no prospect of any. The Great Depression had arrived. For a full six years, he would be out of work; a man in the prime of his life, going from place to place, seeking a day's labor, and rarely finding any. In the Italian neighborhood, men stood on the barren, treeless streets, shaking their heads over the misfortune of it all.

One evening, a man Luigi knew came to the house and gave him some well-meant advice in a low voice: "Luigi, you cannot find work, so you are entitled to relief. Go to the city and you will be looked after." Luigi Stortini — like every other Italian of his day in Sault Ste. Marie — would not countenance the suggestion. There was no honor, no respect, in taking unearned money. A few days later his friend returned and spoke again: "Luigi, there is another way. You can go to work for the city — cleaning the streets, digging the ditches — then the food voucher you get will be pay for work done." Stortini began his life as a city worker.

But on the summer evening in 1931 when he went to receive his first voucher, he was distressed to see that he stood in the ordinary welfare lineup. He continued his work, but his sense of self-esteem and his concern for appearance meant that it was one of his boys who went for the Stortini cheque.

Often in the thirties, the entire family — the parents, three boys, and a girl — would spend the evening at a large swathe of land near the city limits, which had been given to Italian families for their communal garden. Section by section, they made it bloom with the green vegetables and the flame of brilliantly petaled flowers. Its real place in their lives was more practical: they lived through the thirties on the potatoes they would root from the soil each August.[4]

The third Stortini son, born in 1929 in Sault Ste. Marie, was called Raymon. His life, together with those of his parents, provides one of the clearest illustrations of the character and steady ambitions of Italian Canadians in Sault Ste. Marie during the crucial decades from the Depression to the sixties.

In 1942, Raymon was just entering his teens, trying to make

up his mind whether to enter the high school which led to university, or the technical and commercial school with its doorway to an immediate job in the trades or clerical work. He had done well in school, but there seemed a shared view among his Italian schoolmates that university was too high a goal, that the immediacy of a job made technical and commercial school a natural choice. His friends turned in that direction on the first day of enrolment; Ray Stortini went along.

After four boring years he graduated with a commercial diploma, spent a few years as a deckhand on the Great Lakes, then returned to Sault Ste. Marie and worked as an insurance adjuster. His friends noticed that Ray seemed vaguely dissatisfied. "It's not that I hate my work," he told a friend, "It's just that I keep thinking that something else would be more interesting." One summer day in 1952, a YMCA counsellor took him aside and told him it was never too late to think of university; he could enroll under a special program for adults. Raymon shrugged, but sent off an application to the University of Western Ontario, in London. He was pleased when they gave him conditional acceptance as a special student.

Stortini graduated in 1956, at 27 years of age, his degree in liberal arts, but his interests in the law. He enrolled in Toronto's Osgoode Law School, received his degree in 1960, articled under the paternal eye of Roy McMurtry, a future attorney general of Ontario, then practiced criminal law until a day in 1971 when a call from the federal justice minister, John Turner, turned his life in a new direction. Would he, Turner asked, consider an appointment to the bench as a federal judge? He certainly would. In time, Raymon Stortini became Sault Ste. Marie's judge of the county court, sitting on many of the major cases, civil and criminal, for the region of Algoma.

In many ways, Judge Raymon Stortini's path from deckhand to judgeship paralleled, in time and in kind, a path begun by a growing number of Italian Canadians. As Raymon Stortini, second-generation Italian, was making his way upward, so were hundreds of others, though most were in business rather than the professions. They were propelled, like Stortini, by an almost compulsive attitude to work; and by parents who, freed from the obsessive fear of poverty, transferred their energies to the desire for the occupational advance of their children.

Sault Ste. Marie boasted a number of achievers from its old neighborhood. They were among the sports celebrities of the country: the famous Esposito brothers of the NHL, Phil and Tony. They were entering the first rank of business leadership in the nation: Gino Francoline, the entrepreneur of London, Ontario, director of numerous corporations who became Chairman of the Board of Governors of the University of Western Ontario. They were in academic life: Ronald Ianni, who after graduate degrees in law and economics, became President of the University of Windsor.

In part, it was parental desire to see children escape from back-breaking uncertainties of laborer's work, but it was also Italian ambition. As two social scientists from Toronto's York University, Anthony Richmond and Warren Kalback, noted about this generation: "The Canadian-born of Italian origin showed remarkable upward social mobility compared with their foreign-born parents and grandparents. The level of education of the Italians who were born in Canada of foreign parentage came very close to the third-plus generation of British and exceeded that of the French charter group."[5] Most of them grew up, as did so many Italian Canadians, close to the tracks and the unwanted lands, but their vision knew no such boundaries.

It was becoming clear that Italians, perhaps more than any other immigrant group of the fifties and sixties, respected education, so much so that enormous numbers of their children became teachers themselves, a reflection of their reverence for the teacher's place in the old villages. Still, they were by no means alone in their reverence for education. In Quebec, the Francophone community had enshrined its respect for academic life, reflected in the historic traditions of universities such as Laval. Education was made crucial by Francophone nervousness over their position in North American life. By the sixties, Francophones looked into their classrooms, particularly those in Montreal, and found that children, especially those of immigrant parents, were being taught their lessons in English. How could French — a minority language in a vast North American ocean of English — survive, if the very language of the schools was English? This was especially worrying in regard to the many hundreds of Italian children in the city. They came with parents to a city where the dominant culture was French, but in the schools they attended in the Italian neighborhoods, they were taught in English.

French Canadians were not the only Montrealers with convictions on the use of language in the schools. Montreal's Italians felt passionately as well. And they too, especially in the afterglow of Expo 67, had growing confidence in themselves, their rights, their place in Canada. They were developing a unique pride, a subtle belief that, in some ways at least, Montreal's Italia was a special repository of Italian culture in Canada, perhaps because Montreal Italians had to define and confirm Italian life in the midst of the tensions between English and French. The new assertive spirit was to find its most vivid expression in the final weeks of summer, 1969, in a district on the northeastern edge of the city.

It was called St. Leonard. Roughly 35,000 people lived there, almost thirty percent of them Italian, many in the hundreds of duplexes constructed a few years earlier by the company which virtually built the community, the Italian Baroni Brothers. Often an Italian family owned a property and lived in one part while renting the rest to a French family. They got on well; the Italian spirit found natural compatibility with the French. "We admire the English in business," one young Italian writer told a friend, "but we warm in our hearts to the French — their culture, their personality, their style." In the last week of August, just as the year before, conversation among Italian families — those whose children attended the schools of the St. Leonard Roman Catholic School Commission — became anxious.[6]

The previous year, the school commission had voted to phase out English classes in all its elementary schools, in favor of French as the language of instruction. Most Italian parents, while wanting their children to grow up bilingual, wanted their education to be given in English, the language of commerce in the wider world. At the very least, they wanted to choose. The year before, after the sudden decision of the board, they had set up English classes in their homes, teaching about two hundred first graders and paying the bills themselves.

In 1969, there were roughly three hundred first graders with Italian parents. The parents had, through the Association of Parents of St. Leonard, petitioned the provincial government — headed by Union Nationale Premier Jean-Jacques Bertrand — to overrule the School Board and provide the choice of language that had been assured by no less a figure than the previous premier, Daniel Johnson. But nationalist Francophones — seeing the rising tides of immigrants, especially Italians, choosing English as the language of instruction for their children — began to argue that the schools were becoming instruments to undermine the primacy of French culture. The most ardent spokesman was Raymond Lemieux, an articulate architect who was president of a fiery group called Le Mouvement Pour L'Intégration Scolaire.

On August 26, Robert Beale, president of the Association of Parents of St. Leonard, dreading a scene of school opening with no English instruction available for the four hundred first graders, gave warning: "Most of the fathers are construction workers who are depressed because they are out of work. Add discrimination against their kids and you have a very explosive situation." Beale was not exaggerating. That week, his frustrations spilling over, he told Derek Hill, a *Gazette* reporter, that he had tried to see the education minister, Jean-Guy Cardinal, to see if a compromise might be struck for the opening of school in a few days. He had found not just indifference but outright discrimination. "When arguing the St. Leonard situation with Mr. Cardinal's personal secretary," he told Hill, "he gave me the impression that if I wanted English rights, then I should move to Canada. . . ." The tranquil neighborhoods of St. Leonard took on an autumnal chill.

On Wednesday, September 10, after six o'clock, the early evening traffic on Jean Talon Street, the main avenue in St. Leonard, began to slow. Stores were closing, restaurants were quiet and expectant, waiting for the small clusters of Italian families who came out at mid-evening to talk until dark. But there was a silent tension.

Late that afternoon, the radio stations of Montreal reported that Raymond Lemieux, the president of Le Mouvement Pour L'Intégration Scolaire, had been refused a permit to lead his unilingual followers through Jean Talon and on to the school grounds of École Jérôme Le Royer, where they would stage a demonstration in favor of French only in the schools of St. Leonard. Though he had been rebuffed, there were numerous rumors that Lemieux would defy the ban.

At 7:30, at an intersection of Jean Talon near the entrance to St. Leonard, Lemieux appeared. He was wearing a crash helmet and surrounded by his most loyal devotees, but most noticeably, he was followed by a crowd of supporters that stretched so far the end could not be seen. There were more than a thousand of them. Lemieux began his march.

Meanwhile, in a neighborhood deeper inside St. Leonard, a bus driver named Pierre Lafrance turned the ignition and wheeled his eighty-seat bus, packed with helmeted members of the Quebec Provincial Police, toward Jean Talon. Five other buses, similarly filled, moved out behind him. St. Leonard's mayor, Leo Ouellet, raced to his office where the municipal lawyer handed him a legal document he had never thought very much about. It was the Riot Act.

Six busloads of policemen arrived at 4650 Jean Talon at roughly 8:00 p.m., where they formed a blockade four men deep. The Mouvement Pour L'Intégration Scolaire demonstrators, now swelling in number, were by then a half mile away. On the street stood hundreds of people, many Italian, many students.

One of the students was an eighteen-year-old university student of slight stature and strong features whom we'll call Mario Cumbi, who had arrived in Montreal with his parents a few years earlier from southern Italy. He and a friend, Gino, gazed at the crowds. Cumbi, a bright student, was by inclination sympathetic to the feelings of the hundreds of French men and women flooding the streets of the Italian district. After all, he would sometimes explain to his university friends, they were part of the majority in Quebec, yet the language that really counted was not their own, but English.

He and Gino said little as they looked across the street. The crowds waved banners and placards and shouted slogans about Quebec for Quebeckers, French for the schools of St. Leonard. The Italians were quiet, subdued, it seemed.

Suddenly, as if it had fallen with the descending dark, a molotov cocktail exploded on the sidewalk. The Francophone marchers surged across the street, some began swinging sticks, and one grabbed Gino and beat him over the head. For a minute the police seemed paralyzed. In seconds, a once disciplined march became a mob out of control. The marchers dropped their placards and took up the fight, the French attacking the Italians, the Italians either retaliating or being beaten up. Mario ran. Gino fought. Then came the wail of sirens, cruisers, and ambulances, mixed with the most ugly sound of all, the systematic crash of plate-glass on sidewalks as one after another, the shop windows of over a hundred Italian businesses were broken. At exactly 9:04 p.m., Leo Ouelett, mayor of St. Leonard, read the Riot Act, thus placing the entire community under police control and empowering police to arrest any citizen participating in a public gathering.

By 10:30 p.m., the St. Leonard police, the Provincial Police, and hundreds of officers called in from Montreal had gained control. Over a hundred people were taken to hospital, and by midnight, physicians described eighteen of them as being in serious condition. Almost forty people, most of them young people from both the French and Italian groups, were charged. Then, by 2:00 a.m., the whole of Jean Talon between Viau and Lacordaire, its sidewalks carpeted in splintered glass, fell into tragic silence. An Italian businessman looking out through his broken window the next morning told a reporter: "We respect the law. But if the law cannot protect us, then we'll have no option but to leave Quebec."

When they reported the violent night in St. Leonard, the papers varied in certain details, but they were one in their verdict: the Union Nationale government, by stalling on the question of language rights, had precipitated the crisis. The

Gazette was the most decisive of all: "The situation in St. Leonard has been allowed to drift from bad to worse. . . . Mr. Bertrand, for whatever reason, appears to have left the matter to his minister of education, whose evasive and equivocating methods have only assisted the situation to deteriorate."

In particular, it stood firmly by the sentiments of the majority of Italian Canadians in St. Leonard: "Mr. Bertrand supported the long tradition in this province to respect the rights of the minorities. No doubt he has shared Mr. Johnson's awareness that any moves against the natural rights of the New Canadians in Montreal would ruin Montreal's international vocation and bring about a decline of the area on whose progress the whole province depends."

That weekend, in the soft quiet of Saturday morning, a sign painter stood on a chair outside a barbershop in St. Leonard, slowly lettering, first in Italian, then French, then English, the name of the owner. He moved on to another window, then another, and another. In all, 118 shop windows had been broken. On Belanger Street, a man named Antonio Coppola looked forlornly through the broken windows of his pool hall. He spoke in a tight, low voice; "They threw rocks and sticks. We also heard the word 'wop' pretty often. Everybody in the Italian community is pretty mad."

Mario Cumbi, who had run from the melee, told his parents that it was a mean and ugly night, but it was also ridiculous. Why, he asked himself over and over, should the French and Italians fight each other? They should be close in culture and tradition. But Mario, an intellectual boy with high ideas, was a tiny voice in the larger Italian chorus.

At noon on the last day of September, Jean-Jacques Bertrand rose before an overflow audience of the Montreal Canadian Club. He announced that at the next session of the Quebec National Assembly, to open in late October, the government would present legislation that would solve the crisis of St. Leonard. He did not go into detail, but what he said was enough to assure those who listened in wary silence that he was at last ready to stand publicly with the principles of his predecessor Daniel Johnson to protect minority language rights in the province of Quebec. "If it is fair to expect French-speaking people to take more part in every area of Canadian life," he told the members, "it must be equally reasonable to expect greater participation by the English in every area of Quebec life."

A few weeks later, on October 24, Bill 63 was passed, assuring parents freedom of choice in the matter of the language in which their children would be educated. It seemed a superficial victory for the Italian community of St. Leonard, and tinged with ambiguity.

The French majority and the Italian minority may have had, as Mario Cumbi deeply felt, a certain shared history and status, but the presence of a strong, organized English community made the relationship complex and troubled. Were the Italians, now so adamant about their rights to education in English, solidly part of the Anglophone community? Or were they, with their distinct culture, and their tendency to marry within the Francophone community, really closer to the French community in their emotional and intellectual lives?

Or were they entirely separate? And if they were separate, how securely did they fit in a province undergoing revolutionary change in which the dominant forces were the French and English? Was it possible to survive? Could they cast their loyalties sometimes with the English, whose style of business they felt close to, sometimes with the French, whose style of life seemed more compatible with their own?

With the St. Leonard crisis settled, and the children continuing in the schools in which English was still taught, the question of identity began to matter more and more to a small group of Italian men, mostly in business and education. The best known of them was a tall, suave man, who along with his brothers had built a family business of great wealth and had acquired at the same time, a position of influence within the Liberal party. He had an ability to think in political terms, to exert pressure of the right kind at the right time.

His name was Pietro Rizzuto; he later became the first Italian Canadian named to the Canadian Senate. He commanded respect for his business gifts after having established a large company with building and related activities. With a handful of others, he had founded the organization that, as much as any Italian organization ever can, spoke for Quebec Italians: The Federation of Italians of Quebec, known as the FAIQ. Now that a new government was in the National Assembly (the Liberals headed by Robert Bourassa), Rizzuto knew that language policy would once again be up for review and change. There were a number of emerging young Italian thinkers Rizzuto felt he should turn to, mostly in education. Rizzuto gathered them together, asking them to draw up a policy statement acceptable to Italians, that could be presented to the new government of Robert Bourassa. In time, the group dwindled to a handful, but that handful was to have historic impact not just on the language policy of Quebec, but on the move of Italians in Canada to power and influence.

Among them were three young, intellectual, and highly opinionated men — Angelo Montini, William Cusano, and Donat Taddeo, then still in his twenties, who was destined to become a professor at Concordia University and a highly influential participant in the destiny of both Italians and all Quebeckers. All had liberal and reform instincts, yet they were tough-minded and not easily seduced by vague political promises. They resolved to protect the rights of Italians, to have their children taught in English if they so wanted, and to penetrate Quebec political life so that Italians would no longer feel like outsiders as they had in the past.

For much of that winter of 1973 and well into 1974, in a small room in Montreal's Little Italy, the handful of men headed by Angelo Montini sat discussing and writing. They sensed that their position would have relevance far beyond the new language policy, Bill 22, that the Bourassa government was drafting. It would be a foundation for the building of the Italian future in Quebec. In the end, they submitted their paper to Rizzuto. Rizzuto thought it too rigid, too inflexible. He could not, in faith, go along with it. Thus, despite their respect for Rizzuto, the three men broke away from the FAIQ to create their own reform lobby, the Educational Council of Italian Canadians, which asked in its paper that every Italian family in Quebec have the right to choose the language of instruction for its children.

When in the summer of 1974 the Bourassa government announced Bill 22, it shocked Italians. Bill 22 stipulated that to enter an English school, a student must demonstrate competence in English. This would deny parents the right to begin the education of their children in English, and would prove deeply awkward. Children would be tested on English to determine their rights to English-language instruction, a plan which would mean that within a given family, some children might qualify while others would not, with all the upheaval and hurt entailed.

But if Bourassa's policy was awkward, his plan for implementation held a fatal flaw: it would not begin at the opening of the fall term 1974, but the next term, the fall of 1975. That gave Montini and his Educational Council of Italian Canadians, a year in which to bring about a counter-offensive. Within days, Montini, Cusano, Taddeo, and others prepared their plan at the old brown building in Little Italy, Casa d'Italia. They would set up underground schools held on Saturdays in church basements, for the teaching of English to children who would face the tests in the fall of 1975. The group called a meeting of all Italian parents in greater Montreal, those with children in the grades affected.

At the Casa d'Italia one evening in the autumn of 1974, so many parents came to hear what they might do to assure the English education of their children, that two separate meetings had to be held. All listened intently as Montini and Taddeo explained the bill. Names were taken, and classes set up in neighborhood churches. That fall, in the well-worn basements of the old church buildings in the Italian neighborhoods of St. Leonard, St. Michele and St. Lambert, over 1,500 children could be found on Saturday mornings, reciting English phrases and sentences, learning English, and often, to shrewd teachers, rehearsing the questions they might be asked on the ominous tests. But the classes were only a symbol of something formative and historic: the readiness of Italians to take control of their own destiny in Quebec.

Italians were asserting themselves. In the fall of 1975, most of the children qualified for entrance to English schools. In some cases in which children did not, underground classes continued. So, of course, did the debate over language in Quebec, with language bills being repealed and new ones being advanced as governments changed. In 1976, the Bourassa government was defeated and the Parti Québecois elected, and the stern language bill, Bill 101, was drafted under the minister for cultural affairs, Camille Laurin. The victory of the Parti Québecois brought Montreal Italians together in new, almost evangelical solidarity. It united those of the right and the left, those from the peasant villages of the south and the cities of the north, with the certainty that now they must find unity and security together or face the demise of language and culture. They would eventually prevail, though for some, the years of the Parti Québecois would break old dreams of a common emotional bond between French and Italian.

Mario Cumbi, the young man who in that autumn of 1969 had stood on the sidewalk of St. Leonard, was generally pleased to see the PQ take office. He had recently received his doctoral degree in language, and to his delight, had been offered a position as a lecturer in a Francophone university, the Université de Montréal. In the evenings at home, he began to write. Like many Montreal Italians, he held high linguistic ambition for his children — they would speak French to their mother, Italian to their father and English to their neighbors. They would become, like hundreds of Italian children of their generation, fluently trilingual.

Cumbi was pleased to find that the PQ goal of a fully distinct society was still strongly held; despite certain reservations about its most fanatical members, he still felt a certain allegiance to its basic tenets. Even the occasional incident — for example, the day when a student in his class stood up to say that there was no place there for him since he was Italian — did not deter his belief. He put such events down to zealous nationalism, peculiar to a small minority of individuals. He even accepted a position on the committee to further the use of French as the language of education, business, and day-to-day life in Quebec. Cumbi hoped that he might thereby temper some of its more extreme tendencies.

It was in Quebec City that Mario Cumbi finally realized that French Canadian nationalism did not have room for his own Italian heritage. At the front of the meeting stood Camille Laurin, the minister in charge of the language bill. He was defending its more strident aspects, explaining how French would become the only language in Quebec and how over time, other languages would fade in the cause of linguistic purity. He ended his long speech with a cursory explanation of why it was all necessary. As always, he was direct: "Because Quebec needs a law like this one." Cumbi, who had questioned the minister a couple of times before, stood up for the last time. "Mr. Minister," he began, "if you believe this, that there should be French only in Quebec, why did you place me, an Italian Canadian, on this committee?"

The minister looked stonily at Cumbi. He shrugged. He murmured that it was, as he had just said, all necessary for the good of Quebec. But Mario Cumbi was through with the PQ, and in most ways, through with the Quebec nationalism by which he had stood from his youth, and through the sixties and seventies. "All they care about," he said as he left Quebec City that evening, is "'nous, nous, nous.'"

The years of the Quiet Revolution and the threat of Separatism had forged a new reality for the Italians of Quebec. From the small group that met on language rights in Montreal came formidable organizations and formidable leaders. One was Donat Taddeo, later a major figure in the educational life of Montreal, a Dean of Concordia University, a key advisor to Premier Robert Bourassa on ethnocultural issues, and eventually a representative of Quebec in Rome.

The right of Quebec Italians to choose the language for the education of their own children would always be a troubling issue. It would come under review after review. But the drawn-out struggle would forge unexpected strengths. Men such as Montini, Cusano, and Taddeo, who had been young dreamers together, helped their people shape councils and organizations that spoke for them in modern, forceful, and democratic ways. From the parents' association in St. Leonard, to the FAIQ, to the Educational Council of Italian Canadians, the groups were sometimes fractious, but more often effective.

Eventually, the groups came together in the Quebec Congress of Italian Canadians. At about the same time, Ontario formed a similar congress. Thus, in 1974 Canada had its most powerful ethnocultural organization of that day and this: The National Congress of Italian Canadians. The Congress' future was built upon a constitution drawn up by Lino Magagna of Toronto, the man who came to Canada as an uneducated youth barely speaking English, but who later earned his doctorate in engineering and received the Order of Canada. Part of Magagna's legacy would be writ in that constitution, which set out the broad humanitarian goals that have ever guided men of noble intent such as he: "To foster the evolution of a better Canadian society by promoting mutual understanding, goodwill, and cooperation between Canadians of Italian and other origins."[77]

CHAPTER TEN

CANADIANS AND FRIULANI: HANDS ACROSS THE WATER

Robert Harney looked out from his window at the top floor of the Royal York Hotel, to the foot of York Street in Toronto. As far as he could see, Toronto stretching northward was dusted with snow; the walls of low office buildings and brown factories seemed frozen in the bleak Canadian winter, a season he had never seen until that grey morning in 1964. He fell into deep thought. Harney was in his late twenties, a sturdy man with large shoulders and an open, friendly face. What he saw beyond the window touched a chord in his memory, reminding him of his own hometown, Salem, near Boston: the cold, the snow, the early-morning pedestrians drawing their collars tight against the wind. He had not been home to Salem — where he had grown up the eldest in a family of eight — since he finished his undergraduate years at Harvard in 1960 and had gone to California to take his doctorate in Italian history at the University of California at Berkeley.[1]

Now, on this February day in the middle sixties, he was in Toronto — a young man of high academic credentials who had been offered positions at several major universities — at the invitation of the history department of the University of Toronto, to discuss a position as lecturer in Italian history. Harney's eye fell upon a familiar scene in a window on an upper floor in a

198

building opposite him that almost made him believe, for a moment, that indeed he was back home in the textile manufacturing town of Salem: a burly man in his undershirt was standing on the floor of a sweat-shop with rows of women toiling over sewing machines. Harney was transfixed, as if in coming to Toronto he was truly coming home.

After a couple of days on the campus of Victorian buildings and in a city somehow charming for its blanket of snow, Harney's mind was made up. He would advise the head of history at the University of Toronto that he would take the position. He returned in late summer, with his wife and two small children, and settled in a modest walk-up apartment on the western stretches of College Street, then the main thoroughfare of the city's ever-expanding, ever-moving Little Italy.

His coming was unnoticed beyond the classrooms of the university. In his first year, he taught an undergraduate course in European history; he also conducted a seminar for fourth-year honors students on the Risorgimento, the period in which various visionaries attempted to create a unified nation out of a group of factional states, a movement lasting until the 1860s, when unification took place. And he worked diligently to fortify the Italian content of his European history courses, though he sometimes suspected his well-to-do students took the course simply as preparation for their summer trips to Italy.

Harney had few Italian students. He felt, at times, a vague chill within the thick sandstone halls of the university, perhaps because he was an American disdained by nationalists of the day who felt he and others were a threat to the perspective of Canadian academic life; perhaps because he was teaching subjects regarded as of little relevance in the lingering British atmosphere of the University of Toronto; or perhaps because some thought he had come to Canada to escape the American draft to the war in Viet Nam.

Still, he found two aspects of his new life in Toronto extremely rewarding: the experience of teaching itself, and the Italian community of Toronto, then about 300,000 strong, and well on its way to being one of the largest Italian communities outside Italy. It was a culture he was personally and professionally drawn to. As one of his academic friends would say, "Bob has the best Italian community in the world to study outside Italy itself."

Harney plunged into his work with inherited toughness. He had grown up in Salem, in a family of Irish and Jewish background, in an Italian neighborhood. "I'm proud," he would say with a subtle blend of gentleness and combativeness, "of my marginality." He was, people noticed, more at home with working-class Italians than wealthy ones, spending evening after evening in the small cafés of the neighborhoods and drinking family wine at kitchen tables.

But more than anything else, he began to develop by the late sixties a deep affection, a love, really, for a certain group of students — young Italians from the west end of Toronto, by then a series of Little Italies that went beyond the original community around College Street. Harney looked out over his classes each autumn to see more and more such students, from communities on the boundaries of Toronto and beyond them, then beginning to burst with Italian families — Weston, Downsview, Woodbridge, Richmond Hill. A few were shrewd careerists, but many revealed an interest in their past and in the courage and character of their parents, that Harney found touching and memorable.

He began giving more of his time to a special field within the larger subject of Italian history, which most intrigued his mind: Italian emigration. By 1972, he was writing paper after paper, many of which found readers in universities throughout North America and in Europe. Italian emigration was becoming an important academic concern. He travelled, lectured, and was sought out by other ethnic groups so often that his calendar was booked a year in advance. Generations of students, some of whom he taught, others whom he had merely befriended, went on to teach other Italian young people, often at the high-school level. Several became university teachers themselves, of Italian immigration and Italian-Canadian studies: Bruno Ramirez at the University of Montreal, John Zucchi at McGill University, Franc Sturino at York University in Toronto and Franca Iacovetta at the University of Guelph.

By the late seventies, Harney was not only teaching his

courses and writing on Italian immigration history, but also holding an influential job as head of Ontario's vast Multicultural History Society. His writings and lectures brought him international standing as one of a handful of major scholars (including Rudolph Vecolii of the University of Minnesota, Humbert S. Nelli of the University of Kentucky, and Richard Gambino of New York) of Italian emigration. For the range of his approach, which crossed various academic fields, some placed him very near the top. As one of his students, himself a noted academic, said of him: "He is a scholar of world standing. He brings great legitimacy and credibility to Italian Canadian immigration as a field of study. Partly that's because he's a man of many disciplines, not just history. He draws from anthropology and sociology and history."[2] Or as one of the great benefactors of the Italian-Canadian community across Canada, Anthony Fusco of Toronto, put it, "It is like having someone outside the family approve greatly of the family."

Harney approached his subject with certain key historical convictions. Inherent in the culture of this continent in the last century and through most of this one was a deep wariness of the stranger from other shores; but in the case of the Italian, the wariness took on a suspicion that was so deep and difficult, Harney dealt with it as a special phenomenon: Italophobia. "Anti-Italianism," he told a friend, "is unique — like anti-Black and anti-Jew. It is not just general prejudice. It is not like being anti-Ukrainian. Its stands on its own." According to Harney, this fear has been so embedded in our culture that it became all too easy to dismiss any misconduct by Italians as a reflection of some malevolence that was particular to them.

One of his early monographs, widely read inside and outside Italian and academic communities, helped to define the role of men such as Antonio Cordasco, the legendary *padrone* of the turn of the century in Montreal, widely depicted in immigration history as an incarnation of evil. To Harney, Cordasco was far from admirable, yet he had to be seen for what he was: an opportunistic man in an opportunistic era. He was like many others of his day, including the managers of the CPR and their notorious agents, a man who saw his chance and took it.

"Cordasco, then, was a nasty man and certainly did not deserve the excess profits he exacted from the migrant labour force," Harney wrote, "but he did, except perhaps in the spring of 1904, do his job. The sojourners accepted the *padrone* system because they reckoned he provided them the best alternative in their search for cash. . . ."[3] He would not defend Cordasco, but his views on him were not without a measure of understanding, as if Cordasco had been, in a sense, historically inevitable. After all, Harney argued, the conditions of early Canada made it so — the need for cheap and plentiful laborers, ready to go to the bush and the mines, willing to endure terrible conditions for a season or two in return for ready cash, and the understanding that they would then go home, leaving no burden upon the country. To recruit the men, to bring them out, to ship them to the work site, the system required a middleman. Harney saw no reason why Cordasco should not have profited from both the employer (the CPR) and the men, since he served them both. His profits, though, he found outrageous. In the end, Harney puts Cordasco and men like him in careful context:

> Padronism was callous, exploitive and often dishonest, but it fulfilled a function for those migrants who chose to come to America, not as permanent immigrants but in search of cash to improve their conditions in the old country. To understand padronism properly and to give all parts of the system — employer, intermediary, and labor consumer — their due, we must see it as part of the commerce of migration, not as a form of ethnic crime.

That a great number of Robert Harney's students were becoming teachers was admirable, yet it gave Harney pause, and elsewhere in the Italian communities, it provoked nagging worry. Teaching was an admired occupation among Italians, almost stereotypically so. The teacher in the village back home was a man of great prestige. But in the new Canada, there were other professions. It was becoming too clear that Italian young people were not choosing the other professions in numbers proportionate to the size of the Italian population.

In the late sixties, a young man named Felix Rocca graduated at the top of his class in Sarnia, Ontario, went to university,
and would have drifted to teaching had some friends not urged
him to try the law entrance exams. He did well, and became a
lawyer to a large number of working-class Italians in Toronto,
and a community legal advocate in many a worthy cause. "I
fault the Italian family and community," he would say, "for not
suggesting to young people that there are occupations beside
teaching. There is law. There is medicine. There is computer
science. But we are not represented in those vocations in terms
of our numbers."[4]

One of Harney's prized and promising students, Franca
Iacovetta, who became a lecturer in history at the University of
Guelph, addressed the role of Italian women, an aspect of
migration history usually overlooked. In a lecture at York University on Calabrian women in post-war migration, Iacovetta
pointed out that women were often central to the family's economic survival and success. Many, she argued, were the family's
financial managers, as well as household supervisors. They
performed crucial economic tasks, stretching limited budgets,
some working outside the home, bringing in extra work in the
evenings, taking in boarders, and performing Herculean feats
that have been rendered invisible by the attention given to the
Italian family in general.

"One Calabrian woman," reported Iacovetta, "spent her
first year in Toronto working in a laundry, caring for her infant
son, her husband, his father, and his two brothers. She was
nineteen at the time."[5] To Iacovetta, such women were not
passive minions but strong, often assertive individuals, who
displayed tremendous resourcefulness and inner strength.

By the early 1970s, the chief academic inspiration for people
such as Iacovetta, was not only an academic of rising renown,
but a powerful influence within multicultural life in Canada,
especially within Toronto's booming Italian community. Perhaps because Harney was American, an outsider, free from
factional loyalties to one region of Italy over another, he could be
appealed to as one slightly above it all, to whom clubs, associa-

tions, councils, boards and neighborhoods — filled with thousands of men and women who never entered his classroom — could turn for wise and caring counsel.

Toronto's Italian community, Harney often reminded people, was not so much a community as a set of communities. This was not divisive and threatening, so much as natural and enriching. As the communites boomed to number — counting everybody from the oldest of the first generation to the youngest of the many descendants — almost 500,000, a full quarter of the population of greater Toronto, and moved upward in mobility, Harney scrutinized them with the eye of a scientist peering into a microscope. He saw not the simple Little Italy of popular television, but a vast group marked by a very detailed internal character.

"The Italian leadership," he wrote "is often an uncomfortable alliance of prewar Italian Canadians and postwar professionals and technicians. Both groups seem to interpret the issues of North American life in a dizzying variety of ways, and possibilities for misunderstanding (based on transplanted political ideologies, local Ontario politics, Italian regionalism and on which immigrant cohort one comes from) lurk within every community organization." Often members of one organization or club dismiss those who disagree with them as "pawns" or "paid agents" of the Italian consulate, the Italian Communist Party, the Christian Democratic Party, or some other convenient bogey. Yet, according to Harney, such factionalism is not necessarily harmful — and is not unique to Italians. "A community as large and variegated as Toronto Italia cannot be reduced to a political monotone."[6] Neither can Montreal Italia, Vancouver Italia, Sudbury Italia, or Windsor Italia. There is such a range of diversity within Canadian Italia that it defies the casual umbrella descriptives history has applied.

Two of the men Harney came to know well from the various communities of the city's Italian population were men who, in history and style, were exact opposites, but who became quiet protagonists in an event of historic proportion for the Italians of Toronto, and by extension, those of Canada. They were not yet middle-aged: Anthony Fusco, stocky in build and blunt in speech, and Peter Bosa, tall and soft-spoken. They knew each other only slightly.

Fusco was born in Toronto, one of two sons of Joseph Fusco, a fruit dealer who had come to Canada from Sicily in 1911, and operated stores in several parts of Toronto, most in the east end, among the generally British working-class immigrants.[7] Joseph had stood helplessly by in 1940 when Mussolini sided with Hitler, the internment roundup began, and vandals smashed his windows and called his family dirty wops. "Boys," he had told his two sons, "don't forget the great difference between a government and a people. The Italian government is one thing. The people are another." He died in 1947 when Tony was ten. His death meant that both boys, including the older son Joseph, then a pre-med student, put education behind them and went almost immediately to work.

The following spring, on a wet April afternoon, Peter Bosa, then in his twenties, raised in Friuli, the beautiful and more affluent region of northeastern Italy, arrived alone by train in Toronto to join his father, who got him a job in the cutting room of a clothing factory. Bosa, who used English well, remained in the factory job until 1957, then began an insurance business. In 1957, the same year in which he began his business, he started work as a volunteer for the Liberal Party of Canada, in the riding of Davenport, as a campaign worker for Paul Hellyer, and later, for his fellow Italian Charles Caccia.

Meanwhile, in another part of the city and in another Italian culture, Tony Fusco was struggling. Neither he nor his brother did well in the family fruit business. Both tried working for the larger food chains, Tony for Loblaws and Joseph for A&P. It didn't work; both seemed to feel that Italians, by temperament and upbringing, were not destined to work for someone else. They were discouraged. Then, in May 1954, Tony took a voyage that was to alter his entire life. With his widowed mother he went to Italy, the country had had heard so much about as a child. On May 24, aboard the ship the *Vulcania*, he watched the shores of Sicily approach, where his father had left the family home, just outside the city of Palermo, in 1911, returning only to bring back a wife a few years later. Tony spent a full six months there. By luck, he was taken under the wing of a retired historian from the University of Palermo, who showed him ancient ruins that spoke of a past he had known only through his father's memory. He was ecstatic, a youth with an unschooled but keen and curious mind, whose bright eyes held unspoken dreams. "I found my past," he said later, "and it changed my life." Suddenly an ambition was kindled to study and nurture his rich heritage.

That fall he returned to Toronto. He and his brother borrowed a few thousand dollars to buy a battered secondhand truck, the back of which was covered with a ripped canvas tarpaulin. They tried to make a living carting freight, picking it up from the depots, train stations and airports, and delivering it all over the city. Throughout the day and well past midnight, they sweated, lugging boxes, boards, appliances, putting them aboard the old truck, climbing in the cab and driving its clattering body through the streets of downtown Toronto and beyond to the suburbs. They were delivery men. For a while they hauled wax; then, on weekends, because he could speak Italian, Tony got a contract to deliver beer for Molson's in the city's old Little Italy. By 1959, he and his brother had saved enough so that they could borrow to buy a cartage company with a fleet of forty trucks. Tony had ambitions for larger things.

Sometime early in the sixties, Tony Fusco began phoning a few of the larger corporations on Toronto's Bay Street, to solicit work for his cartage company. He was still in his twenties, a bright, self-taught youth who loved opera and literature, but was without the polish of higher education. One day, having gotten past the receptionist in a well-appointed office in a Toronto tower, he encountered an obstacle he would meet over and over again in slightly different form.

"And what is your name, my boy?"

"Fusco, sir. Tony Fusco."

"Fusco, eh? I see. Just what country is Fusco from?"

"From Italy, sir."

"Italy, eh? And what part of Italy?"

"Sicily, sir."

"Oh, really. Sicily. Sicily! Well now, you aren't one of those Mafia chaps are you?"

He would leave, hurt, yet never resentful. Once, he began to laugh before they asked which part of Italy he was from. He would tell them, in advance, that his roots were in the city of Palermo, the very heartland of the Mafia. It was just as well, he figured, to make light of it, and above all, to hold no grudge.

Often he returned to the dusty office that he and his brother kept at 442 Perth Avenue, in a grimy corner of downtown, to explain that it would all take time and patience. "We are different. Our name ends in a vowel. But I have an idea. I believe we can make good of it. We should sell the idea that, having been born in Canada, but enriched by European ancestry, we just might have a bit more to offer than guys who have only one culture to look at business from."

In 1963, frustrated by the policies of the Ontario government — monopolistic when it came to granting new transportation licenses under the PVC Act — he and his brother hit on an idea that would revolutionize commercial transport in Canada and make them very wealthy along the way. It was called freight forwarding. The company bought, at wholesale rates, space on licensed carriers — trucks, trains, tankers — and sold it to industrial users. At first they applied it in Canada only, then in North America. It became trans-Atlantic. In time, dozens of other such companies would be formed, but none would have the success of the company formed by Tony and Joseph Fusco — Apex Forwarding Company, Limited. Before the end of the sixties, it had grossed $50 million a year in sales, with 2,000 employees and added, shortly after, a land development division with properties in several Canadian provinces and American states.

By the late sixties, Fusco, a wealthy man married to a woman he had met in Sicily on his youthful visit, and now the father of four children, had become involved in an effort he believed very necessary: the attempt to bring some unity to the often fractious political and social life of Toronto's Italian communities. He became vice-president of an organization called the Federation of Italian Clubs, which had been spear-headed by a friend he greatly admired. Elio Madonia was a soft-drink manufacturer, and an Italian made more interesting to Fusco because he was also a non-Catholic — in fact, a Protestant evangelical. But Fusco found his job in the Federation discouraging. "The fractious Italian politics are being transferred to Canada so that meetings are full of big talk, much wind, and no action." Moreover, the federation's approach to hurtful publicity was, in his mind, too confrontational. Fusco decided that he did not find politics, either Italian or Canadian, to his liking.

Bosa, in the meantime, found quite the opposite during the same period of the sixties. He was by then in his late forties, and very well placed in the corridors of the Liberal Party in Toronto and Ottawa. And he was highly influential in the affairs of his own regional club — The Club Friulani, and in the life of the wider community of Italians. The sixties had been a decade in which he had made his way steadily deeper into the corridors of influence, first as an assistant to the federal minister of immigration, the first Italian to hold such a position in a federal minister's office. In turn, he became Executive Assistant to Justice Minister Guy Favreau, then to Postmaster General George McIlraith, and to Trade Minister Réné Tremblay. He gained valuable knowledge, not just about policy, but politics. He also caught the eye and the goodwill of the Prime Ministers of the day (who were aware of courting the ever expanding Italian community), Lester Pearson, and more particularly, Pierre Trudeau. Bosa knew and liked Tony Fusco, though their past and their paths were very different. On one fundamental issue among Italian Canadians they were widely divided. It was an issue which mattered so much to Peter Bosa that it became a moral crusade in his life. He had always felt strongly about it ever since he came to Canada, but certain events of the sixties made him impassioned. Bosa would never forget the day a man — a laboring Italian who tended to turn to him on family matters — came to his office in Toronto and, in the manner of a worried parishoner, told him:

"Peter, I am having trouble with my son. I am worried."

Bosa asked what had happened, was the boy in trouble?

"No," the man replied, "he has never been in trouble, he is a good boy. But what he said to me the other night has upset me terribly. Terribly. I don't know what to do to help him."

Bosa asked what the boy had said. The man had trouble replying. His son had seen so much on television and in the papers about Italians as criminals that, late one night, he had come to his father and cried, "Father, I am ashamed to be an Italian."

Bosa did his best. He knew, more than most Italians in Canada, how cruel and wrong the stereotype was — and how harmful. Often he would recall what U.S. Senator Estes Kefauver had said to injured American Italians, after his famous inquiry into organized crime in 1950: because some criminals are Italian does not mean that Italians are criminals.

But words were easy. Bosa knew that in far too many Italian-Candian homes, the boy's anguish, undeserved though it was, was duplicated. From that day, Bosa gave enormous effort to fighting the slur against his people. He knew he was right; history was the proof. Robert Harney, to whom he often turned for guidance, had recognized that it was unjust but ingrained in the mythology of North America. He had said so in one of his early monographs: "Swarthiness and criminality went together in the American mind and the presence of a Joe Hill in the labor violence or a Baby Face Nelson in organized crime, could not erase the stereotypes that weighed so heavily on the Italian population."[8]

In late November, 1971, as the grey chill of winter seeped through his office window in the northwestern section of Toronto, Tony Fusco, weary of the internal division he'd seen in the Federation of Italian Clubs, and wondering what might be done to help bring Italians together, decided to call a meeting of Toronto's Italian business leaders. They met in the old Casa d'Italia in the core of the city's original Little Italy. "If I have anything to give to this community," he told an acquaintance, "it is to get Italians away from intramural squabbles, Friulani against Neapolitan, Calabrian against Sicilian. We need a common cause. I don't want fighting the Mafia image to be that cause. It's too negative. You can't build self-confidence by fighting a negative issue." The community leaders attending that meeting decided to form an association which was incorporated in April, 1971 as The Italian Canadian Benevolent Corporation. And for good reason, its first president was the distinguished elder of an early generation, Joseph Carrier, who began as a shoeshine boy and became a wealthy shoe retailer, and whose endowments to the community were as exemplary as his diplomacy.

Fusco had been impelled by his concern over the false stereotype, but he felt that could not be removed by petitions and pleas to the media and the government. The community must act not negatively, but positively. It must demonstrate its character; that would be enough. What goal could the group set that would be very demanding, almost unattainable, but so rich in reward that it would give the Italians of Toronto new unity, new pride, lasting self-confidence?

The answer, arrived at in a meeting later in the spring of 1971, was a home for the aged of the Italian community — but not just an ordinary home. It must be of such a high standard that it would be not only a home which Italians — with their strong family feeling — would be pleased to see their parents enter, but, as an institution, the fountain from which the pride and unity Fusco felt to be so needed would flow.

While Joseph Carrier provided the necessary stature to the new Italian Canadian Benevolent Corporation as its president, Fusco became his vice-president. He committed himself to lead, with the support of other directors of the benevolent corporation, in the building of Villa Colombo. He decided that before proceeding, the groundwork would be laid with distinctly Canadian business procedures, including market research. Were Italians, given their well-known belief in the family taking care of mothers and fathers to their dying day, ready to support a home for the aged? The research said yes. Times were changing; many Italian grandmothers and grandfathers, at home with children, were being used simply as free day-care service.

Over the next three years, Fusco was a driven man. He worked in his own business office from five o'clock each morning until ten, then drove to the office of the benevolent corporation to oversee planning for Villa Colombo. At four in the afternoon he would be back at his office for three hours. Then, throughout the long evenings, he would attend more Villa Colombo meetings. His health was a constant worry to everyone around him. He visited forty-seven homes for the aged across North America, seeing what could be learned and applied at Villa Colombo.

The location, ten acres of land near Eglinton Avenue, was chosen with the greatest care — strategically placed to serve the several Italian communities spreading like an arc through a corridor of western and northern Metropolitan Toronto. The name, Villa Colombo, was selected to symbolize the broad community and offend no segment. And the building had to be, in the view of Fusco and his colleagues, opulent. "Italians," Fusco liked to say, "are impressed by opulence and success." Villa Colombo would not have merely the requisite rooms (for 192 people), but unmatched amenities. Moreover, its design, primarily by a talented Italian-Canadian architect, Anthony Ferracuti, would be such that those who moved into it would never feel they had left their Italian culture. It would have activities that would keep Italians of every age and level visiting at all hours of the day: a community centre would be attached for meetings and parties open to the entire community; there would be a *piazza*, just as so many of the residents had remembered it in the village back home; there would be a day-care centre, so that the voices of children would remain part of the lives of the elderly. The corridors of the building would be filled with the singing of children. The costs, as the dream itself were astronomical: $4.5 million. It was an unheard-of amount, especially in a community which, in Fusco's opinion, was not noted at that time for its willingness to donate.

Fusco gambled more boldly than ever. In the fall of 1973, he chaired a fund-raising black-tie dinner at Toronto's Inn on the Park, at which the American comedian Jerry Lewis stood at the podium to extract pledges. All evening, men rose in the affluent crowd and put up $50,000 apiece. Before it was over almost 40 men had come up to the front with such pledges. "And to think," Fusco was heard to say, "that at one time, all the boldest fund-raising Italians did was to pay five dollars for a spaghetti dinner." When it was over, they had raised $3 million. Villa Colombo was on its way.

It opened with great fanfare in January, 1976. Of the $4.5 million cost, two-thirds had been assumed by the Italian community of Toronto, the remainder by government. Most was on hand but much needed to be raised, and to maintain it, ongoing fund-raising would be a necessity. The board of directors decided that each spring a telethon would be held. Since it was a home for the aged, what more natural day than Mothers' Day? The first telethon, to raise $200,000, was set for the following May 8. Sophia Loren agreed to be the guest.

On Thursday, May 6, 1976, just before five o'clock, Peter Bosa was putting his coat on to leave his office in Toronto when he was called to the phone for an urgent message. It was a friend of his, a man who came, as Bosa did, from the Friuli region of Italy and was a fellow member of Toronto's large Friuli Club. His news was not good. A few minutes earlier, the radio had carried a report of an earthquake in the northeast of Italy, in the region of Friuli, not far from the provincial capital of Udine. Whole villages and towns were wiped out. Hundreds were certainly dead, but perhaps thousands, for communications links were destroyed. Bosa, like all the Friulani in Canada, was deeply distressed; his sister and her husband lived in Udine, and first reports said the quake, ranging from a severe 6 to a catastrophic 8.9 on the Richter scale, had its epicentre near Udine.

An hour earlier, in the village of Artegna, fifteen miles from Udine, Mario Micossi, an artist, was finishing his evening meal with his mother on the first floor of their three-storey house. It was a large house, built in the 1600s, with twenty rooms, a courtyard, and a small vineyard. At five past nine, the first shock hit. Both leapt up and headed for the door. Outside the cry arose: "*Il Terremoto! Il Terremoto!*" — Earthquake!

They were in the street when their huge house seemed to be tossed into the air. Then the main shock came. It lasted 55 seconds, and was the worst earthquake in Italy since 1915, battering twenty towns and villages, roiling the waters of the canals of Venice some seventy-five miles away. Over one thousand would die. "When the grand shock was over," Micossi told a reporter from the *New Yorker*, "I took my mother into a nearby field and looked back. First, there was an enormous cloud of smoke, and silence; then we heard the first cries for help. I left my mother in the field with some other women and tried to pull people from the ruins. About nine-thirty, help from outside began to arrive — firemen, soldiers, police, people looking for relatives — and our little group in the field increased to about twenty people. We built a big bonfire there and kept it going all night. And then I crawled back into what was left of my house and took out a coat for my mother and three bottles of slivovitz. No one was crying that night; it was only the next morning that you could see people walking through the ruins, picking up a few possessions and crying softly. The Friulani are not spectacular about grief."[9]

In Toronto, Peter Bosa heard within an hour that at least the earthquake was north of Udine, beyond the plains where his relatives lived, and at the foothills of the spectacular mountains that range northward sheltering towns such as Gemona, Buia, Maiano, and Colloredo, each with magnificent ancient steeples and castles, each the home to hundreds of Friulani. Bosa and others were on the phone all night, talking to people in Toronto, Halifax, Vancouver, and elsewhere, members of the fourteen Friuli Clubs in Canada. They were swept by almost uncontrollable fear, for the newspapers had already reported that the call had gone out to Rome for a thousand coffins. On Friday evening, at the large, rambling Friuli Club on Islington Avenue in the city's northwest, several of the community's leaders met to determine what they could do in the way of disaster relief. The outcome of that meeting was revealing of Italian Canadians at several levels.

At first, the men at the meeting wondered if it should be, in fact, an appeal by Friulani to Friulani, rather than a relief program conducted throughout the Italian-Canadian community. They had sensed from their conversations that the Friuli, a proud independent and resourceful people — sometimes described by outsiders as "the people who make the bricks, not the people who lay the bricks" — wanted it to be their own cause. But within half an hour the committee decided that would be wrong from every perspective; it would be too parochial, slightly disdainful, and too apt to limit what mattered most of all, the financial return. They set their Toronto goal at $250,000.

Later, when he got home, Bosa remembered an appointment a couple of days away. Now, in light of the Friuli crisis, he must cancel it: his appearance, as a leader in the Italian community of Toronto, on the Villa Colombo telethon. Bosa picked up the phone and called Anthony Fusco. Fusco listened as Bosa explained his predicament: "I'm sorry. But you know about the disaster. I'm up to my neck in trying to organize fund-raising. I can't go on the telethon for Villa Colombo while I'm trying to raise money for Friuli."

For what seemed a full minute Fusco said nothing. He understood Bosa's problem, but he had his own. It was, after all, the first telethon for Villa Colombo. He needed Bosa because Bosa provided access to some of the greatest affluence of Toronto's Italian community — the Friulani. As chairman of Villa Colombo's board, he received pledge after pledge from businessmen whose roots were in Friuli. On the other end of the phone, Bosa waited through the silence. Fusco said he'd call Bosa back.

What took place in the next half hour was a turning point in the evolution to maturity of the nation's Italian community. Fusco knew more than anyone else how crucial the telethon was for Villa Colombo. But, leaning back in his chair, his eyes closed in thought, he was weighing other considerations with the business intelligence that had made him wealthy, and the commitment to his heritage which had embraced and frustrated him ever since he had gotten involved in the wider life of Italian Canadians.

On that soft spring evening, it all flowed back through his memory. As Peter Bosa, the influential Friulani, waited for his return call, Fusco came to a conclusion. He saw in the distant earthquake disaster both obligation and opportunity: to help the homeless and injured in Friuli, and to help solidify the Italian community of Canada, and the future of Villa Colombo.

It was just past ten when he picked up the phone. He did not call Bosa directly. Instead, he began a series of calls to key members of Villa Colombo's board. To each he made a terse recommendation: the telethon would be turned over to earthquake relief.

On Sunday, May 8, at exactly nine a.m. in the ornate lobby of Villa Colombo, the first telethon began. It was carried on two stations, Toronto's multicultural Channel 47 and the new Global Television Network. At the outset, a sober-voiced announcer said in Italian that in view of the Friuli disaster, every dollar contributed during the next ten hours would be used to help the victims and rebuild communities of Friuli. The goal was $200,000.

Fusco and Bosa and others working behind the cameras knew that while the city's Italians might respond well with telephone contributions, there was a better way yet. They asked that whole families come to Villa Colombo and appear on camera to make their contributions. Within half an hour, traffic was jammed on Eglinton Avenue in both directions, surrounding streets were becoming parking lots, lineups snaked from Villa Colombo's front lobby over the lawns and onto sidewalks. Fusco knew he had a problem. "They all want on TV," he laughed. "Italians are the world's greatest hams." With a couple of shrewd technicians he set up a camera in the lobby with a red light. Dutifully, hundreds of Italians filed past, smiled at the red light, and announced their contribution. It was a success greater than any of them had imagined. By nine that evening, they had raised $758,000 for Friuli.

For Bosa and his Friuli committee, the results were astonishing. When they concluded the campaign with a Mass at Toronto's City Hall, attended by four thousand Italians, their funds had swollen still more, with contributions from schools and churches and, finally, a million dollars from the federal government. All told, in a single month, the city's Italian community, aided by Italians across Canada and the federal government, had amassed over $2 million. Under the strict supervision of a committee on which Bosa and Fusco sat, the money was stewarded to the building of a hundred and eighty-one new houses and two senior citizens' homes in mountainous Friuli towns.

Along the way to construction there were dark criticisms among Toronto Italians over the way the project was managed by Italian municipalities — criticisms of timing, decisions, and the red tape which wraps itself around Italy like a noose.

For Toronto's Italian community, though, the tragedy, so real to some families that they would never fully recover from its heartbreak, had served as one more milestone on the way to a new and cooperative spirit. Late one evening in the fall of that year, Tony Fusco looked out from a restaurant high over Toronto and surveyed the winking cityscape as someone thanked him for his part. He said only: "It brought us together."

CHAPTER ELEVEN

PUT IT IN WRITING: ITALIAN CANADIANS LOOK INWARD

On November 3, 1972, a 747 jetliner slipped beneath morning cloud to land at Malton Airport on the northwestern edge of Toronto. On its silver fuselage was a large ornamental A, for Alitalia, and on board were a small group of airline executives, several Italian politicians, a handful of reporters, and 111 members of the band of the national police force of Italy.[1] The landing was historic: the first flight of the Italian airline to Toronto, the city which, with surrounding communities, had more people of Italian background than Venice itself.

That afternoon, the members of the Carabinieri band, wearing plumed hats and the braid of dress uniform, marched to Toronto's new City Hall where they played for the public in the square. There were a few speeches, including one by Alitalia's Canadian manager, Enrico M. Striano, who knew, though he did not dwell on it publicly, that after years of denial, Italy's international airline, nearing its fiftieth anniversary, had at last been given access to its most lucrative Canadian market. He had already estimated that it would provide Alitalia with up to 50,000 new passenger trips a year — arriving immigrants, but mostly Italian Canadians visiting relatives back home. Mayor William Dennison welcomed Alitalia. It had transported many thousands of Italians to Canada during the wave of postwar migration, but to Montreal only. Now, it would fly regularly each week to the nation's commercial capital.

That evening, over 16,000 Italians streamed into Maple Leaf Gardens for a concert by the Carabinieri band. As the strains of the Italian and Canadian national anthems floated high in the arena, Maria Bergamin, a member of Alitalia's management staff from Montreal, saw something she would always remember. The Italians wept as the anthem of the land they left was played; then they wept for the national anthem of Canada.[2]

Even before that November (when Canadian Pacific Airlines had flights between Rome and Toronto) Toronto's international airport had struck many people as a meeting place of Italian Canadians, filled with men and women coming and going, saying tearful farewells to those leaving, and offering warm embraces to those arriving. "The airport," wrote the respected essayist Robert Thomas Allen, "looks like an Italian bus station." Most of the arriving people settled like those before them in Toronto, or in cities stretching to Niagara Falls in the west or Oshawa in the east.

But Toronto was the magnet. It was becoming, in Allen's eyes, a marvellous, cosmopolitan place, parts of it virtually Italian towns. "The corner of Dufferin and St. Clair," he wrote in the *Canadian* magazine, "the centre of a residential area four miles northwest of the centre of the city, is like a street corner in an Italian industrial town. Movies are Italian. Juke boxes are Italian. Espresso bars display fancy-shaped bottles of Fabbri Orzata Almond Milk, a syrup of almond extract from Bologna . . ."[3] Allen's enthusiasms were a sign of changing attitude as the chill of old Toronto toward Italians gave way to a new almost fashionable and quaint interest in them.

By then there were somewhat similar, though far smaller, Italian communities in dozens upon dozens of places in Canada, including some as unlikely as they were unknown. In Yellowknife, set amid the coldest inhabited territories of Canada, a group of men and women from the beautiful sunny region of Tuscany had changed the personality of the frontier town. They created the most remote of Canada's Little Italies, and did so exactly as Toronto's Little Italy had been created —

by brothers following brothers. Yet in certain ways they were very different: they were small in number, from a single region of Italy, and inclined to adapt quickly to the culture around them.

In 1951, when the local manpower office in Lucca, a Tuscan city, had advertized jobs in Canada, fifteen men from two villages, Vagli Soto and Vagli Sopra, applied. Six were approved and sailed for Canada that July. They arrived in Montreal where, despite their inexperience, an agent for a goldmine in Yellowknife, Consolidated Mining and Smelting Company, recruited them. They left immediately for Edmonton, where, for the first time in their lives, they boarded a plane; it took them to the crude bunkhouses that had been prepared for them in Yellowknife where the temperature, by December, reached minus forty degrees on the Fahrenheit scale. The work was different and hard, but they adapted, and within a couple of years one of them had saved enough to buy a small house and bring his wife and two daughters from Italy. While it would never equal the historic exodus from the village of Vallelonga in Calabria where virtually everyone came to Toronto, the Yellowknife Italian community brought fully half the population of the two villages of Vagli Soto and Vagli Sopra to Canada by 1970.[4]

While it was possible for some Italians, particularly women, in Toronto, Montreal, and even Vancouver to live solely within the immediate Italian community, thus never learning English, it was impossible in Yellowknife. As well, this community made up of people from a common region, had no political division or disputes. Its size — which fluctuated around 250 as people left for the more temperate climate of the south, especially Vancouver — made it an easily-integrated part of Yellowknife. As visiting scholar Valerie Sestieri Lee would comment: "Yellowknife's physiognomy, both physical and social, promoted activity and collaboration in every able and willing individual. Nobody was redundant: to different degrees, admittedly, they all felt useful." There were no famous people in the Italian neighborhood of Yellowknife, which was probably just as well. There may be value, especially for the young, to look with pride to the pantheon of the Italian contribution in Canada, from navigator and explorer Giovanni Caboto just before 1500, to physicist and inventor Guglielmo Marconi just after 1900, and a long line in this century of celebrities of stage and sport from band leader Guy Lombardo and composer Lucio Agostino, to boxer Johnny Greco, hockey star Alec Del Vecchio, and football players Angelo Mosca, Lui Passaglia, Frank Cosentino, and others. But the story of Italian Canadians is not the story of the famous but of solid citizens on ordinary streets.

By the 1970s, almost seventy percent of such immigrants were living in Ontario, the vast majority, through their well-known hard work, their support of each other, and the opportunities in Ontario, having reached financial security, even affluence. Almost ninety percent were homeowners. The average wage of the main wage-earner in an Italian family was well above the national average. And the Italian-Canadians were developing a new sense of security in the Canadian mosaic, a result of the fresh interest the country began to show after 1967 in its cultural diversity, of the numerical and economic strength of the Italian community, and of the emergence of a group of Italian writers and scholars who dedicated themselves to the history and current life of their people.

Yet there were still old problems and new worries, all of which, in a phenomenon characteristic of the country's Italian communities, would not be left to fester alone or to be solved by government. They would be attacked by a platoon of Italian social workers, academics, writers, politicians, and ordinary volunteers, working in such Italian agencies as COSTI where, since its founding in the sixties, thousands had been given everything from new jobs to new languages. As Alberindo Sauro, the second-generation Italian who served as COSTI's executive director in the late seventies, put it: "In the Italian community, there is never a time when Italians are not discovering problems and finding solutions."[5]

One particular problem and the search for its elusive solution preoccupied the minds of a handful of influential Italian Canadians — the stereotype of criminality which haunted, so unfairly they felt, their history in Canada. It was a problem that continued to vex Peter Bosa for years, so much so that, in the view of a few friends, it almost took too much of his time. The stigma of criminality hurt so many because of the unlawful behaviour of so few — a handful of thugs in the United States and Canada whom the media chose to depict as members of "The Mafia" or "Mob."

As he strolled from his office to his car one evening in the Spring of 1974, Bosa mulled over an incident involving a letter he had written to a newspaper a few days before, in the wake of a story dealing with the deliberate fire at an Italian-owned shop in the district of St. Clair Avenue West, near Dufferin Street. The implication was that the fire was the work of professional criminals of Italian background. The story also claimed that, as usual, the people of the Italian community would not talk to police, in keeping with their Mafia-enforced tradition of fearful silence. "Your recent report on organized crime," Bosa wrote the paper, "should have been called organized defamation." The paper did not run his letter.

There were, he knew, a few Italians who felt he took it all too seriously, but he was adamant, and declared that "it has a terrible effect upon our young people." He was not alone in that opinion. A psychiatrist of Italian descent, Dr. Leo Cellini, noticed that young Italian boys in Hamilton, influenced by what they heard and saw through the media about Italians and crime, were forming neighborhood gangs and calling themselves the Mafia. "I'm from their district," Cellini said. "I worked in family practice there. Now I see boys in gangs who believe that being part of a gang is where they rightly belong. Why? Because that is what the media tells them."[6]

Bosa reached his car and turned the radio to the CBC, waiting for an interview program to begin. He had reason to listen. Earlier that week a couple of his friends who felt as Bosa did had agreed to be interviewed about their plan to form an Italian anti-defamation committee. It would counter the false stereotype of their community they felt the media propounded. They would outline the reasons for their committee, then point to the large body of evidence that disproved the notion of widespread criminality among Italians. For example, they knew that as early as 1957, a Report on Criminality among the Foreign Born, commissioned by the federal government, proved by statistical evidence that immigrants in general had a lower rate of crime than the native-born. The statistics showed further that Italians had the lowest crime rate of all, far below immigrants from the United States, the United Kingdom, and Scandanavia. And when compared to the general population, the Italian crime rate was only one-sixth the national average.[7]

Bosa turned up the volume as the interview program began. What he was to hear distressed him deeply. It was not the questions that were asked, nor the answers that were given, but something far more subtle and powerful. When the interview ended, the producers of the program, unknown to the two visitors in the studio, played a piece of music that left a message underlining the very notion they had come on the air to correct — that Italians were inclined to criminality. The producers played the theme from *The Godfather*.[8] For a moment, Bosa thought he would stop the car and run to a telephone to vent his rage. But he paused. Now, he said to himself, those who thought he was overly sensitive would understand the kind of treatment Italians were up against.

Neither Bosa nor any other Italian leader denied the existence of the so-called Mafia; the most exhaustive examinations of its history have been those of North American Italian scholars such as Humbert S. Nelli and Richard Gambino, and its most ardent foes have been Italian investigators, prosecutors, and judges. All knew of its origin and evolution. In the 1870s, shortly after the random collection of states that were to make up Italy were unified, and when the northern member states continued to mistreat and exploit the southern states, bands of brigands roamed the south, mainly Calabria and Sicily, stealing from the rich and establishing local rule by terror. They were ugly and violent; so was the world in which they had come into existence. As a prominent Italian jurist of the 1870s, Diego Trajani, described it before Italy's parliament: "We have in Sicily the laws scoffed at. . . . corruption everywhere, favoritism the rule, justice the exception, crime enthroned where the guardian of public weal should be, criminals in the place of judges. . . "[9]

In the face of this broad injustice, the gangs soon became known as *società onorate*, honored societies, arming themselves with a Robin-Hood pride, and a freedom-fighter rationale. For the remaining years of the 1800s and into the 1900s, these bands, with disdain for authority and pride in violence, became a fact of life in the south of Italy. (The emergence of the word "mafia" to describe them is a matter of some conjecture. It is generally believed to have been an acronym for one or another Italian motto, but used in strict context and in Sicilian dialect it is a term to connote good, not evil; idealism not criminality.)

But the experts in history and criminology agreed the development of organized crime in twentieth-century North America had virtually nothing to do with these roaming bands of criminals in southern Italy. "Every group," Bosa explained, "living in poverty anywhere, in a country, had some of its young people turn to crime. In the United States the Italian ghettos of the turn of the century were no exception. And when young men there turned to crime, it was only natural they began to excuse or glamorize their activity by drawing upon ancient history. Either that, or writers of that period could not resist adding that dimension to their activity." Thus was created the burden that Italians in North America have lived with for a century. It was a treasure-trove for those who wrote books, films, or news, the perfect urban version of the "wild-west" theme that would dominate popular culture for decades. It had all the drama of fiction, but, in the theatre of the news, it was true.

In the same year Bosa was fostering his campaign to undo the stereotype, a leading American scholar, Richard Gambino, the chairman of Italian-American studies at Queens College in New York, neatly summed up the dilemma: "In the past few years, the mafioso rivals the cowboy as the chief figure in American folklore, and the Mafia rivals the old American frontier as a resource for popular entertainment."[10] One of Canada's most respected criminal lawyers, Edward Greenspan of Toronto, has given thought to this issue, not only because he has defended several clients described as members of the Mafia or participants in organized crime, but because he has taken serious interest in the issue of civil liberty.

Greenspan believes, as he wrote in his 1987 book, *Green-span: The Case for the Defense*, that the labels "Mafia bosses" or "members of organized crime" are labels of convenience, but also distortions of truth. He argues that almost all criminal acts, aside from certain rapes and muggings, by nature, involve two or three people and are hence organized. "When criminals conspire, they most often conspire with other criminals. After all, who else would they conspire with?" As for criminals of Italian extraction conspiring with others of their ethnic background, this is not surprising: "It is common for all people who organize activities, in the spheres of both legitimate business and crime, to give some preference to associates of their own ethnic and social roots. . . . this holds true for all nationalities, so it holds true for Italians."

It is Greenspan's conviction that the labelling of criminals of Italian descent as members of a mysterious fraternal order of organized criminals is not only a myth, but a slander against a large community of law-abiding people. "The point is," he claims,

many allegations of crime heard in our courts involve such criminal conspiracies, yet the term 'organized crime' will be attached to only a few — mainly to conspiracies comprising, or at least involving, Italians. Three Torontonians of Anglo-Celtic background accused of passing counterfeit money are likely to be described as three alleged Toronto counterfeiters. Three Torontonians from Calabrian backgrounds accused of doing the same thing are likely to be described as the Mafia. In all my years of practice I have yet to see any cogent evidence of a 'Mafia'. I only saw alleged or convicted criminals who consorted or dealt with other alleged or convicted criminals — some of whom were described as members of organized crime by the prosecuters and the press. They were selected for this 'honour' in such an arbitrary fashion as to be almost whimsical. Criminals so described appeared no different in their case histories from other alleged or convicted criminals who were never described as members of organized crime by anyone. Both groups did exactly the same things, for the same motives and with the same frequency. The only difference I could see was that the first group was Italian (or had Italian associates), while the second group wasn't or didn't.[11]

All of these factors have been in the background of the portrayal in Canada's media of a handful of men, mostly children of Italian immigrants of the early twentieth century in Montreal, Toronto and Hamilton. Along with their ancestry, each of them had one other distinguishing characteristic: they grew up in poverty, alienation, and delinquency, mostly during the Depression. But given their Italian antecedents and the lure of the Mafia myth, some actually became, in the media culture, minor legends in their own time. This dramatic treatment was nowhere more evident than at their funerals.

As is generally the case with the funerals of politicians, clergy, or lawyers, the funerals of criminals are attended by their "colleagues." On a bitterly cold day in the middle of January 1978, Paolo Violi of Montreal, a widely known criminal, was shot dead in a dingy pool-hall restaurant. Later that week, he was buried with the ususal fanfare and, since such funerals have a theatricality that makes them appealing to media coverage, wide publicity.

On the following day, Bosa, reading the report of the funeral in the highly respected *Globe and Mail*, came upon a reference which left him ashen. The paper chose not simply to report the funeral at length, but to note almost with surprise that no representatives of the National Congress of Italian Canadians had attended. Nor, it said, were any representatives of the Sons of Italy present. Bosa took action. He phoned the publisher, and was given an appointment with Brigadier Richard C. Malone. He tried to explain to Malone, an austere man who sat stonily throughout the conversation, that there was no reason for the National Congress of Italian Canadians to even consider attending Violi's funeral. Violi had no connection to the national congress, or to the Sons of Italy, or to any Italian cultural group. Bosa tried his best to remain calm, and above all, courteous. "Mr. Malone," he said, "here was a criminal killed by another criminal. If you were covering the funeral of an Anglo-Saxon criminal, would you see fit to report that no one attended from the Governor General's office?"

"My, you are sensitive," Malone replied. "After all, all we said is that nobody from the Italian Congress attended." He did not seem to grasp the point — that a common criminal had been depicted as an Italian of such rank that leaders of the community would show up at his funeral. Bosa left, bewildered; he wondered if the visit had been worthwhile.

Toward the end of the seventies, when he was a Liberal senator and head of the Canadian Consultative Council on Multiculturalism, Bosa was in a position to do more about the problem. An event in March, 1979, galvanized him. He sat in his Ottawa apartment watching a CBC television program dealing with organized crime, called *Connections*. He did not question the propriety of the CBC's dealing with the subject — it had done so in a similar series in 1977 — so much as the inevitable imputation of criminality to the Italian community. The 1979 program touched on the life of a Toronto man named Paul Volpe, the son of an Italian turn-of-the-century immigrant, whose parents parted in his childhood. Volpe was an early delinquent, in jail in his early twenties. The program dealt extensively with the underworld, the Mafia, and made reference to several men of Italian background.

Bosa flicked off his television set at the end of the program, convinced that while it revealed little Canadians did not already know, it had done great harm by reinforcing, yet again, the undeserved stereotype of Italian criminality. Bosa wanted media people, especially at the CBC, to understand that their portrayals had a social impact he felt they did not recognize. And he wanted to demonstrate, to himself and to his friends, that his twenty years of assertions that media stereotyping had hurt Italians, were correct.

That spring, The Gallup Poll for the first time, surveyed Canadians on their opinions of Italians. The results surprised even Bosa. Federal statistics may well have shown, as they had over the years, that Italians were among the country's most law-abiding citizens, but the public had its own bias. Fully forty percent of Canadians linked Italians with crime. And if Bosa ever needed proof of media influence in forming that opinion, he now had it. The Gallup survey revealed that of those who had seen *Connections*, almost half were convinced that Italians were apt to be criminally linked.[12] Bosa, sitting in his office sur-

rounded by studies and statistics which proved the very opposite, might have been discouraged, but he was philosophical.
The scholar Richard Gambino had written a few years earlier
about the same issue: "Facts do not often dispel bigotry."

Some facts, however, did favor Bosa. They fell into place with
the passage of time, so that a couple of decades after he had
begun his campaign he would come to feel that the old stereotype was passing, as a result of several factors: more public
sensitivity toward all ethnic groups in multicultural Canada;
more concern in media reporting for the rights and feelings of all
racial groups; the decline of Canada's so-called Mafia and its
replacement in the public mind by new worrying criminal
groups; but, most of all, the emergence of Italian Canadians as
people of ever-widening influence in politics, business, and the
arts, who were to be taken seriously at various levels of community life. Newspapers, magazines, and other media had developed interest in the diversity of Italian matters all the way from
cuisine to architecture. The old stigma was becoming history,
largely because Italians themselves overtook it and dispelled it.

Near the end of 1980, The National Congress of Italian
Canadians — then over six years old, with headquarters in
Ottawa and regional congresses across Canada — was gathering confidence and credibility. There were, of course, some
Italians who felt it a bit removed from the ambience of their
communities, too apt to be filled with *prominenti*, but a landmark episode in the final weeks of 1980 gave its critics pause.
The episode came with cost, but it proved that the congress was
not just a windy lobby, but an organization that could rally a
wide constituency and marshall deep compassion.

In the dark of late evening, on Sunday, November 23, the
phone rang in the home of the congress's Toronto President,
Angelo Delfino. It was a friend calling to ask if Delfino had
heard of the tragedy and what, in light of it, he was planning to
do. Delfino, having heard nothing, went to the radio and turned
to the city's Italian station, CHIN.

An earthquake many times greater than the one in Friuli in
1976, had devastated over a hundred towns in southern Italy,
not far from Naples. "Early reports," said the almost stricken

reporter from Naples, "put the death toll in the thousands." An
army general made a heart-stopping estimate: as many as ten
thousand might have died. They were in the regions of Campania and Basilicata, from where huge numbers of Italian Canadians had emigrated, especially to Toronto, and to a lesser extent,
Montreal.[13]

The following evening, Monday, November 24, Delfino sat in
a room in the old Casa d'Italia, in Toronto, surrounded by about
twenty people from the city's Italian organizations — COSTI,
the Italian Immigrant Aid Society, The Italian-Canadian Business Association, The Italian-Canadian Benevolent Corporation, Villa Colombo, and others. He assured them that
throughout the day, the president of the National Congress,
Laureano Leone, a Toronto pharmacist, had been on the phone
to regional members from Vancouver to Halifax. But given
Toronto's large population with origins near the scene of the
disaster, it was natural that the Toronto district of the congress
would be a rallying point for information about the tragedy and
response to it.

Delfino, even if he had tried, could not have conceived on
that grim evening the drama that lay ahead for him, for weeks,
months, even years. It would affect not just his own life, but that
of dozens of others in the Toronto district of the congress and in
its national executive. Almost immediately an ocean of contributions, the overflowing compassion of Toronto Italia, flowed
in. The following day, at hundreds of instant depots in mid-city
and on the fringes, crowds surged with gifts of money — at
stores, banks, clubs, houses. At least three radio and television
campaigns were underway.

Delfino, a soft-voiced man in his late thirties and a teacher
who had recently been made an administrator with the Toronto
Board of Education, was given a leave of absence to cope with
the mammoth task of overseeing the receiving of 80,000 donations, directing their handling, and seeing that every donation
was acknowledged with a receipt. Within a few weeks, the
congress in Toronto alone had collected $3 million; in time, the
national contribution to the rebuilding of the Italian towns,

including private donations and government assistance, reached over $12 million.

For Angelo Delfino, who became not just the head of the Toronto effort but a chairman of the committee that actually directed the rebuilding in Italy, the job would be rewarding but burdensome — in fact, the most burdensome chapter of his entire life. For the congress took a major decision that left it open to criticism: it did not send the money it raised directly to Italy, but put it in the bank, for use at a later date, to rebuild homes and towns.

That decision, arrived at by the national membership, gave adversaries an easy target: millions of dollars were in the bank in Canada while overseas, in Italian towns such as Balvano, Potenza, and Avellino, families were destitute, having lost their relatives (three thousand had died), and standing in need of immediate relief — food, shelter, clothing. Too often, Delfino's phone rang late at night with a question, sometimes from a reporter, sometimes from a curious citizen, always the same refrain: "How come you have millions in the bank in Toronto for the earthquake and haven't sent it to Italy? Can you explain what's going on?"

Delfino would explain, over and over: Italian authorities had told the National Congress very clearly that immediate relief — food, clothing, and so on, was not a primary need. They had, within days, put up temporary shelter, then pre-fabricated housing. There were whole warehouses filled with food and clothing. The desperate need was the one on the horizon: rebuilding decent, permanent homes. "That," Delfino would say, "is what the Italian community did in the wake of the Friuli earthquake, and it was a success. It was a competent operation in which the money received was translated into concrete good for the communities. We are not sending money now for money is not needed now. Many years ago, this was done following an earthquake and there was no accounting for the money once it got to Italy."

It was all sensible and reasonable, but it did not satisfy the emotional desire of people who wanted to feel that their money was putting food on the tables and roofs over the heads of people immediately.

Before the end of 1980, the problem was exacerbated in a meeting with representatives of the Toronto district of the respected International Red Cross. Delfino, along with a couple of his senior volunteers, met at the request of the Red Cross officials, to discuss the role of the Red Cross in the relief effort. Delfino came to the meeting expecting to hear an offer of help. Instead, he got another message: the Red Cross would like the money being raised to be handed over to it for prompt disbursement through its international offices. The Italians were annoyed at the implication that they, despite the business expertise of their group, and the experience they had already had in the Friuli earthquake, were not capable of overseeing the financial campaign and administering its results in the best interests of their people back home.

The Italians and the Red Cross parted company on sad, cool terms. The Red Cross began gathering funds on its own, a tactic which, in the opinion of Delfino and others, reduced the Italian coffers by over $2 million, applied money before it could do maximum good, and contributed to the ongoing confusion among well-intentioned, if not well-informed people, who wanted money sent to Italy whether Italy wanted it then or not. "The lives of the committee handling the rebuilding project," Delfino confided to a friend, "are being totally disrupted by criticism based entirely on misunderstanding. In some ways, it is a nightmare."

Within a year, the National Congress had a professional engineer from Canada on the sites where new housing would be built. He prepared documents on what was needed, and drew up specifications — for homes, for a senior's complex, for an orphanage. In the middle of winter, 1981, Delfino and some of his committee members flew to Italy and, to make certain construction was handled professionally, they interviewed forty prospective builders in the region. The bidding process was meticulous: it was monitored by a committee made up of the town's mayor, the leader of his council's opposition party, the local chief of police, a representative of the region, a lawyer appointed by the Canadian Congress, and a member of Delfino's earthquake committee.

The complications were extensive, given the great distances, the Italian bureaucracy, the regional regulations, the ongoing criticism, but the congress weathered it. Construction in the first of the several towns chosen for rebuilding began in 1982. All projects were finished by the middle of the 1980s. They included housing for a hundred and fifty families, an orphanage, a seniors' home, a number of recreational complexes, and medical facilities for handicapped children.[14]

In the region of great mountains, many hundreds of men, women, and children, some of whom can scarcely recall the terrible day in November 1980 without tears, live in homes and on streets whose names show their lasting gratitude. There are Canada Streets, Canada Squares, Canada Villas. Things happened, for the most part, just as the Congress had wanted. Laureano Leone, the Toronto pharmacist who was president of the National Congress when the disaster struck, always insisted that it had been wise to withstand the pressure to hand over the funds immediately. "Otherwise," he said, "we'd have the Italian comunity saying, 'Hey, where did that money go?' "[15]

For a long time afterward, there was a tinge of sadness in the manner and words of Angelo Delfino, for both the tragedy and the aftermath. One evening, after the buildings were completed, the people moved in, the books audited and approved by the international auditing firm Clarkson-Gordon, he sat alone in the large, empty boardroom of the Columbus Centre, the vast complex of Italian cultural and recreational life in Toronto, not far from Villa Colombo. He was subdued, the long years of effort — from 1980 to 1986 — had taken an inner toll.

"Who would not have considered it a privilege and duty?" he thought as the night wore on. "It was, on the whole, an outstanding success, to raise in such a short time so many millions. But you know, the cost to some of us was very great: in time away from home and family, in time away from work and business, in withstanding criticism based on misunderstanding. So, for the National Congress I believe it was a moral success. In political terms, I don't know. So much of our efforts that might have been given to other things had to be diverted. We may not have gained that much."

It seemed natural that much of the leadership in Italian affairs in Canada in the postwar period would gravitate to the people in business and the professions. Yet at the same time, and with much less public attention, a small band of others began to make a distinctive contribution to the life of Italian communities and the broader fabric of Canada. These were Canada's Italian writers. For the most part, they were men and women whose parents had come in the huge postwar wave of migration. The most striking part of their work — whether that of the poets Pier Giorgio Di Cicco and Mary di Michele, the novelists Maria Ardizzi and Frank Paci, or the essayists Joseph Pivato and Fulvio Caccia — was their readiness not simply to mirror their culture, but to look deeply within it, to try to describe what it meant to be Italian in Canada. Their writings illustrated Shaw's words: "You use a glass mirror to see your face, you use a work of art to see your soul."

In March 1972, a twenty-four-year-old youth, Frank Paci, who was born in Italy but grew up with his parents in the Italian community of Sault Ste. Marie, Ontario, returned to Italy to visit his birthplace and that of his parents. He went to Pesaro, on the beautiful Adriatic coast, where the valleys run on for great distances and the ruins of castles still stand on the slopes of the mountains. For Paci, it was not just a memorable visit, but, as for many young people of Italian background, an experience which changed his life, and gave him a new sense of direction.[16]

Paci, who wanted to be a writer and who had studied at the University of Toronto and been encouraged by Margaret Laurence, now saw clearly the subjects he would deal with and the approach he would take. "The trip was the catalyst," he said later, "that finally made me see that I had to come to terms with my Italian background before I could write anything else. The trip made me appreciate my parents. For the first time I began to see them clearly. Beforehand, I had only seen them in the context of Northern Ontario." Paci returned to Canada shortly and began work on his first published novel. It was called, simply, *The Italians*. "I had in the back of my mind," he said, "to celebrate my parents and others like them, to thank them for what they had done."

It is not common to find novelists who write to celebrate and thank their parents. In the North America of Paci's time the opposite has been much more prevalent. But Paci was following a course which, despite diversity and difference, was very much in keeping with a deep-seated Italian sense of what matters most. The family was the centre. Each of his novels touches upon Italian family life, the commitments of men and women to each other and to their children. But he did not ignore the pain inherent in their Canadian experience — the uprooting from the old land, the settling in a strange culture, the learning of a new language, the profound change that swept through life in the sixties at a time when they were still trying to adapt to life in Canada.

Paci became one of the best known of the writers of Italian origin in Canada, but there were a surprising number of others. Before long, the young poet and essayist Antonio D'Alfonso founded Guernica Editions of Montreal, a small firm specializing in the publication of Italian writing. D'Alfonso estimated that over a hundred people — poets, novelists, essayists, playwrights — were at work on literary projects. "I do not believe immigration killed Italian culture," D'Alfonso said, "but we must work hard to preserve it. That is my whole purpose."[17]

Frank Paci, who also taught school in the Toronto suburb of Etobicoke, was heartened to see, shortly after his first book, that the themes that interested him were the themes that interested numerous other Italian writers — the dislocation of the immigration experience, the sacrifices of parents for chidren, the pressure of growing up Italian in a new culture that was becoming highly secular and highly materialistic. "Only after writing *The Italians*," he once told an interviewer in an issue of the quarterly *Canadian Literature*, "did I see that there were a few others writing about the same theme. I was as isolated as anyone. It was a pleasant surprise, as if I discovered a few others on the lifeboat with me."

Many of these writers in Toronto, Montreal, and Vancouver

banded in local groups, and also formed a national organization. There were some interesting differences, especially between writers who had grown up in the Francophone milieu of Quebec and those who had grown up elsewhere in Canada. They made up a unique writing colony. As Joseph Pivato, one of their number who became a professor of Comparative Literature at Athabasca University in Alberta, noted in his introduction to *Contrasts*, an anthology of Italian-Canadian essays: "Probably more than other ethnic literatures, Italian-Canadian writing does not fit easily into one cultural tradition. It exists in English, French, and Italian and is influenced by all three literary traditions." Pivato urges that Italian writers maintain their identity and resist the tendency to be assimilated: "Exposure to ethnic writing is one way to approach the new reality of multiculturalism. Italian-Canadian literature, as a body of writing, illustrates many of the qualities of a varied ethnic literature in Canada . . . "

The writers shared their work and their opinions, working independently, yet with a common purpose: to define for themselves and others what it meant to be Italian in Canada in the last half of the twentieth century. In several ways, they represented an entirely new, third presence among Canadian writers — not English, not French, but affected by both and originating during the ferment surrounding Quebec in Confederation, when French culture took on new assertiveness.

Marco Micone, a slim, scholarly Montrealer, came with his parents from the south of Italy when he was thirteen in the early fifties. His plays, first written and performed in French, dramatized the pain of trying to adapt to a new country while the heart longed for an old one. The best known of these, *Gens du silence* (Voiceless People), deals with an immigrant family whose members are depicted in almost tragic terms, as victims of an inevitable tide of history over which they had no control, but which determined their empty destiny.[18]

Beneath the shade of the trees of his backyard in Montreal, Micone spoke of the immigration experience of his parents' generation:

Some people have seen my plays as making the immigrant from Italy entirely a victim. But in each of my plays there is someone who rises above it all, who prevails, who is not defeated. Still, I do believe that the immigration experience has been a great hardship. In the first draft of *Voiceless People*, I put it all very starkly: I denounced the power structure in Italy for throwing out my parents and their generation; I denounced the power structure of Canada for exploiting them as cheap labor. I denounced the power structure of the Italian community in Canada for using them for material gain. I later revised this somewhat — for dramatic and theatrical reasons — but my basic convictions remain. You know, it is probably not even right to refer to Italians in Canada as Italians. Immigration has made them something else. Whatever they are, they are not Italian.

A few of the writers emerged early from their identity as "Italian-Canadian writers", to find a place in the mainstream of Canadian work. One was the gifted poet Pier Giorgio Di Cicco, a member of a Catholic order living in King, Ontario. Di Cicco, like a great many others, found that his return trip to Italy, made around the same time as Paci's, had a profound effect. "I went out of curiosity," he later wrote, "and came back to Canada convinced that I had been a man without a country most of my life." In much of his work, Di Cicco mourns the lost beauty of the Italian heritage, which he feels lies buried beneath the ruins of modern materialistic existence in Canada. "They are build-ing Rome in one day in Toronto," he writes in one of his poems, "Multicultural Blues," "and it will disappear in the snows."

In a room on the third floor of a building on the campus of York University in Toronto, several of the writers gathered on a winter Saturday to talk together of their task and their audience. Four of them sat with York University professor Franc Sturino before a small audience: Frank Paci, Mary di Michele, Giorgio Di Cicco, and Antonino Mazza.[19]

They were a serious group, serious about life, about writing, about themselves. They struck a visiting journalist in the audi-ence as unlike many writers of the current generation, for they were modest and humble in style, with nothing of the vanity many writers wear as the costume of their calling. "My vision of what it is to be a writer," said Frank Paci, "has to do with what it

means to be a good human being." He said that his books —
The Italians, Black Madonna, The Father — might be read by
the people of whom he wrote, Italian men and women like his
parents; but he was saddened that this had not happened. "I
was hoping," he said, "that they would read them and see that
someone cared enough to tell their stories." This sensitive, compassionate spirit informed the words of Di Cicco: "My reason
for writing at first was simply that I felt lonely, and was seeking
my voice. Later, my purpose was to bring something gracious
into someone's life." He quoted the poet Pablo Neruda, who
knew the beautiful worth of a poem: "It is that which gives
people hope."

Di Cicco was instrumental in helping found a small poets'
workshop, not all Italian, in Toronto. It was he who introduced
to the group a slight woman of quiet personality, Mary di
Michele — whom almost everyone called Mary di Miss Shelley,
but whose last name was, in fact, pronounced "Meek-eh-lay."
She was born in Italy, grew up in Toronto, and graduated with a
master's degree in English and Creative Writing from the University of Windsor, where she had come under the influence of
the well-known American novelist Joyce Carol Oates. Beginning
in the late seventies, Mary di Michele published several collec-
tions of poetry. An early volume, *Bread and Chocolate*, dealt
with the familiar theme of Italian immigration and the family.
But some of her later work carried her in different and surprising directions. A collection called *Necessary Sugar* showed a
maturing perspective that caught wide attention from people
who might have expected a young Italian woman to stay within
traditional themes. Mary di Michele did not; her writing took on
a strong feminist dimension. It was widely read and seriously
regarded; she won the CBC's literary award for poetry, and
received numerous invitations to be a guest lecturer in universities across the country. She acquired a solid reputation among
Canadian poets. On that Saturday, as the writers spoke of their
regret that too often they were confiningly Italian-Canadian
writers, a member of the audience said he had just returned
from a university in the United States where Mary di Michele
was being studied, not as an Italian-Canadian writer, but as a

poet of standing. As the *Globe and Mail's* literary critic, William French, observed: "She is clearly one of the more gifted poets of the country. If she continues to develop as well as she has thus far she will be one of our major poets."[20]

If the writers of Italian origin were courageous enough to draw the immigrant experience in honest detail — its painful dimensions, not just its laudable achievements — so were numerous other Italian Canadians, in social work, education, and medicine. By the seventies it was as if such people, aware of problems beneath the family surface, were unwilling to wait for outside agencies to deal with them, but wanted Italian Canadians to do so themselves. There were a few, who, out of old pride, would cultivate a veneer of idealistic serenity, even to themselves. They could point to the facts of high incomes, fine homes, and a generation of young people entering the universities.

But in both the writing colony and among the social workers, there was readiness to look deeper and to speak honestly. Such people recognized the external accomplishments. But they were aware of internal difficulties, wanted to understand them more fully, and deal with them.

On a clear day in early fall, 1974, in an office near St. Clair and Dufferin in Toronto, a counsellor and therapist named Dr. Saverio Pagliuso, sat opposite a man who had come to seek his help. Pagliuso, an affable, gentle man, had come from Calabria to Canada as a youth in the early fifties. On this autumn afternoon, he sensed that the man across from him — anxious and flushed, and troubled in speech — was suffering from alcoholism. He knew that if he did not stop drinking, he would probably die. Pagliuso rose to watch the man leave his office, convinced that the future was dark. Within weeks, the man was dead. Pagliuso was sad and angry. He knew that too many such Italian men suffered from excessive drinking, which he felt was brought on by problems related to their immigrant experience. Neither the community in general, nor the Italian community in particular, Pagliuso felt, recognized the problem or seemed ready to face it.

Pagliuso decided it was time that the issues were set out in a candid form. He would write a report, directed to the Addiction

Research Foundation of Ontario, for whom he did therapeutic work, to persuade it to train more people to work specifically among Italian Canadians. He was, he said, appalled by the lack of services directed to Italian immigrants. He was putting it on paper, he told a friend, with some hesitancy, but out of great urgency. "I am doing this," he wrote in a note, "on the assumption that it is only by revealing the very soul of a group that a proper foundation is laid for any future action."

HOME IS WHERE THE HEART IS — BUT WHERE IS THE HEART?

Saverio Pagliuso had good cause to worry. In his home in one of Toronto's Italian districts, not far from the corner of St. Clair Avenue and Dufferin Street, he rolled a sheet of paper into the typewriter, and prepared to write the report he felt would go to the heart of certain problems he saw in Italian families that had come to Canada as he had, in the fifties. He paused. He stood up, strolled to the window bathed in late afternoon light, and looked down the street past the rose gardens which even then, on the last day of September, 1974, were as if they had just bloomed.

He wondered, looking at the placid facades of the tiny houses, how many of the people inside would descend in fury upon him for what he was about to write, how many would claim that by revealing things best kept within the private walls of the Italian family, he was bringing embarrassment upon his own people. He knew them so well — knew, above all, their pride. He was one of them, having spent his childhood in the village of Melito in Calabria, and coming to Windsor, Ontario in the early fifties where his father spent his lifetime as a factory worker. Saverio grew up, took degrees in philosophy at Windsor

239

and Toronto, and a doctorate from the University of Waterloo, and taught a few years at York University in Toronto. As his interest in his people and their problems deepened, he began to spend more and more time as their counsellor, therapist and friend, first through the Italian Immigrant Aid Society to which so many turned, later through the Addiction Research Foundation of Ontario. He knew his people intimately, and had been in touch with many others, who knew their people. Pagliuso concluded that even if people turned on him in misdirected anger, he must plead with agencies to provide more trained workers, fluent in Italian, to deal with the problems he was meeting. He returned to his typewriter, put the word "Confidential" at the top of the first page and began to type.[1] For fifty pages, like a surgeon before a class in anatomy, Pagliuso laid bare the Italian family as he saw it.

Once, he had returned to the old village in Calabria, where he had a sad meeting with a boyhood friend, a poet who took him at dusk on a walk past silent, aging houses, most of them enveloped in silence since their occupants had moved to Canada. "He recited a poem," Pagliuso wrote, "on the immigrant: 'The uprootedness of those who leave; the abandonment of those who are left; lonely old age at home, and the struggle to find new roots in foreign soil.'"

It was this movement of history, inevitable but painful, that was at the heart of an illness afflicting too many Italian families in Toronto, and by obvious extension, Canada: "To understand them is to understand the tragedy in their lives and the lives of their loved ones whether here or in Italy. And to understand this tragedy is the first step in understanding the upheaval that drives some to distraction, others to alcohol, and many of their children to drugs."

He estimated that over eighty percent of the Italians in Toronto came from the south, and the south was another world — almost medieval, just then beginning to enter the twentieth century. It held to customs so deeply ingrained that they were almost impossible to change in the space of a lifetime. In his own village of Melito, he recalled, no one ever married in the month of May, a custom so old it was ancient in the days of Rome. This embrace with the past was especially noticeable in matters of the family, relationships between husbands and wives, fathers and daughters, mothers and sons. It touched the family in ways innumerable and not always perceptible to even the quantitative methods of the sociological researcher.

For example, he pointed out, when a man married a woman in the south, the ancient beliefs decreed that the real tie remained to the family into which each had been born: "The man's closest ties are with his paternal family — the bloodline — not his wife. It is the same for the woman. The idea that a man shall leave his father and cleave to his wife and the two shall become one flesh, is a completely foreign concept. The war of the sexes becomes acutely tragic, with [unpredictable] and sometimes monstrous consequences [for] the children, who are the battleground."

As he wrote, Pagliuso recalled an incident when a distant relative made a gossipy comment to him about her own husband, excusing it with the remark, "It's okay because we are family, he is not." He told a friend that in the modern world such a view is almost insane, but among too many southern Italians it was strong. "It is further complicated," he wrote, "by the fact that the so-called bloodline runs on both sides. So the husband remains closer to his family, but the wife remains closer to hers. Their marriage is made difficult from the beginning." As for the woman and her rights, he wrote, "The woman is the centre of the home. She is the one that gives that subtle 'homey character' to the house. Yet it is not her home, as she is subject to her husband — and his bloodline — no less than their children. Her children, the children she has produced, are not her children but fuel for the greater glory of her husband's family name."

The husband's position in marriage has problems created by the pull between old loyalty and new. Where does he place his heart? He seeks fulfillment — a sense of worth, for instance — in his marriage. But given the fact that his wife's loyalty is still to her family, he is often kept at emotional distance. "He finds," wrote Pagliuso, "that the centre of his home is his wife and that in the savage struggle of the sexes, the children inevitably take the side of their mother. He finds himself alone. Pushed away by the children and his wife, he is emotionally pulled closer to his

no-longer existing clan. He slowly becomes the donkey of the
family . . ."

This history is made more complex by the experience of
immigration, which to Pagliuso was a voyage made by men
always on behalf of their families and, in view of their limited
education and resources, an act of tremendous courage: "It is
as though you or I were to pack a suitcase, and with a few dollars
in our pocket, go to Siberia in search of fortune."

But the voyage carries seeds of future pain:

> He has left behind all his material posessions, but he is yoked to
> the full burden of his pyscho-social baggage. He tries to live as
> close as possible to Little Italy so the shock to his system will not
> be too great. Then his family arrives. As I have stated, he has not
> counted on anything other than economic change, so he jeal-
> ously guards against any strange new influences disrupting his
> family life. He does not want his wife to work, for this would
> indicate that he is not a good provider. He watches his daughter
> like a hawk, so she will not lose her 'honor'. And his sons must
> respect him and submit to his authority — this is the right way,
> the only way.

For an Italian from the south, emigrating to Toronto was like
being born again. The bloodline of the past was cut off. The
new customs and different ethical categories, the pressures of
making a living and getting ahead, meant that women must go
to work. This opened the door to female independence and all
that followed in its wake. The father finds that his boys go to
work while still at school, earn money, enjoy freedom, may even
move out of the house while still teenagers, as Pagliuso himself
did in Windsor, much to the chagrin of his father. The girls live
in two worlds, trying at home to stay within the old culture of
submission, at school tasting new freedoms, going on dates,
thinking of careers. Many men, said Pagliuso, are left devastated. They had not bargained for this: "His wife is no longer 'his',
his children go their own way, he is completely lost."

From his office at the Addiction Research Foundation, Pagliuso observed more and more Italian men, very few of them
drinkers when they came, drifting into excess, many drinking on
the job to help cope with their anxiety over what was happening

at home. One man came to him, he recalled, after seeing a non-Italian psychologist because of his worry — an obsession, really — that his wife, now working, was having an affair. The psychologist told the man to accept the fact that life was different now, that he had his life, and his wife had hers. To Pagliuso this was an appalling way to deal with the complex Italian psyche. "The guy could not understand what kind of moron this was talking about his wife having a life of her own. They had formed a family. You are not an individual existing by yourself. In fact, in the dialect of many southern Italians, there is not even a concept such as 'my life' or 'my rights.'"

Women were now drinking, and while only a few were leaving their husbands out of frustration with the old customs and in search of the new independence, it was probably just a matter of a decade before many more began to. The situation with children was the real shock: heavy drinking, even the use of heroin, was becoming common. "I believe," he wrote, "St. Clair and Dufferin to be the major centre for the distribution of heroin; occasionally one can see transactions taking place on the street." It distressed him greatly, it hurt him to report it, but he was, as he had said earlier, laying bare the soul of the community in the hope of getting help from the people able to offer it — the Addiction Research Foundation, the Italian community, the social agencies.

He felt, like others, that the economic contribution of Italians to Toronto was a fact that justified their receiving better social service for their tax dollars:

> One is appalled by the lack of services directed to Italian immigrants by government-funded agencies. It is clear now that the immigrant requires more help than the established native. A number of men have come to me for whom I have been able to do little or nothing because they do not fit into any existing program. The same lack is evident in the desperation of parents with addicted teenagers who have no one to talk to in their own language.

Pagliuso asked for more training of Foundation staff, more help for Italian priests who were still the most trusted counsellors, and an opportunity to explain, more specifically, the kind of

programs needed. But even before that, he wanted to see the
groundwork laid among Italians themselves: "Italian immigrants need gradually to be taught that there is nothing shame-
ful about needing help to resolve difficulties arising within the
family — the new family that they are evolving in Toronto."

Pagliuso was only one of a number of people in his community and field to sense that beyond the laudable successes — the
material well-being, the admired families, the beginning of
widespread popularity — the Italian-Canadian communities
had human frailties.

Renzo Carboni, a Toronto physician who had been born in
the mountains of Calabria, and studied medicine in Italy and
Canada, saw in that same period a worrying trend among men
who had come to Canada in the fifties, worked hard in construction, and become prone to emotional disturbances that
showed up in brooding family issues. "Often," he told a public
audience of concerned Italians, "they are related to family
issues and are not major issues, but to Italians, especially those
from the south, even minor ones are enough to make him very
upset — his 'nerves', his 'stomach' his 'system.' All of this is
psychosomatic."[2]

Sometimes, in the late seventies, Carboni, whose practice in
Toronto was almost exclusively Italian, and who spent much of
his time as a physician at Villa Colombo, shared his opinions
with Franca Carella, a tall, poised woman, who had spent her
early Canadian years in Alberta in nursing, then came to
Toronto where she took an interest in wider issues of the Italian
community and health. She was, by then, Director of Social
Services at Villa Colombo. "Franca," Carboni would say to her,
"the degree of psychosomatic illness is really very concerning.
We must do something about it." Carellas's reply was very
candid, and while understood by Carboni, it was not calculated
to gain easy popularity among some Italian Canadians.[3]

"The trauma of immigration," she said, "is only one part of
the reason for all of this. There is something else. There is
something missing among too many Italians. They came here in
the fifties with a vision — making money and owning a house.
They got the house. It became a castle. Then they gave their

children everything they never had — clothes, cars, trips. But too many forgot that while we wear five-hundred-dollar boots on our feet, our heads and hearts can be empty. What about the inner person? We are forgetting the emotional needs of people."

Out in the Italian neighborhoods, working men and women, not trained like Pagliuso, Carboni, and Carella, were coming to the same conclusion. Gino Vatri, who came to Toronto from the north of Italy at the tail end of the migration in the late sixties to make a living as a machine operator, and whose wife was a schoolteacher, sat with a few friends not long after Pagliuso wrote his epistle and wondered about the same issues. His wife, Santa, an articulate woman, put it forthrightly: "I see the confusion in the children at school. Do you know what the problem is? Too many have been given too much. Go to some weddings and you will see it. Once I could go to a shower and take pillow cases from Eatons. Now it must be silverware from Birks."[4] Sometimes, even to ordinary Italians, it seemed as if in leaving Italy they had left the richest part of their heritage behind, to replace it with the superficial trinkets of the new land.

One of the communities' best known social workers, Frank Orlando, recalled leaving as a small boy with his mother in the early sixties and the long train trip from his home in Calabria to the city of Naples. It was as if, he thought to himself, looking out the window, with every turn of the wheel, part of himself and all that he was was staying behind. In North Bay, Ontario, he who had been reading by the time he began school in Calabria, was baffled to find people regarding him as a peasant boy. Worse, he was astonished that Italians — people who had come from a land rich in culture — seemed to want to get their children out to work as soon as possible. "I was shocked," he would say later in his life, "at the values, that Italians there did not treasure education and culture. So I was alone in my ambitions. It was sink or swim. I guess I swam, and by the time I received my masters [degree] in criminology from the University of Toronto, most people would say I succeeded. But I wonder about the cost to a child's internal life — the trauma of leaving, the cold welcome, the emphasis upon working for money and material things."[5]

By the late seventies, throughout Toronto's booming Italian communities, the men and women who examined the deeper things of their people shared identical concerns. Gregory Grande, an articulate man who came in his late teens to Toronto with only a handful of English words, and was catapulted into the University of Toronto from which he got two degrees and went on to a doctorate, became, like his friend Orlando, a social worker with the Toronto Board of Education.[6]

He looked out over the community from his position as one of the key board members of COSTI-IIAS and concluded: "We must have a centre for Italian family counselling. The family, when the great migration flow took place in the fifties and sixties, was clearly defined. But in North America, the family was then going through vast changes. And not only in North America. Back home in Italy also."

About a year after he had come to Canada, Grande was shocked to see his younger brothers going to school in jeans and T-shirts. He had gone to high school in Calabria wearing a white shirt and tie, and could not understand the new informalities of dress in Canadian schools. A few years later, he returned to Calabria, went to his old school, and found the students in jeans and T-shirts. "Italy too has changed," he said, "but the Italian immigrant in Canada is tied to a vision of Italy that has faded."

By the opening of the eighties, there were numerous offices in Canada's largest Italian centres, where day after day, the flow of Italians, mostly men, filled the offices of Italian social workers, psychologists, and physicians. Invariably, no matter what the city, Italians were being helped by Italians who spoke their language, sensed their problems, and offered their services without charge. The people spoke of their health, which led them to talk of their lives. In Vancouver, the problems seemed fewer, perhaps because the Italian population was smaller, perhaps because so many came from the north of Italy where the old customs of which Saverio Pagliuso wrote were not persistent. In Montreal at the time, the old Casa d'Italia, once the site of police raids in 1940, was now the place to which troubled Italians, including battered women, could turn for counselling through an organization set up by the community to provide services of all kinds — from monetary help for needy people to counselling for young people at Saturday schools. Luciana Soavee, a deeply committed woman, set up a special program to help handicapped youngsters of Italian descent find their just place in the school and community.

In Toronto, Renzo Carboni, then deeply engrossed in the practice of neurology, and Franca Carella, were convinced that tens of thousands of Italians needed basic information about the mind and the body. In June, 1983, they took the step of launching a health magazine — *Vita Sana* (Your Health). They met regularly in Carboni's small office in Toronto's Italian northwest where, late into the evenings they wrote articles that described, in the most basic Italian, simple anatomy and practices for maintaining health.

The magazine, amateurish in its early appearance, was picked up free of charge once a month by thousands of people, at the church or the club or the local store. It tried to reassure the worried Italian man or woman that surgery for removal of appendix or gall bladder did not mean incapacitation for life.

Carboni went on the air. "Too many of our people can't read," he told Carella, "or else they won't read." In 1983, with the magazine picking up, he got in his car each Tuesday morning and drove through the maze of streets in western Toronto to College Street, where above a family grocery store, one of the city's legendary figures of Italian descent, Johnny Lombardi, operated the radio station CHIN. Carboni climbed the stairs, and found his way through the jumble of hallways and tiny offices to a small studio. Just past ten o'clock, he'd don a set of headphones, flick on his microphone, and announce the topic of the day on which he would take questions for the next two hours. He did the program for six years, then — finding the pressures of medical practice, publishing, and broadcasting too much for one man — he stepped aside, and Franca Carella became not only publisher of *Vita Sana*, but the host of the health program on CHIN.

"The subject for this morning," she would say over CHIN, "is the importance of the formative years in a child's life." She would speak for five minutes, then open the phones for questions. It was in the early eighties that she began to detect a disturbing undercurrent in some of the her callers' voices as if the question was only a cover for a deeper, more troubling matter. "I cannot give my name," a woman would say, "but I would like to ask a question. How can I tell if my son is on drugs?"

Franca Carella, got in touch with a Toronto psychologist of Italian descent, Gianni Carparelli. He, too, looked over the landscape of Italian family life, especially the youth, and while he saw much that encouraged him, — children holding values of love and respect toward parents — he saw, as Carella did, drug use that worried him. Soon, he and Carella could be found on Tuesday nights in a small, out-of-the-way room in the huge Columbus Centre, surrounded by Italian teenagers who confessed their dependencies and came together with two trusted adults of their own community to find their cure. In time she could count well over a hundred teenagers whom she had helped end their addictions. "There is so much that is good for all of us in Italian family life," she said one evening, "that we can't rest until we find help for them all. Each one."

The problems of family life and personal addictions were far from unique to Italian Canadians; they afflicted every group of Canadians in the seventies and eighties. But toward the beginning of the eighties, some people within the country's Italian communities began to notice a trend they felt was more pronounced among their own people than any other. One evening, aboard a plane that had just taken off for Rome from Toronto, an Italian immigrant named Olivo Mellozzi spoke of himself as one of its prime examples.

"I do not know where I belong anymore," said Mellozzi, a slight man whose dark eyes looked out sadly over his glasses at the passenger sitting next to him on the Alitalia jet. "I came to Canada in 1955. Then I came back to Italy in 1970. Then I returned to Canada in 1978, but only stayed a little over a year. I returned to Italy. Then in 1980, I came back to Canada. But by then my children were lonely for Italy. So I went back to Italy and I have stayed there since. But I am worried. Not for myself, but for my children. I do not know what is ahead for them, I just do not know." It was the middle of May, 1987. Olivo Mellozzi was heading home to Italy, after visiting Toronto yet again.[7]

Mellozzi was fifty-four at the time, and as he told his story to the man beside him — a writer on one of several trips to Italy, this time to visit people like Mellozzi who had gone home — his story lifted the curtain on one of the most striking episodes in the entire history of Italian emigration to Canada: the return to the old country of thousands of Italian Canadians in the eighties. They were men and women who, in expressing the reason for their return, chose the language of economic opportunity — "a better life." The true reason was the ineffable one echoed by the Canadian writer Morley Callaghan: "All of life is a longing for home."

When Olivo Mellozzi came with the stream of migration of 1955, he settled in Toronto where his brother had come before him, in the heart of the old Little Italy, where the footprints of Italian migration were on every street. Soon he bought a house at 165 Petrie Street and moved up from his first job in a laundry to practice his trade: making fine shoes. He took English at night school and on free evenings strolled down Yonge Street, or wandered to the corner of College and Spadina where he and his friends would take in the show at the Victory Burlesque. Before long, he had brought out a young woman from Italy and married her.

Olivo Mellozzi liked Toronto, but in the bleak Januaries of the sixties, when winter seemed to punish the streets of Little Italy, he rose in the dark for the trek to the factory in Brampton and found himself dreaming of Italy — the sun-washed village, the familiar square, the blue canopy of sky. In early 1966, he went to work one morning to be told the factory was closing. He found another job, but for some reason, both he and his wife began to think more and more of Italy. In the evenings, his wife spoke of her parents. Sometimes he was sure that in the dark of the bedroom, he could hear her weep. By 1969, they had made up their minds. Olivo sold his house to his brother Marino, withdrew his savings, and, with his wife expecting their second child, went back to his hometown, about 120 kilometres from Rome.

He was only repeating the saga of tens of thousands of Italians before him in the century, who came to the Canadian forests and railways, but always as sojourners, planning on returning to Italy even as they left. But Olivo's decison was different: he had come to stay, like most of his contemporaries. And in the very year in which he made his return, so many others began doing likewise, that a new migration phenomenon began: the return of the Italian immigrant. Some called it reimmigration, others, repatriation. It would continue for twenty years as Italians sold their homes, mainly in Toronto, but also in Montreal and Vancouver, and returned to the land they left.

Olivo Mellozzi found a small house on a hill back home, a job in his trade, and felt for that first year that he had made the right decison. For one thing, the conditions that led him to leave Italy in 1955 had changed for the better — not a lot, but enough to make the future brighter than the past. At work, it was often the talk of the shop floor — that small companies, such as the one he worked for making shoes, were beginning to move the economy forward, creating exports, investment, and jobs in the process. So much remained to be done — the country seemed to be strangling on its own bureaucracy and too heavily dependent on imports — but for once, it seemed reasonable to hope that opportunity was ahead. Economists, particularly in Rome and northern Italy, were predicting an actual growth in the economy. Before the decade ended, Italy would be spoken of, not as the land of despairing peasants, but as the nation of economic miracle.

As the famous former Prime Minister Amintore Fanfani put it: "*Canta che ti passa*" — "sing and let it blow over." Italy had cancerous bureaucracy, but enormous creativity. By the 1980s, one of its conglomerates of over 1,000 diverse industries was generating revenues of $40 billion a year, ranking third in the Fortune 500. As Joseph Carraro, the gifted Catholic priest who helped found COSTI and later worked for the Italian labor movement helping Toronto Italians get their pensions from Italy, put it: "There are two Italies — the Italy of bureaucracy and the Italy of the private sector. The latter is dynamic, energetic, creative. We have been the greatest merchants, the greatest explorers, the greatest artisans. There is only one Sistine Chapel."[8]

Still, something seemed amiss in Olivo Mellozzi's life back in Italy. His job was acceptable, his wife happier, his two children doing well. But he had begun to feel strain — his days seemed filled with anxiety and his nights were often fitful and sleepless. He left the house in the morning for the factory and by the time he arrived, his hands would be sweating, his limbs filled with new, strange aches. One night he sat up late wondering what was wrong, and gradually came to the conclusion that he was not worrying for himself, but for his two children, one born in Toronto, the other in Italy. They mattered more than his job; what of their future? The country might be improving, but not that much. It did not have the opportunities for the young that Canada offered. One day in the spring of 1978, after he had been back in Italy seven years, Olivo Mellozzi sat in the last light of the evening writing a letter to his brother in Toronto. "I am coming out," he said, "to look for a job in Toronto."

His wife and children did not want to leave but eventually he persuaded them that it was for the better — he'd make more money, the children would have a better future and, as for his wife, she would get used to it. They arrived in Toronto on a warm spring afternoon in 1980, and moved back into the house he had left and sold to his brother. He got work in his field. But before long, he realized that it was a mistake.

Sometimes he would return from work to find his wife in tears, longing for home. The children, within a few months, were so upset that Olivo himself took ill. "They are all so sad," he told a friend, "that I, too, cry for them." In the fall of 1980, he made up his mind once more that for the sake of the family, he would return to Italy. He remained there, but every so often, he came back to Canada, to Toronto to see his brother Marino and his ailing parents whom he had brought to Canada himself in the late fifties, and who had found their peace there.

Gregory Grande once gave a lecture at York University in Toronto to a group of men and women with special interest in Italian immigration. The subject was the return of many Italian

Canadians to Italy. Grande had just returned from one of his
own frequent visits to the south of Italy near the village of
Vallelonga and had met many who had returned. In his view,
they returned because, one way or another, they had not found a
true home in Canada: "They had never really felt they belonged
to Canadian society; they felt they could return to Italy and,
because they had earned a fair bit of money in Canada, live
more comfortably there. A lot of them have a positive economic
impact on the small towns. Often they build houses just like the
ones they had in Woodbridge and Downsview — complete with
the arches."

Others, who had remained in Italy and saw them return,
noticed that many came in search of an Italy they remembered,
but which had disappeared. "Many of them seem frozen in
time," said Peter Gentile, a young English teacher in the town of
Vibo Valenti, not far from the Calabrian city of Cosenza. "They
think they will meet the same people and they do not. They
think they will go to the square as they did twenty years ago. But
people do not go to the square anymore. Italy has changed and
its people have changed with it. So, many of those who return
seem rather sad, finding that only the sun and the weather are
as they remember."[9]

In the spring of 1987, the town of Maiarato in Calabria, not far
from Vibo Valenti and near the tip of southern Italy, was baking
in days of seemingly unending sun. Along the cobbles of the
street, shadows fell upon old walls and the afternoon itself
seemed to have slipped into sleep. Some 2,500 people live in
Maiarato, but so many left for Canada in the fifties that, in
Toronto, there was an active Maiarato Club throughout the
sixties. Then in the seventies, whole families began returning
and when, in the spring of 1987, they tried to explain why, it
was often difficult for them to find words.

In a small house of immaculate rooms, where a bouquet of
wild flowers rested on top of the televison set, an elderly woman
named Marie Antonia Pietro, sat wondering why she really left
Canada.[10] She may have been convinced, like so many other
women of her age and generation, that some of the ills that

came with age — the weakening back, the shortness of breath, the loss of energy — could be cured, if only she returned to the clear air in the land of her childhood. Her friends often spoke of it. Now, on this spring morning in 1987, she had been sitting for long hours before the television. "We went to Canada in 1964," she told a visitor, "to Toronto. My sister was there. Life was good. But I worked so hard. Then my sister decided she would go home. I felt very alone. I came back too." She fell into a sombre silence. When asked if the return had been a happy one, she at first said nothing. Then, looking up slightly, she murmured, "No."

In the nearby field where the land runs onto marsh and then into a sloping green forest, a small factory stood, the soft hum of machines drifting through an open doorway. A handful of men and women were at work, making brooms. Paul Costa — forty-six-years old, trim, with a soft deep voice and a quiet confidence — was explaining to a visitor why, after ten years in Canada and still in the prime of his life, he had returned to Calabria, not to retire, but to build a career.

"I remember," he said with a shrug, "how I would often think of home when I was in Toronto. The town. The old friends. And in Toronto, how hard I worked. I went in 1965. Sometimes it seemed that all I did was work. In one month, just after I went to Canada, I had six jobs — sometimes three at once. Then I bought a grocery store. I would get up at 5 o'clock in the morning to be at the food terminal to get food to sell. Then I would work until eleven o'clock at night. In Toronto you live to work. Around 1973, I decided I wanted to come home. First I began a factory to make jeans. It had problems. Now we make brooms. But it is hard to be in business in Italy. So many business problems. In Toronto, business is done differently. If my factory could be in Toronto, I would love to go back. But that is not to be. Not now."

For all the men and women who had returned to Maiarato, the common impulse, at least the conscious one, had been the one expressed by Paul Costa — the longing for something in life other than the dawn-to-dark drugery of the culture of Mammon in Toronto. Each, it seemed, had found in Canada a prosperous existence and an unfulfilling life. The magnet of materialism had given its reward and the reward was incomplete. "I was working all the time," said Rego Mancheti, "nothing else but work. I did not even see my friends." And Gregory Sivaggio, who worked in Toronto first as a baker, then an excavator, before coming back in the seventies, put it in different words with the same melancholy tone: "If you want the "good life" of Toronto, you work, work, work. It all depends on what you want. Money is not everything, but in Toronto it seems to be."

But the return to the old country was never the way they had dreamt it might be. The town, for so many, had changed. Or was it they who had changed? They had found work, they had obtained a good house, the weather was beautiful, but here, as in Canada, there was something unattained, something intangible to do with family, friends, peace of mind. They who had loved the town and longed for it, now found themselves strangers within its walls.

On the afternoon when Rego Mancheti spoke of rejecting the endless treadmill of empty work in Canada for the ideal life of the old town in Italy, she ended with a sentiment that could be heard time and time again in Italian villages where the returning Italians of Canada had tried to find a place: "The friends I had before I went to Canada are still here, but they are not my friends anymore. They have changed. I don't know what it is. They seem to have a different mentality. When I see them I say hello. Mostly that is all. They are different." Or perhaps she, who had spent so many years in Canada, is different. Perhaps the small town, like the waters of a harbor behind a departing ship, had closed behind her when she left so many years before.

Italy itself, even in the south, had changed in ways that even those who left could never have dreamt possible. Its newly secular spirit was reflected, for example, in the startling number of annual abortions: 350,000 in 1986.[11]

Luciano Coraggio, an urbane Roman who was part of a final, elite wave of migration in the early seventies, settled in Montreal to become editor of the city's leading Italian paper *Il Corriere Italiano*. He regarded their return as almost always a sad mistake: "I have never gone back since I left. I want to live with the

Rome I left forever clear in my memory. Those who return find a new Italy, not the one they expect and long to find. And they find new Italians. The land and the people they left are no more."[12]

In Maiarato, the women who returned, even more than the men, seemed enveloped in disappointment. A soft-spoken, courageous woman named Antonia Redropal, who had come back to Maiarato from Pittsburgh in 1973 and had been unhappy ever since, said, "It was a mistake. All of the people who came back here from Canada or America would tell you the same thing if they were willing to speak openly. Life is better over there. Here there are too many petty jealousies, too much dullness, too little future." Her husband had gone back to Pittsburgh and found work. She longed to join him. Her eyes said she would.

It is a full day's journey on the *autostrada* from the lush lands of Calabria to the mountain peaks of the north and the towns cradled in the great hilly land of the region of Trentino. Beyond the historic city of Trento, the road climbs and winds through cloudless air, through a town called Cles, and then, beyond a curving sweep of roadway from which Cles becomes a speck to the eye, the land seems to end in the town of Revo.

Just over a thousand people live in this town of ancient rust-brown houses and jumbled, short streets that look out over an unending carpet of mountains. There is one hotel, the Hotel Revo, with a small shadowed bar and a corner dining room. One afternoon in the spring of 1987, a slight, dark-haired woman with expressive eyes stood at the bar alongside two men. A few others sat at tables, playing chess. Her name was Mrs. Rossi. She spoke in a calm but declarative style, and what she said echoed the words of men and women a world away in the Italian south.

"We lived in Downsview just outside the city of Toronto. My husband was a carpenter. I had two jobs — one in a factory during the week, the other waiting on tables in a banquet hall on weekends. We came back to Revo in 1979. It was difficult at first. The first two years were the hardest."[13] She paused, looked toward the dark corner where the old men sat and murmured. "The people were different. They did not think as we thought. People who go abroad to Canada discover a different way of thinking — no envy, no jealousy. But we were very realistic about coming back. We knew it would be difficult. But you know, we came back from Canada better people because of Canada. I learned to socialize in Canada. I learned to work outside the home. I learned to live without gossip."

She looked up, and in the doorway stood her teenage daughter, Franca, her slender frame silouhetted against the brilliant blue of the afternoon sky. Franca was fourteen, a pretty girl with delicate features and eyes that seemed to gather the light. "Franca," her mother said softly, "is still finding it difficult. In Toronto, after all, she could go out by herself. Naturally she cannot here. She compares everything to Toronto. And everything does not compare favorably." Franca came in and stood beside her mother. Someone asked her what it was that she missed about Toronto. Her shoulders stiffened. Her voice had a slightly defiant edge. "Everything," she said.

Her mother said that there were numerous people in Revo who had come back from Canada. One she knew, Thomas Regatti, lived just a few houses away. Her daughter, she said, would be pleased to show the way to his home. Franca led, complaining as she went that she had no one to speak English with and as a consequence, was losing the language. She wanted to go back to Toronto, the sooner the better. She climbed a set of brick steps at a sparkling new house and tapped gently on the door. A tall man appeared, dressed in jeans and work shirt. "You are from Toronto?", Thomas Regatti asked, his eyes alight. "How are the Leafs?"

Regatti, who is in his middle fifties, grew up in Revo, knowing all the while that though it was beautiful, it was poor, so poor he would have to go abroad. People had been doing so for generations. In 1956, it was his turn. "I remember it so well," he said, "I landed in Toronto and went to live at 664 Davenport Road. I got my first job at a restaurant. Have you ever heard of Old Angelo's?"

He became quickly a warehouseman in the food industry,

spending almost twenty years with Dominion Stores, much of them as a foreman. But in 1981, he felt the longing for the land he'd left. "I left this town when I was nineteen," he said. "I planned to come back in five years. Well five years became twenty-five. One day in Toronto in 1981, I found myself saying to no one in particular, 'It's time to go home.'" What was behind the feeling? For a moment Regatti looked perplexed. "I don't exactly know," he replied, "except that I had a deep desire that my bones would rest in Italy. And at that time, my children were still very young, one five, the other six. So I knew it would not be a hardship for them to adjust. Not if I left then."

He got up. Someone had come to the window; they exchanged a few words. He came back, pushed his hand through his greying hair, and continued: "I should mention that I was helped by the fact that my father had an orchard and it is mine now. We grow the best Delicious apples in the world, right here in the valley. The altitude, the air, the atmosphere is what makes it possible. So I do reasonably well through apples. But, yes, I still miss part of Canadian life. I miss the Leafs. I was their greatest fan. In some ways here, to tell you the truth, the people are different. Or maybe it isn't the people. Maybe it is me. I mean this is a small town. They still look through the shutters. Sometimes it is hard to adjust to that. And to the terrible slowness of the government. You go from office to office to office. My wife filled out the income tax form and sent it in four years ago. A couple of months ago she got her return. So in a sense, I am still adjusting. But I am here for good. I still remember how I felt when I went to my supervisor at Dominion Stores that day in 1981 to tell him I was quitting to go back to Italy. He said to me: 'Don't quit, take a leave of absence.' But I refused that idea. I knew that if I came back to Italy, and still had a job to return to in Canada, I would be on the plane before long." Regatti got up, and invited his guests to come to the door at the back of his kitchen. He led them to the deck beyond the door. Softly, the bell, just a few yards away in a tower two centuries old, began to toll. The horizon, at eye level, seemed to run on forever. The valley itself descended from the yard of his house, down through the tiny village, through orchards and meadows and the roads of the Alps to a green floor that seemed a day's journey away. "That," said Regatti, "is why I am here."

It was quite late in the afternoon. In the Hotel Revo, the men were beginning to head home one by one, for the evening meal. One sturdy, weathered man paused to speak to the visitors. He seemed proud to give his full name: "I am Beneto John Rossi." Then, as if anxious to tell of his experience, he said that he had gone to Canada in 1955, settling in Toronto, and working for ten years as a barman, first at a tavern called The Brown Derby, then at an old and favored bar in the The Walker House at the foot of University Avenue. He had come back to Revo in 1965 at the urging of his wife who was sure the air would help her health. He paused; it was clear that he had something more to say, but only if he were asked. Someone wondered aloud whether he ever thought of going back to Toronto. "To tell you the truth," he replied, "if my wife would return with me, I would be on the plane tonight. Tonight." Why did he miss Toronto so much? Suddenly, his eyes began to glisten. "The people," he said, "The people. In Toronto, for me, every day was a good day."

Men such as Rossi have been making the return trek to Italy ever since the first of their kin left it. But since the seventies, the stream has quickened. In the early eighties, virtually as many Italians left Canada as entered. In 1982, 2,455 arrived and 2,145 left; in 1983, 1,785 arrived and 2,299 left; in 1984, 1,432 arrived and 1,715 left. As Canada's economy improved toward the middle eighties, the homeward flow slowed, but it did not cease.[14]

By the end of the decade, according to the Italian Embassy in Ottawa, over 10,000 Italians had gone home. The Italian government, mindful of the hardships that drove its citizens to emigrate in the first place, feels a sincere if modest obligation to help them now that times are better. In the city of Trento, in the early spring of 1987, an official of the region's immigration department sat in a white, sun-washed restaurant, steps from the site of the historic Council of Trent of the sixteenth century, and explained the program that his province, like provinces elsewhere, provided for the "returnees". For those who needed help, it paid half the family air fare from Canada to Italy, helped move the furniture, and provided each wage earner with the equivalent of a few hundred dollars. If they were unable to find work or support in Italy, the case with very few, it offered social assistance. But the problems of returning Italians were seldom economic.

To the south, ranged by the same alpine peaks that break the sky over Revo, sits the town of Taio. There, a sturdy, tall man with reddish hair, Gino Inama, found himself in one of the more stressful periods of his recently tumultuous life.[15] It was three years since he had come back to his hometown, filled with optimism at the prospect of running a business with members of his family. His wife, a Scottish woman he had met in Toronto, came with him, as did his two Canadian-born children. It took only a few months for Gino Inama to realize that his dream was not just an idle fantasy, but almost a nightmare. The printing business did not go well, nor did the relationships in Taio. His wife and children went back to Canada; Inama remained in Taio disconsolate, spending two years selling time-share chalets in the ski resorts of the Alps and doing well, but all the while wondering where he should be, and what he would do about his family situation. His voice cracked when a friend asked him if he would remain in Italy or return to Canada. "I am doing well here in my work so I want to stay," he said. "But for my family I should be in Canada. I simply don't know what to do."

On that spring day in 1987, he sat at a small table in a tiny Taio restaurant, looking out to the mountains, sipping coffee and smoking cigarettes, and tracing the disappointment of his return: "I knew it would be difficult — but not this difficult. In Canada I had a successful career in real estate, nearly twenty-five years in the Toronto market. I served a term as president of the club for people from this entire region — Trentini. No wonder that one day my wife said to me: 'In Canada you were a somebody. Here you are a nobody.' She saw me try my best to take part in the local associations here. They were cool to me. They called me an American. Here in the town I grew up in, I am a stranger. I am not one of them. My children went back to Canada and then, to be with them, my wife felt she had to go. I will go back soon and I will have to make a decision. Either they come back with me or else I will go to Canada and try to rebuild my career."

He seemed honestly perplexed, as if life had become so tangled he could not sort it out. "Maybe," he began again, "maybe they should come here. You see, I have a good job. And my son, who is perfectly bilingual, could find good work because of his skill with language. My daughter is intelligent and resourceful. And I believe if my wife tried again . . ." His voice trailed off. He lit another cigarette. "But let me tell you something. It is not easy to work in real estate here. The paperwork is terrible, phenomenal. In Canada I did my own income tax. Never here. Some people find it so terrible they never bother filing their income tax. And the government never gets around to them." If it was all so bad, why did he keep wondering if he might stay and persuade his family yet again to stay with him? He shrugged and replied quickly: "Well, of course, life is not all paperwork."

In July of 1987, Gino Inama arrived at Pearson International Airport in Toronto, was met by his wife Elizabeth, and drove to her apartment on Kipling Avenue in the city's northwest. By then, Elizabeth had re-established herself with the bank for which she had worked before her move with Gino to Italy; their son was working and about to be married, and their daughter was in high school. It was clear that all three had found their place once again in Canada.

One day shortly after he arrived, Gino went for a long walk with Elizabeth. They headed to a park where, in early afternoon, only a few people were strolling. There, sitting on a bench, they raised the subject of their future. Cautiously, Gino put the case for the family's return to Italy: his job was good, his son would get a good job in view of his skill in English and Italian, his daughter would receive an excellent European university education. Would Elizabeth give it one more try? His wife said nothing. She looked at him. She said she understood his feelings, she respected them, but her mind was made up — she was staying in Canada. A few days later, Inama flew back to Italy where, for the remainder of summer and fall, he spent his days, sadly, doggedly, winding up business, selling the house, saying poignant farewells, and preparing to return in the fall to Canada to look for work. In October, 1987, he was back in Toronto. He was fifty-five years old and he was starting all over again.

In the first week of January, 1988, Gino Inama began working in real estate once more, representing a company in Toronto called Ideal Real Estate, and specializing in commercial and industrial property. He seemed driven, arriving at the office before seven in the morning and rarely going home for evenings. He spent much of his time on the northern and eastern edges of Toronto, where he assembled and sold land for development. He did well: by December he had earned commissions in the vicinity of $500,000. He was, he said, fortunate in getting back into real estate at a time when Toronto was entering a new boom. Sometimes, he told a friend, the dreams of Taio, and what might have been, crept to the edge of his mind, but he told himself it was all the past, all history. He must live for the future.

That August he began to feel a strange ache in his right shoulder. He dismissed it as rheumatism. It did not leave and so he consulted his physician. The doctor sent him to two specialists for more thorough testing. The results were revealing and troubling: he had an ulcer, an inflamed intestine, and a very high cholestrol level. "You are a victim of stress," one of the physicians told him. "You are to go on a strict diet for the cholesterol. And I want you to begin a four-week rest right now." Inama flew immediately to Taio. He spent a month on the farm of his sister and found, for the first time in many months, deep peace of mind. His pains and aches vanished. Then he came back to his work in Toronto, where by the end of the year, he put together a parcel of land for which a developer offered many millions. "I am home," he told a friend on a cold winter morning. "I am back where I must stay for good." A few days later he flew to Taio for a ten-day visit.

In the summer in which Inama was re-establishing himself, a small, dark man in an immaculate grey suit, Leonardo Lalla, arrived from Italy at the large suburb of Scarborough, near Toronto. Lalla, who held doctorates in the humanities and in veterinary medicine, was the mayor of Monteleone, not far from

Naples, a town of short streets with a view of the low, silent hills. While his visit to Toronto was social, it was also official, since like other mayors he would speak at a banquet for the many people from Montelone living in Toronto, bringing greetings and news from back home.

Ever since Leonardo Lalla had become mayor of Monteleone, he had seen people come back home from Canada hoping to find happiness and tranquility in the old town. Too many, Lalla felt, found disappointment. He knew, even as he left for Canada that July, that he would find among those who came out to meet him and hear him, a number dreaming of going home again. Lalla did not have the heart or the will to deter them. But, he knew that too often, it was not a good idea.

One day in Scarborough, he sat with a handful of men from Monteleone in the living room of one of them. Someone raised the question: how did he feel toward the idea of people going back? He hesitated. What he said seemed to reveal yet another turn in the wheel of the Italian immigration experience. He said that, truly, he understood how people felt. And the people of Monteleone like to see anyone come home to visit. That was why the town was planning, the very next summer, a special homecoming celebration for a group from Toronto.

Perhaps, Lalla seemed to be saying, that was the best way. After all, the world was now a smaller place. And Italians in Canada had done so well that they could afford to come home for visits, not once or twice, but many times. Perhaps, in fact, it would do them well to visit often. "I sense," he said with great diplomacy, "that the people from Monteleone have acquired much of the world's goods in Canada. Of course, there is more to being a truly rich person than material goods. There is culture. There is a worldview. That is why we invite our people back for visits and when they retire, perhaps to spend part of each year with us."[16]

As he spoke, Leonardo Lalla looked around the room at the men from Monteleone — a businessman, a retired tailor, two who still worked in construction — each of them prosperous, a couple of them with sons who were young business executives. They were silent, each looking at Lalla, then glancing through the wide living-room window at the empty street. In their silence there was an unuttered admission that their destiny was indeed not back home in the Neapolitan hills, but in the city history had chosen for them, and to which they must belong.

At a corner about eight miles from where Lalla spoke, in the heart of Canada's best known Little Italy — the intersection of Dufferin Street and Eglinton Avenue West — stands a discount grocery store called Valdi's. Beside the store entrance is a doorway opening upon a narrow stairway that leads to the floor over the store. The walls of the second floor have an old, fragile look; the floor creaks. A door to the left rattles open upon a waiting room in which twelve straight-backed chairs line the walls. There are posters on the wall, scenes from Italy Five Italian men sit in total silence. Now and then, a woman appears from behind the opaque glass doorway to the inner office. She calls a name, a man stands, and, with a decided limp from an old injury, makes his way shyly through the doorway. This is the office of INAS-Canada, an acronym standing for National Institute of Social Assistance.

The men, once inside, explain why they qualify for a pension from Italy — they served in the Army as youths or else they worked in Italy for the requisite length of time before they came to Canada. Each year, over a thousand men troop into the spartan office, fill out an application, and usually receive a pension from Italy of about four hundred dollars a month.

Often, the director of the office hears the men himself. It is that kind of office, and he is that kind of man. This is Joseph Carraro. Four decades after coming to Canada as a Catholic priest, over a quarter-century after helping found the organization COSTI, Carraro is no longer a priest; he is married and the father of several children, but he is still a selfless worker among the people he dedicated himself to long ago. He shakes hands, grasping each man by the shoulder, and ushering him into the office with the cluttered desk, and the shelves lined with books on economics and philosophy.

There is a tiredness around his eyes, as if the battles of the past have left him not despairing, but weary. In the middle of a

January afternoon in 1989, Carraro is in a reflective mood, wondering where the life of Italians in Canada has led and where it may yet lead. Several months earlier, he spoke his worry that somehow, despite all the achievement of material welfare and growing goodwill, something of depth was missing from the life of Italian Canadians, particularly those in Toronto. Why, he wondered, were there not more Italian young people in the mainstream professions — in medicine, law, computer science, engineering? Why, he wondered, were there not more Italian-Canadian young people achieving — as Asian young people obviously were — so much so early in music?

He was candid. "It is because the Italian community is too often a community built around the buck. Making it big in material well-being has come to mean too much. It has meant that education has suffered greatly. Where are our Italian young people in computer science, in architecture, in surgery? We have, as Italians, arrived in a material sense. Some are still deprived and that is very sad. But a great many are financially well-off, many extremely well-off. We will pay for this in the decades ahead. Why? Because we are enjoying materialism now without regard to the consequences. Young people see their fathers having made a lot of money without education. But their fathers were too busy struggling to pay off the mortage to get an education. Now they feel that Daddy will give them a job. In fact, Daddy may even give them a company of their own. Well, sometime beyond the year 2000, we may begin to wonder when we go to our bankers, our physicians, our lawyers, where are the Italians? We have failed somewhere. As soon as this problem of Italian young people not aiming for higher education was detected a decade ago, Italian opinion-formers ought to have been doing something about it. Too many young people of potential have simply settled for the easy dollar."[17]

He stood up. He urged the visitor to keep it all in perspective, for after all, there was more about Italians in Canada to be appreciated than to be regretted. Most of all, he said, Italians have become truly and deeply Italian *Canadians*, no longer outsiders, not assimilated either, but integrated, moving more and more within the character of Canada itself. Canada had become, in the decades since its centennial in 1967, not just a land of English and French, but a mosaic of cultures. Italians, perhaps more than any other group, had found a joyful place within that mosaic: "We are no longer the people from Italy. We are Italian but we are truly Canadian. We really are. And as each year goes by we will be showing how deeply we are a part of the destiny of the nation."

Carraro stood for a moment. He sighed, shook hands, and turned, making his way back into the waiting room with the faded posters of fading villages. As he went, there seemed about him, even in his tiredness, a serenity of purpose, as if he had long ago found his place and made his peace with the new land and the expansive horizon of its future.

ENDNOTES

CHAPTER ONE

1. The main source material for this chapter is testimony provided at The Royal Commission into the Immigration of Italian Labourers to Montreal and the Alleged Fraudulent Practices of Employment Agencies (Ottawa, 1905), and the Report of the Commissioner, Judge John Winchester, both of which are located in the Robarts Library, University of Toronto. Also examined were various newspaper reports of the time, most of which appeared in *The Gazette* in winter, spring and summer of 1904. Scholarly evaluations of the period are contained in "The Italians of Montreal," a paper by Professor Bruno Ramirez. The role in history of men such as Antonio Cordasco is examined in detail in various papers by Professor Robert Harney, notably "The Padrone System," and "Sojourners in the Canadian North, 1885-1920." All are in the library of the Multicultural History Society of Toronto. Supplementary documents include numerous pieces of correspondence between Cordasco and his agents and clients, much of which was obtained through the Public Archives of Canada, Ottawa. Descriptive material on the Montreal Courthouse is based on historical monographs in the Montreal City Archives and on an article in *The Gazette* of Montreal, August 9, 1979.

2 All references to John Winchester are drawn from the *Dictionary of Canadian Biography*, the Toronto *Star*, May 9, 1919, and the Toronto *Globe*, May 9, 1919.

3. See the Report of the Deputy Minister of Labour, the *Labour Gazette*, June, 1906.

4. See "Canada as a Target of Trade and Emigration in Post-unification Italian Writing" by Nicoletta Sevio, in *Arrangiarsi, The Italian Immigration Experience in Canada*, edited by Roberto Perin and Franc Sturino, Guernica, 1989.

5. Descriptions of the club car, dining car, railway line and service provided through consultation with the former corporate historian and archivist of Canadian Pacific Limited, Omer Lavallée , CM, of Montreal.

6. From correspondence included in the Report of the Commissioner, Judge John Winchester, 1905.

CHAPTER TWO

1. See *History of Thunder Bay* by Joseph Mauro, published by the City of Thunder Bay; and the Fort William *Daily Times-Journal*, September 16, 1905. Descriptive material surrounding Laurier's trip and visit provided through consultation with Omer Lavallée, CM.

2. Biographical data on the three community leaders of the Lakehead is contained in documents of the Thunder Bay Historical Society, the Port Arthur *News-Chronicle* and the *Daily Times-Journal* of the period.

3. S.C. Young's widely expressed convictions on the potential of the Lakehead are amplified in his report to the Fort William Board of Trade, October, 1905.

4. For a detailed examination of the Benevolent Society, see "Community in the Making, a case study of a Benevolent Society in Fort William's Little Italy," by Antonio Pucci at the Thunder Bay Historical Museum.

5. A thorough and absorbing study of labor history and unrest in northern Ontario, which informs much of my treatment of the period, is "Community and Conflict: a Study of the Working Class and its Relationships at the Canadian Lakehead, 1903-1913," a master's thesis by Jean Morrison presented at Lakehead University in 1974. See also the valued insights of "The Italian Community in Fort William's East End in the early Twentieth Century," master's thesis by Antonio Pucci, presented at Lakehead University in 1977.

6. *Daily News*, August, 16, 1909; also, an oral-history interview with J.M. DiGiacomo, by the Thunder Bay Labour History Project, 1972, in which he recalls the crush of workers fighting for the disk: "A small man like me, only 14, my ribs would just be about broken."

7. All reportage on various conflicts between workers and police is, unless otherwise indicated, drawn from material in the Fort William *Daily Times-Journal* and the Port Arthur *Daily News* of the period.

8. Reportage on the trials and sentencing of the Deprenzo brothers is drawn from newspaper reports of the time, and the private notations of Mr. Justice Middleton, which were deciphered for the author by Geoffrey Brohier of Toronto.

9. Information on the roles of the Reverend J.M. Shaver and Mrs. Shaver at Wesley Institute is drawn from biographical material and articles in the *Missionary Bulletin* of the period at the United Church Archives, Victoria University, Toronto. Also examined were reports on Port Arthur and Fort Williams complied for the national bodies of the Methodist and Presbyterian Churches in 1913 by Bryce Stewart.

10. Based on two interviews with the late Hubert Badani in September, 1984.

CHAPTER THREE

1. The Memoirs of Ernest Jones, quoted in *Toronto Remembered; a Celebration of the City*, by William Kilbourn, Stoddart, 1984.

2. See *Of Toronto the Good*, by C.S. Clark, originally published in 1897, reprinted in 1970.

3. See "The Italian Immigrants of the St. John's Ward, 1875-1915" by John Zucchi; *Immigrants: A portrait of the Urban Experience, 1890-1930* by Robert Harney and Harold Troper; and "Chiaroscuro: Italians in Toronto 1885-1915," by Robert Harney, *Italian Americana*, Spring, 1945. All are in the library of the Multicultural History Society of Ontario, Toronto.

4. From "The Redemption of the City," an address to the General Assembly of the Presbyterian Church of Canada, 1913.

5. *Canada and the Canadian Question*. Edited by Carl Berger, University of Toronto Press. First published in 1891.

6. *Rupert Brooke in Canada*, PMA Books, Toronto, 1978.

7. "Toronto's Melting Pot," by Margaret Bell, *The Canadian Magazine*, May-October, 1913.

8. "The Drama of the Ward by Augustus Bridle," the *Canadian Magazine*, November, 1919. Mr. Bridle, a widely read observer of the time, was merely reflecting prevalent sentiment when he wrote that "a Methodist church in the ward, Old Agnes Street Church, which had become a Yiddish theatre, had been a stronghold of Methodism among the swarming foreigners."

9. "Hot roast for Italians," letter in *Jack Canuck*, June 1, 1912. The following quotation is from "Italians degrade their women," another article in the same issue.

10. From the report of the medical officer of health, Charles J. Hastings, M.D., 1911, Toronto City Archives.

11. See "What is 'the Ward' going to do with Toronto?" a report to the Bureau of Municipal Research, 1918, Toronto City Archives.

12. Most of the reportage on the late James Franceschini is based on unpublished biographical material by Leslie Roberts of Montreal, supplemented with papers provided by the Franceschini family, interviews with his nephew, James Franceschini, along with papers of the late Frank Ryan, Ottawa, and the recollections of Kay Ryan.

13. Recollections of the late Charles Robson and Robson Leather factory were provided in an interview with his son, James Robson, of Oshawa, Ontario.

CHAPTER FOUR

1. See "Interning all Italians under suspicion — Mr. King," by H.R. Armstrong, Toronto *Star*, June 11, 1940.

2. From Norman Robertson's covering memorandum to Superintendant E.W. Bavin, Intelligence Section, Royal Canadian Mounted Police, Ottawa, September 5, 1939; Norman Robertson's memorandum as chairman of a committee including Superintendant Bavin and J.F. MacNeill, K.C., of the federal Department of Justice, was provided through the Canadian Security Intelligence Service under the *Access to Information Act*. For amplification of Robertson's difficult role see *A Man of Influence: Norman Robertson and Canadian Statecraft, 1929 – 1968*, by J.L. Granatstein, Deneau Publishers, Toronto.

3. Secret memorandum from Assistant Commissioner R.R. Tait, May 2, 1940, provided by the Canadian Security Intelligence Service under the *Access to Information Act*.

4. All references to the late Luigi Pancaro are based upon several interviews and papers provided by Dr. Pancaro and his widow.

5. All references to events in the town of Dominion, Nova Scotia in the summer of 1940 are based on interviews with residents, arranged through the courtesy of Professor Lino Polegatto, The University College of Cape Breton, Sydney. Interviews were conducted in the first week of June, 1983, with Mario Ravanello, Ralph Gatto, and Camella and Luigi Scattalon; also Domenic Nardoccio. Papers reviewed included the town history, *Dominion N.S., 1906 – 1981*, several newspapers of the area and time, and a brief essay, "The Italian Community in Dominion," by Emilio Vaninetti, located at The Beaton Institute, University College of Cape Breton.

Also examined were speeches of the day by Clarence Gillis, MP, Cape Breton South; in particular the speech of November 18, 1940 in which he said, in part: "We all remember the hysteria that was caused when the Italians entered the war and in Nova Scotia these Italians were pushed out of their employment . . . My considered opinion is that if an attempt were made at this time to force these men into the mine, there are likely to be serious repercussions." In *Saturday Night* magazine, December 28, 1940, the writer W.D. Hamilton expressed dismay with the action of the miners: "Take, for instance, the case of the coal miners on Cape Breton Island who continue to deprive the country of thousands of tons of coal which therefore have to be imported from the United States because they refuse to go into the mines with aliens."

6. Interviews with various Italian families in the city of Hamilton, Ontario, were arranged through the courtesy of Mr. Zaffiro's son, Nicholas Zaffiro, Q.C. (Nellida Pattaracchia is the wife of Nicholas Zaffiro.) The interviews took place in December, 1983.

7. Interview with Berlino Colangelo, Hamilton, Ontario, March 18, 1983.

8. Mr. Farquharson's article, "Several hundred held in Mounties Roundup of Italians in Canada," June 12, 1940 was one of a number of comprehensive pieces on the subject in the *Globe and Mail* in the summer of 1940. The *Globe and Mail* opposed the roundup and criticized the internment on its editorial page.

9. House of Commons Debates, 1940, 1, 667, cited by Ramsay Cook in "Canadian Freedom in Wartime", an essay in *His Own Man*, from *Essays in Honour of A.R.M. Lower*. Edited by W.H. Heick and Roger Graham, McGill-Queen's Universtiy Press, 1974.

10. From a memorandum from G.L. Jennings, Assistant Commisioner, RCMP, March 23, 1936.

11. From a memorandum by Norman Robertson to O.K. Skelton, August 28, 1939, in which he reports the counsel of the RCMP to outlaw all organizations thought to have become identified with Nazi propaganda, and to suppress any ethnic publications thought to have been so identified.

12. From Mackenzie King's diary, November 16, 1939, as cited in *Man of Influence: Norman Robertson and Canadian Statecraft, 1929 – 1968*, by J.L. Granatstein.

13. See "City Policeman, two professors held as Italians. . . ." Toronto *Star*, June 11, 1940.

14. From an interview with Alino Astri, Toronto, Ontario, July 20, 1986.

15. The *Globe and Mail*, June 8, 1940.

16. Canadian Press report in the London *Free Press*, June 12, 1940.

17. The internment, its place in the history of Italians in Canada and its impact upon their communities is dealt with lucidly and comprehensively in a master's thesis by Joseph Ciccocelli, University of Western Ontario, 1977: "The Innocuous Enemy Alien: Italians in Canada during World War Two." A list of internees and their communities of origin was provided by Luigi G. Pennacchio, a historical researcher, of Toronto; descriptive material on Camp Petawawa was provided by camp officials at Petawawa, Ontario. See also "Brief History of Petawawa," including a report of a Red Cross inspection carried out in September 16, 1940, located in the camp archives.

18. Precise numbers for Italian internees are difficult to ascertain as the number varied with new arrivals and recent releases. According to Joseph Ciccocelli the number varied from the camp number of 597 shortly after the Italians arrived, to the figure of 700 estimated by an internee, the late Donato Sansone, M.D., of Toronto.

19. All references to Mrs. Guagnelli's experiences are based on an interview with her in Niagara Falls, Ontario, November 29, 1985.

20. All references to the Reverend Libero Sauro are based upon papers and correspondence provided by his son, Alberindo Sauro, of Toronto, Ontario.

21. All references to Mr. Frenza are based upon an interview with him in Montreal, Quebec, April 6, 1984.

22. References to James Franceschini are based on the unpublished biography by Leslie Roberts, papers from his nephew James Franceschini, Toronto, and recollections of Mr. Franceschini by the late Luigi Pancaro, M.D.

23. The group, made up largely of clergy and lay people of the United Church of Canada, was represented in its dealings with Ottawa by the late A.R.M. Lower.

24. See "Non-Punitive Punishment," by B.K. Sandwell, *Saturday Night*, June 28, 1941. Also, "Democracy Defends Itself," by Sandwell, *Saturday Night*, July 13, 1940.

25. Material pertaining to Frank Ferri is based on an interview with him in Hamilton, Ontario, July 19, 1983.

26. References to Dr. Scozzafave's term in Camp Petawawa are based on an interview with his daughter, Mary Lou Mellilo, in Welland, Ontario, December 12, 1986. "He was not a political person at all," she remembers, "But as the best-educated Italian in the community he was vulnerable. We lived beside the Welland canal so there were actually rumours that my father was going to blow up the canal."

CHAPTER FIVE

1. See various studies, in particular, "Post-War Immigrants in the changing metropolis with special reference to Toronto's Italian population," a doctoral thesis in sociology by Samuel Sidlofsky, University of Toronto, 1969, in which the years 1940 to 1945 are dealt with as "The Difficult Years."

2. The Department of Labour Yearbook, cited by David Croll in December 1949, reported only 250 Italian immigrants between 1945 and 1947. (While there were numerous small Italian communities before and immediately after World War II, Canada's Italian life was lived mainly in Montreal with its roughly 23,000 citizens, Toronto with about 15,000 and Vancouver with somewhat less than 10,000.)

3. The *Globe and Mail*, June 17, 1943.

4. All references are from the papers and recollections of James Franceschini of Toronto, and in particular, the unpublished biography cited above.

5. See House of Commons speech by David Croll, *Hansard*, December 9, 1949.

6. See "Contours of post-war Italian immigration to Toronto," an essay by Franc Sturino, *Polyphony*, Spring/Summer, 1984.

7. From a lecture by Franca Iacovetta, February 2, 1989: "Italian contract labour, a pre-history of Italian construction workers in post-war Toronto," delivered in the lecture series, New Voices in Italian-Canadian Studies, presented by the Mariano Elia Chair in Italian-Canadian Studies, York University, Toronto.

8. From interviews with the Reverend Enrico Battiston, and with Rodolpho Hoffer in Azzano Decimo, Friuli, May 21, 1984.

9. Based upon an interview with Tulio de Rubeis and other officials of L'Aquila on May 22, 1984.

10. *The Italians*, by Luigi Barzini, Atheneum, 1964. For amplification of Barzini's opinion of the disadvantaged south, see his essay "La Problema del Mezzogiorno," in the same volume.

11. Statistics about Vallelonga are from the office of the Mayor and Municipal clerk, Vallelonga, Calabria, Italy. All references to Antonio Galati (in the following pages) are from an interview with him on July 4, 1987, and from information supplied by Bruno Suppa, Toronto, whose recollections of Vallelonga inform this chapter, along with the author's visit in May, 1984.

12. Interviews with Mayor Francesco Costantino and several former citizens of Vallelonga, Toronto, July 15, 1987.

CHAPTER SIX

1. *The New City, a prejudiced view of Toronto*, by Pierre Berton, The Macmillan Company of Canada, 1961, reflects the vigorous economic spirit of the late fifties in Toronto.

2. For extensive examination of the post-war Italian influx into Toronto, see "Contours of Post-War Italian immigration to Toronto," by Dr. Franc Sturino, York University, Toronto, 1984, at the Multicultural History Society of Ontario Archives. Sturino calculates that between 1950 and 1965, roughly 23,000 Italians a year arrived in Toronto.

3. See "Metro's Progress: An Address to the Toronto Real Estate Board," Toronto 1955, in booklet form at the City of Toronto Archives.

4. Information on Sam Ruscica and his sponsorship of numerous Italian laborers, is based on interviews with his son, Frank Ruscica, in Toronto, Ontario, July 21, 1987, along with correspondence and documents provided by Frank Ruscica.

5. Interview with Joseph Gennaro, Toronto, Ontario, October 7, 1982.

6. See "The Italian Community in Toronto," an essay by Robert Harney in *Two Nations, Many Cultures, Ethnic Groups in Canada* (Toronto: Prentice-Hall of Canada, 1979).

7. See "The Italians of Montreal," by Jeremy Boissevain, a study carried out for the Bilingual and Bicultural Commission, 1970.

8. Historical references to the Italian population of British Columbia are based on censuses of Canada, various editions of *Il Marco Polo*, 1975 and 1976, *The Italians of Western Canada* (Guinti; Marzocco, Vancouver, 1977), with an English translation by Jean Meyer; and several interviews with Italians of Western Canada, most notably Anna Terrana, coordinator of the Italian Cultural Centre, in August, 1987. See also issues of the centre's newspaper, *Il Centro*, published quarterly.

9. Biographical data and quotations from the late Angelo Branca are drawn from the engaging biography of Mr. Justice Branca: *Angelo Branca: Gladiator of the Courts*, by Vincent Moore, Douglas and McIntryre, Vancouver, 1981.

10. See *The Italians of Western Canada*, "How a community centre is born," by Giovanni Germano, and other chapters in the book.

11. See *The Italians of Western Canada*, "The Idea of the Centre; the negotiations and bureaucratic dealings with the municipal government and the provincial government of British Columbia."

12. "Petition," *Il Marco Polo*, January 31, 1977.

13. From an interview with Mario Pastro, Vancouver, February 14, 1989.

CHAPTER SEVEN

1. E. Smith, Fair Wage Officer for the city of Toronto, in a press statement given March 19, 1960. Much of the information in the following pages is based on an interview with the Honourable Frank Drea, September 29, 1987, Toronto.

2. Details on the events at Hogg's Hollow are based largely on the following sources: articles and editorials in the Toronto *Telegram*, March 18, March 25, 1960; the coroner's verdict in the Hogg's Hollow enquiry, April 2, 1960, which said, in part: "The evidence is clear that similar conditions exist in an irresponsible segment of the industry engaged in sub-surface construction;" an interview with John Boddy, retired chief of the North York Fire Department, North York, Ontario, September 8, 1987; and an interview with fireman Alex Baird, Toronto, Ontario, September 12, 1987.

3. Submission of the Ontario Federation of Labour to The Select Committee of the Legislature, May, 1958.

4. The *Globe and Mail*, April 5, 1960.

5. Information on the inquiry came from the report of Coroner D.K. McAteer, April 2, 1960, and the Drea interview cited above.

6. The *Telegram*, March 21, April 2, April 5, 1960.

7. The events of both strikes were widely covered in Toronto papers of the time. The reportage here is largely based upon coverage in the *Globe and Mail*, August 3 to August 14, 1960; May 30 to July 14, 1961, by the paper's labor specialist, Wilfred List, whose reporting was impartial and thorough.

8. Dr. Eugene Faludi, planning consultant, quoted in *Sweethearts*, by Catharine Wismer, James Lorimer & Company, Toronto, 1980.

9. The events of John Stefanini's life were recounted in various interviews with him in 1987, and in the Drea interview cited above.

10. The *Globe and Mail*, August 6, 1960. See also the *Globe and Mail*, May 29, July 17, 1961, and the Toronto *Star*, July 29, 1961.

11. Interview with John Stefanini. The view that Premier Leslie Frost promised union leaders an arbitration board, additional safety inspectors, and a royal commission in return for a return to work, is supported in a paper by Frank Colantonio, a participant in the events of 1960 and 1961, at the Multicultural History Society of Ontario Archives, Toronto.

CHAPTER EIGHT

1. Reportage on the commission is drawn from *The Report of The Royal Commission on Labour-Management Relations in the Construction Industry*, March 1962, from various submissions contained in the proceedings located at the Ontario Archives, Toronto, and from newspaper reports of the day and interviews with Carl Goldenberg, (February 29, 1988) and Tom Eberlee, (October 12, 1987).

2. All references to the statements of the Honourable Leslie Rowntree, Minister of Labour, are from *Hansard*, Ontario Legislature, March 19, 1963; February 13, 1964.

3. In taking this view he was in line with another of Carl Goldenberg's observations on the discontent of the day in the Toronto construction industry: "Although both parties have shown irresponsibility in the house-building industry, it does not follow that disregard for the law by one party justifies unlawful acts by the other."

4. See a profile of Lou Myles by Kenneth Bagnell, *Leisure Ways* magazine, April, 1986.

5. References to Charles Caccia, Joseph Carraro, and COSTI, are based upon reference materials from COSTI and interviews with Charles Caccia, (March 1988), Joseph Carraro, (February 1988), Bruno Suppa, (June 23, 1982 and July 15, 1987).

6. By 1989, COSTI — joining forces with the Italian Immigrant Aid Society of Toronto — was reaching tens of thousands of immigrants and others of every ethnocultural group from Italians to Vietnamese with services of virtually every kind from language training to family counselling. It enriches the life of much of Toronto.

7. Interview with Lino Magagna, CM, August 2, 1985, Toronto.

8. In his essay, "Italophobia: An English-speaking malady?" (Studi Emigrazione, Roma, 1985), historian Robert Harney cites the British scholar R. Foerster writing in 1919: "No one can follow the fortunes of the Italians abroad without being struck by a sort of contempt in which they are often held. Dago, gringo, carcamano, badola, cincali, macaroni — how long the list of epithets might be!"

9. 1946 figures from the Canadian Institute of Public Opinion pole, 1955 figures from a similiar survey cited in N. Tienhaara, *Canadian Views on Immigration and Population*, Ottawa, 1974, quoted in Harney.

10. References to the experience of Franc Sturino are based upon an interview with him, February 5, 1988. The Mariano A. Elia chair was established in 1984, following a gift of $350,000 from Mariano Anthony Elia of Toronto who came to Canada from Calabria as a child in 1929, became a prosperous developer and a strong advocate of the study of Italian-Canadian history.

11. From the preface to *The Vertical Mosaic: An Analysis of Social Class and Power in Canada*, by John Porter, University of Toronto Press.

CHAPTER NINE

1. *The Vertical Mosaic*, p. 168.

2. The estimate of 450,000 is based upon the census of Canada, 1961. At the date of publication, the figure is over 700,000 (*The Census of Canada, 1986*, Supply and Services Canada, 1986).

3. Historical profile of Sault Ste. Marie is drawn from a variety of sources, including "Francis Hector Clergue and the rise of Sault Ste. Marie as an Industrial Centre," by Margaret Van Every, *Ontario History*, 1964, Number 3; Sault Ste. Marie, by Katherine Punch, *Canadian Geographic Journal*, December 1966; "The Story of Sault Ste. Marie," by F. Clever Bald, *The Beaver*, Autumn 1955; and *Stories of the Past; 300 years of Soo History*, located in the Sault Ste. Marie Public Library.

4. The stories of Luigi Stortini and Judge Raymon Stortini, are based on an interview with Judge Stortini, March 23, 1988.

5. "Factors in the Adjustment of Immigrants and their Descendants," by Anthony H. Richmond and Warren E. Kalback, Statistics Canada, 1980.

6. The events of September 1969 in St. Leonard are based on various newspaper reports of the period in *The Gazette* and the Montreal *Star*, two books, *Le débat linguistique au Québec*, by Donat J. Taddeo and Raymond C. Taras (Les Presses de L'Université de Montréal, 1987), and *Issues in Cultural Diversity*, by Harold Troper and Lee Palmer, The Ontario Institute for Studies in Education, 1976, as well as interviews with several observers of September, 1969 and the aftermath, including Donat J. Taddeo, Montreal, June, 1988. Mario Cumbi is the pseudonymn for one of the observers of the confrontation of September 10.

7. From Article Two of the orignal by-laws of the congress. Magagna was invested with the Order of Canada in May 1988, cited as the founder and first Vice-President of the National Congress of Italian Canadians.

CHAPTER TEN

1. Biographical material from Robert Harney based on an interview with him in Toronto, September, 1987.

2. Interview with Franc Sturino, Toronto, February 5, 1988. The following quotation is from one of several interviews with Anthony Fusco, the first on August 4, 1988.

3. This and the following excerpt from "The Padrone System and Sojourners in the Canadian North, 1885–1920," by Robert Harney, a paper presented to the American Italian Historical Association, Cleveland, Ohio, October 27 & 28, 1978.

4. Interview with Felix Rocca, Toronto, July 10, 1985.

5. Lecture by Franca Iacovetta, York University, Toronto, September 27, 1986.

6. *Little Italy Now*, by Robert Harney, Attenzione, Toronto, December, 1979.

7. Biographical references to Anthony Fusco, Toronto based on interviews with him, the first of which took place on August 4, 1988, and on supplementary interviews with others of Toronto Italia. All biographical references to Peter Bosa, Toronto, based on interviews with him, the first of which took place, April 8, 1988, and on papers from Peter Bosa.

8. *The Italian Experience in America, A Handbook for Teachers of Italian*, by Robert Harney, The American Association of Teachers of Italian, 1976.

9. The *New Yorker*, August 17, 1976.

CHAPTER ELEVEN

1. From the *Winged Arrow*, Canada, January, 1973, an Alitalia publication.

2. Interview with Maria Bergamin, Montreal, July 13, 1988.

3. "From Italy with Joy," by Robert Thomas Allen, *The Canadian Magazine*, November 8, 1969.

4. For a detailed monograph on the Yellowknife community see, "From Tuscany to the Northwest Territories: the Italian community of Yellowknife," by Valerie Sestieri Lee, *Canadian Ethnic Studies*, XIX, 1, 1987.

5. Interview with Alberindo Sauro, Toronto, June 23, 1982.

6. Interview with Leo Cellini, Hamilton, Ontario, October 20, 1983.

7. A study of a four-year period beginning in 1951 and carried out by the Judicial Section, Health and Welfare Division, Dominion Bureau of Statistics, (Public Archives of Canada, Ottawa). A study in the early seventies, done for the department of the solicitor general, reached generally similiar conclusions.

8. Bosa interview and a letter from the CBC President of the day, A.W. Johnson, to Peter Bosa expressing regret for the choice of music.

9. *The Business of Crime*, by Humbert S. Nelli, Oxford University Press, 1976.

10. *Blood of my Blood: The dilemma of the Italian-Americans*, by Richard Gambino, Doubleday & Company, New York, 1974.

11. *Greenspan: The Case for the Defense*, by Edward Greenspan and George Jonas, Macmillan of Canada, 1987. The *Globe and Mail* story described on page 225 was entitled "They

sent flowers and regrets — for Violi funeral," The *Globe and Mail*, January 28, 1978.

12. Gallup Poll, May 1979. The Poll revealed that 47 percent of those who viewed the program linked Italians with crime, while 37 percent of those who did not watch the program held that view.

13. Reportage on the earthquake of 1980 is drawn from news reports of the time, documents of the National Congress of Italian Canadians, including "Report Number 28, Visit to Italy, September 23-26, 1984", lists of assignees entitled to receive housing built and donated by the national congress; the video production "Via Canada," Les Productions Voilà; a letter to contributors to the financial campaign signed by Angelo Delfino, autumn, 1986 and an interview with Angelo Delfino, February 23, 1989, Toronto.

14. When all building projects in both regions were complete, one of the town mayors, Salvatore Torsiello of Laviano, urged understanding by Canadians of the time involved: "Our Canadian compatriots must understand that the delays and difficulties we've encountered do not result from the intent of the administration and certainly not the Congress of Italian Canadians or its President. These are difficulties inherent to the realization of public works in this country. Public works have their own time frame which is not necessarily our individual time frame." And Antonio Picerno, who with his wife and two children moved into one of the new Canadian homes in Balvano, told a Toronto *Star* reporter in July 1984: "If everybody had used their money to build houses we'd be better off."

15. Dr. Laureano Leone quoted in the Toronto *Star*, Sunday, July 15, 1984.

16. Biographical data and quotations on Frank Paci are from *Canadian Literature*, Volume 106, Fall, 1985.

17. An interview with Antonio D'Alfonso, Montreal, July 14, 1988.

18. Interview with Marco Micone, Montreal, July 13, 1988.

19. The writers appeared at The Toronto Circle, Symposium on Italian-Canadian Writing, March 18, 1989, at Founders College, York University, Toronto. Sponsored by The Mariano A. Elia Chair in Italian-Canadian Studies.

20. From a conversation with the author, September 8, 1988.

CHAPTER TWELVE

1. This account of Dr. Saverio Pagliuso's views is based upon various private papers provided by him, in particular that dated September 30, 1974, and an interview with him on May 12, 1985.

2. A lecture by Dr. Renzo Carboni delivered in the Mariano A. Elia Lecture series, Columbus Centre, Toronto, April 2, 1986.

3. Material on the work of Franca Carella is drawn from various issues of the publication *Vita Sana*, and from an interview with her September 21, 1988, Toronto.

4. An Interview with Mr. and Mrs. Gino Vatri, March 30, 1984, Toronto.

5. An interview with Frank Orlando, May 21, 1985, Toronto.

6. Various interviews with Dr. Gregory Grande, in particular that conducted on May 20, 1985, Toronto, and a lecture given at York University, Toronto, September 27, 1986.

7. An interview with Olivo Mellozzi, May 16, 1987.

8. An interview with Joseph Carraro, January 12, 1989.

9. An interview with Peter Gentile, Vibo Valenti, May 18, 1987.

10. All comments by residents of Maiarato made in interviews on May 17, 18, 1987, in Maiarato.

11. Statistic from the column, "A national contempt for the law," by Peter Newman, *Maclean's*, December, 1987.

12. Interview with Dr. Luciano Coraggio, Montreal, June 23, 1988.

13. All comments from residents of Revo made in interviews in Revo on May 21, 1987.

14. Statistics provided by the Italian Embassy in Ottawa, Canada, December, 1988.

15. The saga of Gino Inama is based on numerous interviews with him, the first in Taio, Italy on May 21, 1987, the last in Toronto, on Januray 20, 1989.

16. An interview with Leonardo Lalla, Scarborough, Ontario, August 5, 1987.

17. The interview with Joseph Carraro of January 12, 1989.

BIBLIOGRAPHY

BOOKS:

Angelo Branca: Gladiator of the Courts, by Vincent Moore. Douglas & McIntyre, Vancouver, 1981.

Blood of my Blood: The dilemma of the Italian Americans, by Richard Gambino. New York, Doubleday and Company, 1974.

Contrasts: Comparative Essays on Italian-Canadian Writing, edited by Joseph Pivato. Guernica Editions, 1985.

Immigrants, A Portrait of the Urban Experience: 1890 – 1930, by Robert F. Harney and Harold Troper. Van Nostrand Reinhold, Toronto, 1975.

Issues in Cultural Diversity, by Harold Troper and Lee Palmer. The Ontario Institute for Studies in Education, Toronto, 1976.

Italians in Canada, by A.V. Spada. Riviera Press, Montreal, 1969.

La Ville Sans Femmes, by Mario Duliani. Société des Editions Pascal, Montreal, 1945.

Mayor Howland, The Citizens' Candidate, by Desmond Morton. Hakkert, 1973.

Man of Influence: Norman Robertson and Canadian Statecraft 1929-1968, by J.L. Granatstein. Deneau Publishers, Ottawa, 1981.

Of Toronto the Good: a social study, by C.S. Clark. Toronto Publishing Company, Montreal, 1889. Reprinted by Coles, 1970.

Rupert Brooke in Canada: 1887-1915. PMA Books, Toronto, 1978.

Strangers Within Our Gates, or Coming Canadians, by James S. Woodsworth. University of Toronto Press, 1972.

Studi Emigrazione/Etudes Migrations, Centro Studi Emigrazione, Roma, 1985.

Italians in Toronto, by John Zucchi. McGill-Queen's University Press, 1989.

The Enemy that Never Was: A History of Japanese-Canadians, by Ken Adachi. McClelland and Stewart, Toronto, 1976.

277

The Horsemen, by Clifford W. Harvison. McClelland and Stewart, Toronto, 1967.

The Italians of Montreal: social adjustment in a plural society, by Jeremy Boissevain. Queen's Printer, Ottawa, 1970.

The Italians of Western Canada: How a Community Centre is Born, by Giovanni Germano. Giunti, Florence.

The Italians, by Luigi Barzini. Atheneum, New York, 1964.

The Business of Crime: Italians and Syndicate Crime in the United States, by Humbert S. Nelli. Oxford University Press, New York, 1976.

The New City: a prejudiced view of Toronto, by Pierre Berton. The Macmillan Company of Canada Limited, Toronto, 1961.

The Vertical Mosaic: An analysis of social class and power in Canada, by John Porter. University of Toronto Press, 1965.

Toronto Remembered: a Celebration of the City, by William Kilbourn. Stoddart, Toronto, 1984.

THESES:

Ciccocelli, Joseph Anthony. "The Innocuous Enemy Alien: Italians in Canada during World War Two." Master's thesis, University of Western Ontario, 1977.

Morrison, Jean. "Community and Conflict: a study of the Working Class and its Relationship at the Canadian Lakehead, 1903-1913." Master's thesis, Lakehead University, Thunder Bay, Ontario, 1974.

Pucci, Anthony. "The Italian Community in Fort William's East End in the early Twentieth Century." Master's thesis, Lakehead University, Thunder Bay, Ontario, 1977.

Sidlofsky, Samuel. "Post-War Immigrants in the Changing Metropolis with Special Reference to Toronto's Italian Population." Ph. D. diss., University of Toronto, 1969.

Sturino, Franc. "Inside the Chain: A Case Study in Southern Italian Migration to North America, 1880-1930." Ph. D. diss., University of Toronto, 1981.

MONOGRAPHS, ESSAYS FROM SCHOLARLY JOURNALS, AND ARTICLES FROM MAGAZINES:

Allen, Robert Thomas. "Portrait of Little Italy." *Maclean's*, March 21, 1964. "From Italy with Love (Some Lessons In Living)." *The Canadian Magazine*, November 8, 1969.

Bell, Margaret. "Toronto's Melting Pot." *The Canadian Magazine*, May-October, 1913.

Bell, Daniel. "Crime as an American Way of Life." *The Antioch Review*, March, 1953.

Bridle, Augustus. "The Drama of the Ward." *The Canadian Magazine*, November, 1919.

Harney, Robert F. "The Padrone and the Immigrant." *Canadian Review of American Studies*, 1974.

——— "Ambiente and Social Class in North American Little Italies." *Canadian Review of Studies in Nationalism*, 1975.

——— *The Italian Experience in America: handbook for teachers of Italian*. American Association of Teachers of Italian, 1976.

——— "The Commerce of Migration." *Canadian Ethnic Studies*, 1977.

——— "Italians in Canada." Occasional papers on ethnic and immigration studies, Multicultural History Society of Ontario, Toronto.

———— "Montreal's King of Italian Labour: a Case Study of Padronism." *Journal of Canadian Labour Studies*, 1979.

———— "If one were to write a history of Postwar Toronto Italia." Multicultural History Society of Ontario, 1987.

Jansen, Clifford J. *Community Organization of Italians in Toronto, The Canadian Ethnic Mosaic*. McClelland and Stewart, 1978.

———— "Education and Social Mobility of Immigrants: a pilot study focusing on Italians in Vancouver." The Institute for Behavioural Research, 1981.

Lyon, W. J. *Brief History of CFB Petawawa*. Camp Petawawa, Ontario, 1982.

Pennacchio, Luigi G. "Fascism and the World War: The Impact on Toronto's Italians." A postgraduate dissertation and basis of a lecture in the Mariano Elia series, York University, Toronto, February 9, 1989.

Pagliuso, Saverio. "Private brief on problems and needs within Toronto's Italian-Canadian community." Report submitted to the Addiction Research Foundation of Ontario, 1974.

Pucci, Antonio. "At the forefront of militancy: Italians in Canada at the turn of the century." *Studi Emigrazione/Etudes Migrations*, Rome, 1985.

Ramirez, Bruno, and Del Balzo, Michele. *The Italians of Montreal: from sojourning to settlement, 1900–1921*. Montreal, 1980.

Sturino, Franc. "Family and Kin Cohesion among South Italian immigrants in Toronto," and "The Italian Immigrant Woman in North America." Toronto, 1978; "Contours of Post-War Italian Immigration to Toronto." Toronto, 1984.

Wood, S.T. "Tools for Treachery." *Royal Canadian Mounted Police Quarterly*, April, 1941.

Zucchi, John. "The Immigrants of St. John's Ward: Patterns of Settlement and Neighborhood Formation." Multicultural History Society of Ontario, 1978.

NEWSPAPERS:

Canadian newspapers served not only as sources for information on the experience of Italian Canadians in history, but as mirrors of the attitudes of their time. Those quoted are cited in various footnotes and were of great value. They include issues of the Port Arthur *Daily News* and the Fort William *Daily Times-Journal* in the years of labour unrest in the Lakehead, both of which were examined on microfilms in the Public Library of Thunder Bay, Ontario.

Editions of various newspapers dealing with the internments of 1940 were examined at either the Metropolitan Toronto Reference Library or the reference library of North York, Ontario, and include the *Globe and Mail*, the Toronto *Star*, the *Telegram*, the Montreal *Star*, *The Gazette*, the Hamilton *Spectator*, the Winnipeg *Free Press*. The issues involved in the strikes in the construction industry of the early sixties in Toronto were reviewed in that city's three daily papers, the *Globe and Mail*, the Toronto *Star*, the *Telegram*. Events leading up to and including the crisis of St. Leonard were reviewed in the pages of the *The Gazette*.

INDEX